MW01234071

I AM NOT WHITE

One Man's Journey from Whiteness to Oneness.

Richard Pellegrino

Global Work Institute

ISBN: 979-8-218-23104-0

DEDICATION

Dedicated to the memory of my parents, Tony & Louise, who provided the loving foundation for my future service to humanity And to my family and "intentional community" who give me the love and support daily to serve: My dedicated and loving Wife of forty years and Eight Grown Children, each of whom make me proud (and who periodically feed me ☺), plus seven Grandchildren (so far; hint ☺). And to my extended "Beloved Community", a work in progress which gives us all hope! (You know who you are!)

CONTENTS

INTRODUCTION

Disclaimer: I know that I am identified as "white" in this nation and world. I know that this identification and "branding" affords me considerable unearned privileges and opportunities which those who are not "branded" as "white" do not possess. That is the current reality, however it is a perverted, distorted, deluded, and false, man-made, American-and-European-manufactured, reality --- not an authentic one. The sub-title of this memoir could have been "One man's journey from delusion and false identity to his authentic self."

So, I share my story of awakening (or "awokening") with the hope that it may help you discover your authentic self and identity, and then act on that discovery in ways that bring us closer to our collective authentic reality of oneness. But first, so that we are on the same page, let's start with some definitions:

DEFINITIONS

Whiteness, along with the entire notion of distinct "*races*," is a fabricated description and false identity devised by European slavers and subsequently adopted by Americans. Its purpose was to rationalize the abhorrent practice of the transatlantic slave trade and the enslavement of Africans with darker skin, thereby fostering the illusion and fallacy of white supremacy. In her book "*Caste: The Origin of our Discontents*," author Isabel Wilkerson provides a concise history of the origins of American "*whiteness*." During the 1800s and early 1900s, each new immigrant arriving in the United States—most of whom are the ancestors of present-day Americans—encountered an existing social hierarchy established through slavery. This hierarchy placed individuals with extreme differences in pigmentation at opposing ends. Each immigrant had to navigate this hierarchy and determine their position within their new society. At some point in this process, Europeans underwent a transformation, assuming an identity as "*white*" that had not existed before nor had been necessary. They assimilated into a novel creation—an overarching category encompassing all individuals arriving in the New World from Europe. It was through becoming American that they became white. In their countries of origin such as Ireland or Italy, these individuals may have possessed various social or racial identities but being white was not one of them. As James Baldwin astutely remarked, *"No one was white before he/she came to America."*

-**Beloved Community:** A community in which everyone is cared for, absent of poverty, hunger, and hate and infused with oneness, equity, and peace. (*Rev. Martin Luther King Jr. popularized the term during his lifetime of activism and imbued it with new meaning, fueled by his faith that such a community was, in fact, possible.*)

-**Triple Evils of Society:** *"The Triple Evils of POVERTY, RACISM and MILITARISM are forms of violence that exist in a vicious cycle. They are interrelated, all-inclusive, and stand as barriers to our living in the Beloved Community. When we work to remedy one evil, we affect all evils."* -MLK[1]

-**Woke:** Awakened, Enlightened, and Aware of the authentic realities of our existence here on Earth, the main one being the essential ONENESS of all living things, our interconnectedness and interdependence, and the fact that every individual, nation, and culture is both unique and exceptional in their own way, with not one superior to another. (Note: Yes, we are using the

---

[1] From "Where Do We Go From Here: Chaos or Community?" by Dr. Martin Luther King Jr.; Boston: Beacon Press, 1967. For more on the Triple Evils, Beloved Community and King Philosophy of Non-Violent Social Change read https://thekingcenter.org/about-tkc/the-king-philosophy/

popularized "Woke" concept, regardless of any connotations it may conjure, as it means, in our context, "awakening, wakefulness, and enlightenment" to the false, American & European manufactured socio-economic and political indoctrination and propaganda, as well as to our own personal self-awareness and development as wholistic beings, in relation to all living things. And besides, we find it hilarious that anyone would not want to be woke versus being asleep.)

-Woke EQualizers: A movement of superheroes who have committed to non-violently EQualizing bullies and bullying in all its forms, including the *Triple Evils* (institutionalized bullying), and who are building *Beloved Community* to protect and defend those bullied and rid the world of bullying and the Triple Evils of racism, poverty, and militarism forever, through the solutions of "Beloved Community" oneness, equity, and peace.

- EQualized/EQualizing: Whenever someone, some group, or some nation expresses in thought, word, or deed unfounded superiority claims over another—based on their race, gender, nationality, religious beliefs, sexual orientation, age, etc.—that is the foundation of bullying and they will be shown through non-violent but firm, direct words and deeds that they are not superior and actually suffer an inferiority complex, self-hate, and delusions of grandeur due to the fact that they have to invent fake superiority claims to feel good about themselves or their country. In a word, they are *EQualized*. In a personal sense, EQualizers will also EQualize themselves daily to stay humble and make sure that they are not exalting themselves above others, by listening to and learning from anyone and everyone, especially those they disagree with, and trying to bring empathy, healing, and unity in the spirit of oneness and reconciliation. However, sometimes they may have to exercise "tough love" in order to defend individuals and groups from immediate bullying, but the ultimate goal is still always healing and reconciliation.

-EQ: EQualizing Quotient, or the degree to which you stand up to and call out bullying in all its forms.[2]

Why are you reading this book? Here are some good reasons:

1. If you are on your own journey toward the *"Beloved Community"* of greater "wokefulness," awakening, and enlightenment, and wish to learn from and possibly join others who are on similar paths.

---

[2] "EQ" is also Emotional intelligence (otherwise known as emotional quotient or EQ): the ability to understand, use, and manage your own emotions in positive ways to relieve stress, communicate effectively, empathize with others, overcome challenges, and defuse conflict, all important aspects of and tools for effective "EQualizing."

2. If you are searching for "*meaning*" and "*authenticity*" while trying to make sense out of what is going on, not only in your own life but in the world around you and beyond.

3. If you want to learn more about "woke" concepts and practices such as **oneness, justice, equity, anti-racism, equality, servant-leadership, sovereignty, self-determination, authentic freedom, independent investigation of truth, reconciliation, unity in diversity, intersectionality, decolonization, minimalism, progressive revelation, economic democracy, and community resilience and sustainability.**

4. If you want to check out if this book should be burned or banned because it is too "*woke*" and you prefer to be asleep yourself or keep others sleeping so you can control and bully them. (And please do try to ban or burn this as that will only make it a forbidden fruit and more appealing to others, especially youth ☺.)

5. If you know or think you may know the author—and that goes for his "*intentional community*" family of eight grown children, seven grandchildren (so far), extended family of siblings, cousins and in-laws, plus thousands of friends, colleagues, collaborators worldwide (altogether a multitude)-- and want to find out what really makes him tick (or tock), how he got that way, and why he is called "*the Woke Equalizer.*"

6. Or, and this is our favorite, if you would like to become a "*Woke EQualizer*" warrior and peacemaker yourself, fighting the triple evils and building Beloved Community.

(Note: There are several different suggested ways that you can read this book; feel free to pick one which suits you:

1) You can either read the whole enchilada (and hopefully not suffer indigestion ☺.)

2) You can read just the Introduction and Epilogue (as we've packed both with enough wisdom and action items to get you started on this path).

3) You can read just the Introduction, the last chapter/scene which covers only the new millennium, 21st Century, where so much cool stuff has happened, and the Epilogue.

4) You can read the Introduction, and then skip to the chapter/scene/decade in which you were born (since they are broken into decades starting with the fifty's and ending now) and read till the end, and Epilogue.

So, besides all the above, here is what you will learn if you read on through real life stories and learnings from my somewhat storied life adventures, experiences, and path to self-discovery and self-determination, and discovery of the true realities of the world--which took me halfway around the world.

How did a "white" Italian-American, baby-boomer, born and bred in the 1950's, 60's and 70's, in a completely segregated, blue-collar (literally, with a policeman father) New York community, in a bubble of extreme unearned "white privilege" and "white supremacy", come to be *" the Woke EQualizer"* helping to start a *"woke revolution"*, building *"Beloved Communities"*, fighting the *"triple evils"*, and fiercely advocating for the civil and human rights of all peoples, especially women and "BIPOC" (Black, Indigenous, and People of Color)-- through living, teaching and learning on Native American reservations, in rural and urban Black and Brown ghettoes, in "global south" countries (Caribbean islands, so-called "third world"), while simultaneously fathering and providing for a multi-racial family of ten (plus seven grandchildren, so far), serving in most major civil rights organizations under and with many prominent civil rights leaders, building coalitions, authoring related books and articles, featured and interviewed in many national and local media, leading protests, rallies and other direct actions--- and continuing to do all of the above, and more, today, including continually learning to become a better *"Woke warrior and EQualizer"*. (*Whew, did I really do all that?* That was more than a run-on sentence but a run-on life. 😊)

This list of experiences and accomplishments is shared not to gain any accolades, (though I am extremely grateful to have experienced them) but to give you, the reader, a glimpse into the stories and lessons learned which will be shared in the following pages to help you with your journey of self-actualization. (To become **"EQualized"** and an effective **"EQualizer"** one must stay humble[3] and not exalt yourself, or your nation, or your religion, or your "successes" above others.)

So, buckle your seatbelts and get ready to take off on this journey and adventure together with me, building *"Beloved Community"* and **EQualizing** bullies. Cheers!

Rich Pellegrino

(P.S. Note from Rich "the Equalizer" Pellegrino: This book is written as a narrative which is someone else telling the story; that is, my story told by my friends and family at The Global Woke Institute---and I approve this message

---

[3] Two of my favorite quotes regarding humility from Chinese prophet and founder of Taoism, Lao Tzu: "The reason why rivers and seas are able to be lords over a hundred mountain streams, is that they know how to keep below them. That is why they are able to reign over all the mountain streams." "All streams flow to the sea because it is lower than they are. Humility gives it its power. If you want to govern the people, you must place yourself below them. If you want to lead the people, you must learn how to follow them. "

and story.)

1 **THE FABULOUS FIFTIES**
"Separate but Un-Equal"

Born and branded "white" into the "fabulous fifties", a decade called that by some who enjoyed the relative prosperity, technological advances (e.g., TV vs. radio), and post-war peace of that time, but also a period of a rampant terror and racism for people of color in the entire country, especially the "Jim Crow"[4] South and the "Sundown Towns"[5] of the North and Mid-West, Rich didn't have a clue (and he wouldn't until in his twenties two decades later) about the real America, the real world, and his real self (because of the propaganda he was force-fed until able to think for his self). He was the first-born of four, born after his mother suffered several miscarriages and then took the drug Thalidomide to ease the pregnancy, later found to sometimes produce disastrous results in newborns (including premature death, birth defects and developmental disabilities). Plus, he was a "forceps baby," (forcefully pulled out of his mother's womb by forceps), which caused his malleable head and skull to be cone-shaped and pointed which had to be massaged by his parents for months to attain a normal shape. (When going "bad" and doing "wrong" in his teen years he half-jokingly blamed the trauma of his birth and early infancy, saying *"I'm a thalidomide and forceps baby—what's your excuse?!"* 😊)

His second-generation Italian immigrant American family was in the privileged group, enjoying the status of passing as "white" along with many of the unearned privileges associated with that. "Many" and not "all" of those privileges because Italians and other southern Europeans were still viewed as second-class "white" citizens because of their Mediterranean olive-shaded skin and "illegal" immigrant status—they were derogatorily called "WOPS,"

---

[4] For more on Jim Crow laws and this period https://en.wikipedia.org/wiki/Jim_Crow_laws ,and to learn how slavery was never really abolished see the movies "13ᵗʰ" by Ava DuVernay and "Slavery by Another Name" (book and movie), by Douglas A. Blackmon.
[5] For more on Sundown Towns https://en.wikipedia.org/wiki/Sundown_town , which basically meant that "colored people" had to leave town by sundown"; also see the movie "Green Book."

which means "without papers." (So, one wonders how Italian and other immigrant descendants today, many of whom came here "without papers" and illegally, look down upon so-called illegal immigrants from south of the border and elsewhere. They apparently forgot where they came from and somehow feel better about themselves when bullying others—which is why Rich **EQualizes** them by reminding them of their origins. In fact, he wrote a book to remind them, called *"Immigrant Survival Manual"*. **They are EQualized!**)

His family started out in a predominantly Italian neighborhood in Queens, New York City, and moved out to the Long Island suburbs when he was five because the Puerto Ricans started moving in and "invading" their Italian neighborhood. (This, he learned much later, is how the North is, even to this day, with many segregated neighborhoods, both in the cities and suburbs, even more so than the South. The Southern states were eventually forced to integrate due to the civil rights legislation abolishing Jim Crow segregation laws there, but the Northern neighborhoods still largely remain segregated to this day.) Before moving to the suburbs, he used to enjoy riding the train, especially going to Yankee stadium in the Bronx to watch his baseball heroes play. (He was such an obsessed fan that he really believed his actions at home affected the team's outcomes—whether they won or lost—on the field.) Eating his favorite Italian food at Mario's restaurant, walking distance from his apartment building ---veal parmigiana-- that is, if he didn't fill up on the warm Italian bread they served first, was another favorite activity. (Later in life, after learning that veal was from baby lambs, he switched to chicken parmigiana, and now, favoring a more vegetarian diet, it's eggplant parmigiana. But warm Italian bread remains one of his addictions. In fact, while some have a "beer belly, he claims a "bread belly." 😊)

Moving to the Long Island suburbs, Rich started a completely segregated, suburban life at school age, the eldest of four, with all the expectations that he would follow in his parents' conservative, patriotic, Catholic, completely assimilated American and Italian traditions. As the oldest, not only were the family expectations for "success" placed upon his shoulders, but he was spoiled, especially by his maternal grandparents (who were bilingual, educated Italian immigrants, literally "off the boat"), who had professional, lucrative positions with New York companies.

At the age of five he definitely did not want to leave the comforts of home to the unknowns of kindergarten and literally had to be dragged kicking and screaming into the school and classroom by his mom and teacher. However, once settled in, he was an excellent student. (One memory, which made him so proud at the time and a kind of celebrity in his class, was when his father, a New York City police officer--an "officer friendly" who walked and patrolled a beat in Queens--came in his class in full uniform to speak to the children. This began his lifelong love/hate relationship with law enforce-ment, including entering the profession briefly, which he is still very involved in through his social justice advocacy work attempting to build bridges of trust between the police and communities of color, while ***EQualizing*** those police who are bullies with badges.) Also, he was blessed with a quick intellect and easily aced subjects and learning throughout elementary, and later, other grades, making him somewhat of a nerd and a target for bullies.(Later, when he used that innate intellect to question everything, he was told by his parents and other authority figures—including priests and some teachers-- that he was too smart for his own good, as their definition of smarts and success was to not rock the boat, not question everything, but blindly accept tradition and just succeed materially and family-wise within those established boundaries, no matter how corrupt and racist they were. And that is why, even today, when conservative racists decry higher, university education, critical race the-ories, and anything which produces too much independent thinking and chal-lenge to the status quo, he **Equalizes them!**)

This nerdiness attracted a fair share of bullying by those who were not so gifted (though they had gifts they were not aware of, as we all do) and had to hide their inferiority complexes by acting tough and superior. Not only was he an object of their bullying but so were many others, as bullying at the time was more a norm than an exception. So, at an early age, he had to learn how to neutralize or ***EQualize*** bullies, not only to defend himself but others who were more defenseless, laying the groundwork for his future ***EQualizing*** and lifelong battle against bullies at all levels. (Later in life he would realize that these bullies were learning their inferiority/superiority complexes and resulting bullying behaviors from almost every segment of American soci-ety—parents, teachers, principals, politicians, law enforcement, military, cor-porations, churches, temples, etc.---as the whole country and its systems and institutions are founded upon and sustained by bullying and worse.)

One very important realization Rich later had regarding this beginning period of his life, and a very important one: He was loved. His parents and family loved him and showed it through both the quantity and quality of time they spent caring for him—in other words he was not at all neglected or abused. Even though he was taught some destructive biases and prejudices, mainly by example rather than words, which may be considered a form of abuse, it was not conscious or deliberate and was based on blind tradition rather than intention. They also taught him many good values—especially the value of family as a foundation—and he felt secure, nurtured, and loved which gave his life a strong foundation and enabled him later in life to learn more accurate truths about people and life in general on his own—even if some were radically different than or even opposing to some of the tradi-tional "truths" his parents and grandparents held. And that provided him with the continued conviction and courage to **EQualize** bullies at all levels.

(Research now shows that individual racism and other forms of bullying be-haviors, while often taught to children at a young age either intentionally or unintentionally by parents and significant others, are more directly the result of neglect and/or abuse at a young age, causing low self-esteem and inferior-ity complexes resulting in racist, supremacist, and other bullying behaviors to hide that insecurity and inferiority.[6] Therefore, Rich marvels at and admires those people he met through the years, sometimes in the front lines of advo-cacy for the victims of state-sponsored bullying and other injustices, who did not have such a strong family foundation, perhaps losing one or both parents at a young age or suffering abuse and/or neglect at the hands of parents or other caregivers, and are still able to love and forgive and defend others—they are among his true saints and heroes!)

Rich also came to realize later in life that white identified people in Amer-ica, including himself, are trained and conditioned from a young age, directly and indirectly, to develop a "supremacist, sovereign psyche", meaning, in part, that they are the rulers, that the rest of society is there to serve them, and therefore they are superior. So, they view and process everything and everyone through that lens, mostly unconsciously. And, if things go wrong and don't work out for them and they are not on top and relatively unscathed by life's challenges, even when they succumb to addictions, criminal and even abusive behaviors, it is due, they believe, to bad luck or a failure on the part of the system, universe, or God to protect and reward them for being inher-ently superior, with little or no personal responsibility or accountability for their actions or choices and an ultimate sense of entitlement. Just like children think they are the center of the universe, many white branded folks don't ever grow out of that due to this intense conditioning.

This is not to make excuses for white folks' despicable behaviors but may help BIPOC folks understand why something like *"Black Lives Matter,"* or Obama's presidency, or Kaepernick's *"Take a Knee,"* or anything which simi-larly shatters their illusions and delusions of grandeur, is such a threat to their very identities built upon the complete falsehoods of superiority and suprem-acy. This is why many white folks, who have not overcome these illusions

---

[6] Craig, W.M. (1998). "The relationship among bullying, victimization, depression, anxiety, and aggression in elementary school children". Personality and Individual Differ-ences. **24** (1): 123–130. doi:10.1016/S0191-8869(97)00145-1.
10.1007/s10964-010-9610-x. PMID 21161351. S2CID 207206722. Archived from the origi-nal (PDF) on 2012-05-25.
^ Ball, H.A. (Jan 2008). "Genetic and environmental influences on victims, bullies and bully-victims in childhood". Journal of Child Psychology and Psychiatry. **49** (1): 104–12. doi:10.1111/j.1469-7610.2007.01821.x. PMID 18181884.
^ Jump up to:[a] [b] [c] Cook, Clayton R.; Williams, Kirk R.; Guerra, Nancy G.; Kim, Tia E.; Sadek, Shelly (2010). "Predictors of Bullying and Victimization in Childhood and Adoles-cence: A Meta-analytic Investigation" (PDF). School Psychology Quarterly. **25** (2): 65–83. CiteSeerX 10.1.1.617.7810. doi:10.1037/a0020149. Archived (PDF) from the original on 2014-03-07. Retrieved 2013-10-28.

and delusions, will support and idolize as cult heroes such despicable figures like Trump, and why he can never accept defeat. Or why white police officers who routinely brutalize people of color. And why "Christian" white folks supported and participated in other white folks' commission of every manner of atrocity towards people of color, like public lynching, which were white family entertainment events. And white-state-sponsored genocide of Native Americans and the brutal enslavement of Blacks—both American holocausts. And today, the American foreign policy of oppression and murder of peoples of color worldwide in its empire building and maintaining quest. This is how their universe is ordered as they have been conditioned to believe for centuries. (Rich realizes that he would have been the same were it not for his experiences outlined throughout this book, starting in his adolescence, including shock treatments like drug use and addiction, which literally shocked him out of his supremacy illusions and delusions, and therefore which, though   painful,   he   is   grateful   for.)

To close out this period, while Rich was enjoying his elementary school life in a protected and privileged bubble, watching mainly cartoons on the newest invention—black & white TV--outside of his protected bubble of white privilege and supremacy, in 50's America, Black & White didn't mix so well. (For example, he was told that if he swam in the same pool with Black kids then their color would wash off on him; well eventually, he dove in, full body and mind!) More seriously: Emmet Till was lynched, Jim Crow was alive and thriving in the South, Sundown Towns were spreading across the country, the U.S. entered the Vietnam war (which would last 20 years), McCarthyism[7] was in full force demonizing and ruining people's careers and lives with unfounded (communist) accusations, and white families' wealth began to climb as they were given incentives and aid (welfare) to purchase homes, as Black families were denied such aid, including Black veterans of the world wars, and were red-lined into substandard housing and neighborhoods. (Meanwhile, music—the universal language—was always present and both soothing and inspirational, laying the groundwork for Rich's future musical passion and performances.)

Some of the "woke" musical artists of the 50's which he followed included Ray Charles; Buddy Holly; Everly Brothers; Perry Como; Dean Martin, Sammy Davis; Coasters, Platters; Isley Brothers; Four Tops; Elvis; Woody Guthrie; Billie Holiday; Diana Ross.

---

[7] The practice of making unfounded accusations of subversion and treason, especially when related to communism and socialism—two of the contrived boogeymen of the time-- and still to this day. https://en.wikipedia.org/wiki/McCarthyism

2 THE SWINGING SIXTIES
"Counterculture Revolution Begins"

And then it all changed. Well, not Rich's white privilege (which has never ended), and neither his white bubble and "separate but unequal" status (that would take some years and major upheavals to unravel) but this was the decade and age of questioning (questioning everything which was taught to them by previous generations, because, frankly, the traditional American "land of the free and home of the brave" narrative—that Americans could do no wrong, were superior and exceptional above all other peoples, told and taught in what were really Americana fables, all started to unravel.)

Every attempt that 60s and 70s American society made to fill the void, to replace the lies of the past, to advance and begin actually fulfilling its destiny penned in the Declaration of Independence---that ALL are created equal (not just white folks and Americans), and ALL are entitled to pursue life, liberty and happiness—with equity AND THEN equality, was met, once again, with violent repression and murder (just as any such attempts at progress and the actual founding and settling of America had been birthed in violence in the decades and centuries before.)

John F. Kennedy was elected President, the first Catholic and youngest man to hold that office. When he openly espoused more progressive and universal principles, including ending Jim Crow segregation, he was assassinated, as was his brother and would-be successor, Robert Kennedy. News of these assassinations were announced over Rich's school public address system, and he and his classmates were shocked but were still too young and sheltered to understand what was happening. Dr. Martin Luther King Jr., who led a successful, non-violent, civil rights movement and revolution to grant Blacks and all Americans equal opportunities in all areas of endeavor, ultimately getting dozens of new laws passed (but not before many men, women and even children were brutalized and murdered by state-sponsored and protected terrorists), was assassinated, likely coordinated by the FBI, sparking riots in cities across the nation. (Later in life, after studying the life and works of MLK, Rich would come to revere him as a prophet and a "founding father" of the new or renewed America which finally, under his leadership and that of his deputies, attempted to start living up to its ideals as expressed in the Declaration of Independence.) Again, though sheltered in their bubbles, Rich and classmates were shocked to hear these "assassination" announcements during their school days, with some children in tears though still unaware of these events' significance but realizing something was wrong in their hearts.

Other Black leaders, who did not espouse non-violence as Dr. King had, formed armed militias, the most famous being the **Black Panther Party for Self Defense,** which not only protected the Black neighborhoods from the terroristic police and other thugs who were on the police payroll (who were also caught distributing drugs and guns to the populace at the urging of the state to try and stir up havoc in the community). The Panthers also helped feed, clothe, and house the people—a prime example of mutual aid. Many of them were assassinated by racist and corrupt law enforcement on behalf of the state, including one of the Panther leaders in Chicago, Fred Hampton. One after another, those who stood up for justice, equality, and freedom were either mowed down or jailed on bogus charges for decades. (It was later proven that the FBI and its delusional and terroristic leader, J. Edgar Hoover, orchestrated these assassinations, executions, and infiltrations[8], in conjunction with local law enforcement agencies around the country, to try and suppress the cultural awakening and revolution which was taking place. But their racist, corrupt, and terroristic actions actually poured gas on the flames of change, as the new generation would no longer tolerate their corruption.)

That police violence and repression, and the escalation of the Vietnam war by elite elected representatives and their corporate sponsors who drafted young people to be the fodder for their empire building, were the last straws. They helped spark a counter-culture revolution comprised of those who refused to abide by the old racist, corrupt, and terroristic order, including the strange bedfellows of hippies, flower children, anti-war and civil rights activists, Black Power organizations (like the Panthers and Nation of Islam), Student Nonviolent Coordinating Committee (SNCC), Southern Christian Leadership Conference (SCLC), National Association for the Advancement of Colored People (NAACP), Women's Lib, United Farm Workers, American Indian Movement (AIM), and more. All had differing tactics, from non-violent to violent revolution, and everything in between, but all were opposed

---

[8] COINTELPRO was a series of covert and illegal projects conducted by the United States Federal Bureau of Investigation aimed at surveilling, infiltrating, discrediting, and disrupting domestic American political and social justice organizations. https://en.wikipedia.org/wiki/COINTELPRO#:~:text=COINTELPRO%20(syllabic%20abbreviation%20derived%20from,disrupting%20domestic%20American%20political%20organizations.

to the war, racism, and state-sponsored terrorism, and many took to the streets and disrupted business as usual. (Eventually, Rich was among them and fully immersed as a soldier in this "awakening" and revolution, but first he had to emerge from his white bubble.)

So, in the early sixties, while Rich was still in elementary school, he was still firmly secure and sheltered in the delusional bubble of white privilege, supremacy, and ignorance of the real world—only shattered periodically and briefly by the announcements of the assassinations and by the air raid drills when he and classmates had to hide and crouch under their desks to instill the fear of the other boogey-men—the Russians—who they were told were out to get them. In fact, almost every problem in society at the time was blamed on the Russians; if the tomatoes in your garden weren't robust enough, it was those "damn Russians" poisoning the atmosphere.

Rich's grandparents took him regularly to Yankee baseball games, his family went on vacations to their summer home in New Hampshire which his grandparents co-owned, and they often visited cousins in the city, really immune to and insulated from any of the controversies going on around them. (And before climate change was even a thing, when his family first moved to the Long Island suburbs the winter snows were so deep they could build snow tunnels which the neighborhood kids could walk upright in, however every few years those diminished until there were hardly any major snow falls.)

The Bubble Breaks

Then came middle school, the pre-teen and teen years, and everything in Rich's world began to change, as he changed too. He started to care about how he looked-and wanted the latest "counter-culture" styles—pointy shoes with higher heels, adopted from Hispanic and Black cultures—and the "British invasion" of pop and rock bands with their distinctive dress styles including "bell bottoms," and, of course, longer hair. He wanted it all as he desperately wanted to fit in (especially since he was viewed as a nerd and therefore a bit of an outcast), but his conservative parents wanted none of it, forcefully removing any such apparel he acquired and even forcefully holding him down and cutting his hair. So, he started hiding and storing any such items he could in his lockers at school rather than taking them home.

At his parents' urging, and with the hopes that he would become a "jock" (athlete) rather than a "freak" (hippie), he enrolled in middle school wrestling sports. Although he usually hung out with older friends in the neighborhood and had already been introduced to the euphoria of drinking alcohol as a pre-teen, playing sports introduced him to a new level of mind and body altering substances. (Most people may not realize that many young people begin drug abuse in both sports and the military, then and now.) His middle-school wrestling coach brought mixed "screwdriver" drinks (vodka and orange juice) to their matches so they would feel no pain when wrestling their opponents. But one day a fellow teammate introduced Rich and other teammates to amphetamine pills ('speed') so that they could get a similar effect as the alcohol without the nausea or other, mainly stomach, side effects. (However, they weren't aware of one of the side effects of the "speed", so the first time they all used it one could hear screams coming from the locker room, as it shrinks the male genitals, only temporarily, but these macho boys didn't know that! 🙂.)

That was his introduction to hard drugs—he began using speed before even smoking pot (marijuana), and unaware that he may be predisposed to becoming an addict, he became addicted to it—the first of many drugs and addictions which would follow. In fact, he became physically addicted to every known narcotic drug of the time---uppers, downers, heroin, cocaine, etc., and psychologically addicted to marijuana, LSD, and other hallucinogenic drugs. During his entire adolescence he was high on one or the other drug nearly every day! When taking an "upper" then he needed a "downer" to come down, and so the cycles went, always seeking the next level of drug-induced euphoria.

During this time Rich's family vacationed at the New York City police department resort for officers' families, located in the Catskill mountains. Before that he had sold small amounts of drugs and pot casually, but at the police resort he met some of the biggest drug dealers in New York, all adolescent children of police officers, who were relatively immune from being busted because of the "blue wall" against arresting offspring of fellow officers. So now "blue privilege" was added to his "white privilege", and he joined the ranks of more established drug dealers, many of whom did not use the drugs themselves but just made money selling them. However, as an addict, Rich both used and sold the drugs, daily.

Rich inducted his younger brother and sister into his small "drug cartel," and while his parents suspected what he was doing they turned a blind eye, not wanting to believe it. He dealt drugs up and down the East Coast, from New York to Miami, and became such an adept "street pharmacist" that he carried a Physicians' Desk Reference book which had pictures, descriptions, and side effects of every drug manufactured—so that he could explain to his customers what to do and not do to avoid OD's (overdoses). The few times the cops caught him they let him go when they saw that he had his father's police badge with his identification.

There were many drug-induced adventures during this period, which included wild, drug-filled parties with famous rock bands and musicians that he was invited to because he worked in record stores and also was a drummer in a band, with large bowls of cocaine, worth thousands of dollars, passed around among the guests. Rich supplied his high school teachers with drugs and had a violent altercation with his father when he discovered that Rich was selling drugs out of his home. He ran away and hitchhiked to Miami, and eventually was arrested there and placed in juvenile detention until his parents bailed him out and flew him home. He then learned that his schoolmate and friend, Richie Diener, had been shot and killed by his father over his drug use and dealing. (Later, Richie's story was made into a TV movie, which briefly depicted Rich and his family and helped launch his counseling career some years later after he was clean).

Rich's bubble was broken, at least cracked open a bit, never to be restored again! But he only partially emerged through the cracks and was not to have a friend of color for almost another ten years. That's how solid the racial separation was and how impermeable the bubble was and is still for many. Though they would protest and march together, even deal and use drugs together, and work jobs together, Rich would still never visit friends of color at their homes, in their neighborhoods, or they at his, until many years later. (Even recently, a documentary filmmaker in North Carolina was producing a film on race relations from the perspectives of both conservatives and liberals and was surprised to find that many white self-described liberals whom he interviewed had never had a close Black friend in their whole lives. This is still likely the norm rather than the exception, in most communities.)

Upon entering high school, which had several thousand students only a few of whom were Black, Rich, like many adolescents of that era, began to question everything that his parents, schools, churches, politicians, and every other institution had taught him, but he continued living in their racial separation bubbles, even though, intellectually, he knew racism and prejudice were wrong. Though he was immersed in using various drugs daily—as were many if not most athletes—he tried out and was accepted in freshman football, playing the position of "tight end". However, that and his overall athletic "career" was shortened by two incidents. In one of their first games, he caught a pass and proceeded to run the wrong way scoring a touchback for the other team (duh) . And then, on a much more serious note, the Kent State murders happened, and changed everything--to be continued in the next 70s chapter.

The soundtrack of the 60's included the woke artists: Beatles; Supremes; Dionne Warwick; Aretha Franklin; Carole King; James Taylor; Bob Dylan; Ten Years After; Jimi Hendrix; Eric Clapton; Rolling Stones; Bob Marley; Lionel Ritchie; Smokey Robinson; Country Joe & the Fish; Carlos Santana; Richie Havens; Mamas & The Papas; Janis Joplin; Jim Morrison & the Doors: Jackson Five. Many of them performed at the Woodstock Music Festival in 1969 (which Rich attempted to run away to and attend—at the age of 15— however his parents literally locked him in his room, preventing any escape. However, in the following years, he attended other similar but smaller rock festivals on the East Coast.)

3 SEVERANCE SEVENTIES
"Breaking the Chains"

The counter-culture revolution which began in the sixties was in full swing in the 1970s, and so was Rich, now having reached the age of sixteen at its opening. This decade was characterized by continued national protests, mainly against the Viet- Nam war still (until its end in 1975), as the main civil rights battles of the sixties had already been won and legislation passed to protect the equal rights of African Americans (though it would take years for those laws to be respected and enforced in the South—a battle which is still being waged over 50 years later).

The Women's Liberation, LGBTQ Rights, and Environmental/Green movements were also still in full swing, bringing about new legislation such as Title IX laws which prohibited sexual discrimination in schools and sports for the first time, ever. On a global scale, this period was characterized by frequent coups, domestic conflicts, and civil wars which arose from or were related to decolonization and the global struggle between the West and mainly Southeast Asia, the Mideast, and Africa.[9]

At home, the battle lines were being drawn between the white, conservative, (so-called) Christian right (including "white supremacists" and "white nationalists"), and the people of color, the Jews, and Commies (Communists). Anyone who spoke up for equal rights ---Blacks, Chicanos, Native Americans, Women, LGTBQ, Jews, white progressives, etc.-- were labeled by the white right as Commies, enemies of America and anti-American. (That hasn't changed 50 years later, and the white right still targets all of them as

---

[9] To understand past and present American foreign policy of oppression, colonization, and empire-building, you must read William Blum's works, "Rogue State" https://williamblum.org/books/rogue-state/ , "Killing Hope: U.S. Military and CIA Interventions Since World War II" https://williamblum.org/books/killing-hope , and retired Marine Major General Smedley Butler's "War is a Racket" https://en.wikipedia.org/wiki/War_Is_a_Racket

their boogeymen and uses any chance to bully them using violent rhetoric often producing violent acts of extremism and murder. This is why Rich and the organizations he helped found believe that the white right, white supremacists, white nationalists, and their supporters, are all domestic terrorists who have infiltrated every level of government, law enforcement, and society, *who must be called out and EQualized!)*

Episode One: Emergence

On May 4, 1970, the Kent State shootings, also known as the May 4th Massacre or the Kent State Massacre, resulted in the murders of four and wounding of nine unarmed Kent State University students by the Ohio National Guard in Kent, Ohio. The killings took place during a peace rally opposing the expansion of the Vietnam war into Cambodia by United States military forces, as well as protesting the National Guard's presence on campus. The incident marked the first time that a student had been killed in an anti-war gathering in United States history.

This shocking incident was the last straw for Rich, and his bubble finally burst wide open. At his high school, the administration refused to fly the flag at half-mast for the murdered student protesters, as other schools around the state and nation did, so some of the students decided to lower it themselves, Rich among them. When assembling at the flagpole they were met by a group of student "jocks" (athletes) who were there to prevent the "hippies" and "freaks" from their mission. Rich and a few other students, who were both "jocks" and "hippies" had to decide which side they were on and decided to protect the hippies from the jocks, with force if necessary, so that the flag could be lowered. This confused the jocks and threw them into disarray, and the mission was accomplished.

After that, there was no turning back; it was a turning point. Rich was now a committed hippie, no longer a jock, and quit the team and school sports to pursue his new-found ideals and commitments to social justice, anti-racism, and peace. (Interestingly, over fifty years later, pro-football player Colin Kaepernick suffered the same fate, at a far greater cost to his career, when he "took a knee" during the playing of the national anthem to protest police brutality against Black folks.)

Episode Two: Glory Years 1970 to 1975

The next five years, 1970-75, were to be Rich's glory years (ages 16 to 21) --his emancipation and emergence from the "matrix" by ingesting the "red pill"[10] for the discovery of both his true self and his true environment—a new birth, though not without a lot of labor and some pain and turmoil. That would set him on a path to becoming and being the *"Woke EQualizer,"* forever. During this period, he would protest the war in Washington D.C. at the nation's Capital with tens of thousands, and be arrested in the largest mass arrest in U.S. history; travel throughout Europe twice (once for pleasure and once on a spiritual quest); hitchhike this entire country, coast to coast; attend many rock and Grateful Dead concerts and festivals, while continuing his intensive drug use and dealing; be arrested for selling narcotics to under-cover federal agents, facing multiple felonies and years in prison; dated and befriended his first Black and Jewish girl-friends; graduated high school among the top ten percent of his class (in spite of all the above); witnessed the *"Death of Richie"*, his friend, murdered by his father and made into a TV-movie of the same title in which Rich was briefly portrayed; enrolled in the martial arts (Tai Kwon Do) with a national champion sensei straight from Korea; enrolled in Transcendental Meditation (TM) with its founder Mahari-shi Mahesh Yogi; quit using and selling narcotic drugs through the assistance of martial arts, TM, and other spiritual means; moved to upstate New York to the Adirondack Mountains near Canada; engaged in the intensive study of religions, mystical and spiritual practices and philosophies, embracing most, including but not limited to Buddhist, Hindu, Christian, Amerindian, Muslim, and Bahai; enrolled in college to become a Counselor. (Read about each of these adventures in the following episodes.)

Episode Three: D.C. Protest: Largest Mass Arrest in U.S History

In May 1971, at the age of sixteen, Rich traveled to Washington D.C. with tens of thousands of others from around the country to join one of the many mass protests of the Vietnam war and the Nixon administration's prolonging of it. This was a civil disobedience protest, organized by the more militant members of the anti-war movement, designed to completely disrupt every-thing in D.C., both at the Capitol and in the business and residential districts. It was decided that small groups of protesters would block major intersec-tions and bridges in the capitol, under the slogan, *"If the government won't stop the war, we'll stop the government."*

---

[10] From the 1999 film, "The Matrix" in which humanity is unknowingly trapped inside a simulated real-ity, controlled by the elite, the Matrix, and the resistance offers potential rebels a choice between two pills: red to reveal the truth about the Matrix, and blue to forget everything and return to their former passive life of acceptance of the status quo. https://en.wikipedia.org/wiki/The_Matrix

Rich was part of a team that was to sit-in at the Department of Justice and the FBI headquarters to demand all the illegal surveillance records they were keeping on protestors and activists around the country. President Nixon, who later had to resign in disgrace due to his many criminal activities, ordered thousands of military and national guard troops to supplement the thousands of Capitol and D.C. police. They swept the city arresting anyone who looked like a protestor, violating everyone's civil rights and making the largest mass arrest in U.S. history, converting the Washington Redskins football stadium into a jail to hold the arrestees. Rich was among those arrested. (Later, the ACLU sued the government for this gross violation of civil rights and a class action settlement was paid to all the arrestees, however Rich was not among the recipients since he had used a fake ID, a common practice at the time.)[11]

Episode Four: First European Pilgrimage

Rich's maternal grandparents, who had retired and moved back to Italy, invited him to visit them, all expenses paid. So, he packed his bags the summer of '71 (at the age of 17) and flew from New York to Amsterdam first so that he could visit more of Europe while on his way to Italy. Amsterdam was one of the favorite destinations for young people worldwide since marijuana was legal and readily available there. Upon arrival, Rich checked into one of the many inexpensive youth hostels, dormitory style lodging, with the equivalent of today's cannabis dispensaries on site. He rented a Vespa motorbike to ride and see the sights.

At the hostel he met Cloe, a mixed Black, Jewish American who was there with her boyfriend, both also from NY. He and Cloe hit it off so well she surprisingly ditched her boyfriend and joined Rich for his travels. On a visit to the windmills in the Dutch countryside they had a slight accident and the Vespa ended up in one of the many canals there, with Rich and Cloe slightly bruised and mended by the local Red Cross office nurses.

They then took the train to Paris and checked into a hotel there. Rich tried to use the broken French he had learned in school however the Parisians he encountered acted offended, and one post office clerk explained, *"Monsieur, if you cannot speak our language correctly, speak English, as most of us are bilingual."* (He witnessed them treating French-speaking Canadians the same way, so didn't feel so bad.) Rich and Cloe visited an outdoor café to eat lunch and ordered a pizza to share. When the check came it was exorbitant, Rich protested, and the waiter marked it down. Rick still protested and it was marked down again. Finally, the waiter called the gendarmes (police), and they all

---

[11] Read more of the story of the historic May Day Protest and arrests at https://en.wikipedia.org/wiki/1971_May_Day_protests

negotiated a reasonable price. (Rich later learned that Americans were treated this way in many places, because everyone thought they were relatively wealthy, so there was a "sliding scale" of prices for American tourists which often had to be negotiated down. Plus, there was, and still is, the "ugly American" syndrome, with many Americans often thinking and acting like they were better than others and entitled to preferential treatment, while being disrespectful of local cultural practices and norms. So, they sometimes needed to be and were *EQualized* by the locals.) Rich and Cloe visited more of the sites in Paris and then, when checking out of the hotel, were shocked at the exorbitant surcharges the hotel levied on their collect calls to their families in the States. So, Rich, never being one to back down when faced with injustice, again refused to pay, but this time the towering Libyan clerk wouldn't budge and called the gendarmes. Before the police could arrive, Rich and Cloe grabbed their bags and dashed out the door, leaving those charges unpaid.

They decided to hitchhike a ride to Italy, so they found a popular spot for getting a ride and were lucky to get picked up by an Italian man in a Maserati sports car who was driving all the way to Rome, through the beautiful Swiss Alps. That was an exciting trip on both the highways and breath-taking mountain roads, which took about thirteen hours. (One thing Rich noticed was that the highways had separate lanes and sections for motorcycles and bicycles, rendering them much safer than those in America.) Upon arrival in Rome, they boarded a train for their final destination of Pescara on the Italian east coast and Adriatic Sea, where Rich's grandparents resided. Halfway to their destination the conductors yelled *"sciopero,"* (*pronounced SHO-per-oh*), which means "strike," and the train halted in the middle of nowhere. The workers then walked off on one of the many planned Italian labor strikes leaving passengers stranded until the strike was over or replacement workers arrived. (Rich learned that this was a commonplace occurrence in Italy. Once, while on a long-distance call to the States, the operator interrupted him, saying *"sciopero,,"* and the call was disconnected. These strikes are meant to be disruptive and harassing, and were apparently effective as Italy, like most of Europe, has some of the fairest and most progressive pro-labor laws and practices now, far more advanced than those in America –*they are EQual-ized*[12]).

One of the first things Rich noticed was an interesting dichotomy regarding Italian racism: how aggressively Italian men were attracted to and pursued dark-skinned Cloe. As she and Rich walked through the towns, men came up to talk and flirt with Cloe as if Rich was invisible, and, on the other hand,

---

[12] For more on Italy's and Europe's progressive labor laws and practices, watch the movie, *"Where to Invade Next"* by Michael Moore https://en.wikipedia.org/wiki/Where_to_Invade_Next .

how prejudiced, racist, and discriminatory many were toward her as well, apparently viewing her as inferior and as a sex object only. (This shouldn't have been surprising though, since the same is true in America---how white men view Black women, and really, how most men view and treat most women, as inferior and as playthings—*they are* **EQualized**. But this was the first time Rich had befriended a Black woman, so he really didn't have a clue how they were treated.) Cloe, being the free spirit she was, enjoyed the Italian men's attention and, since Rich's grandparents nearly disowned him for bringing a Black girlfriend to their town, she stayed in a nearby hotel and attracted some suitors to keep her entertained while Rich was busy with his family.

Feeling unwelcome though, Cloe soon flew home to New York and Rich was free to explore his family roots and relatives with his cousin Anna from Bologna in northern Italy. (To his surprise she was blond haired and blue eyed, looking more German than Italian. Rich would later learn that the reason his skin and that of his southern Italian side of the family was "olive-colored" was not because of all the olives they ate—though substantial—but because the north African, darker-skinned "Moors" and Arabs had ruled and intermarried with southern Italians back in the 800s, while the northern Italians were more Germanic in appearance, though all Italians have been passing as white for centuries. However, when Italians first arrived in America, they and other southern Europeans were discriminated against by the whiter northern European, WASP--white, Anglo-Saxon, Protestant--Americans. Later, while Rich was traveling in the southern U.S., when white racists learned Rich was Italian they would sometimes refer to him as a "Yankee nigger," or a "sand nigger." So, ironically, those ignorant folks exposed what most Italians were trying to hide, and it never offended Rich because he was happier to be associated with Blacks and other people of color than ignorant white racists—*they are* **EQualized.**)

During the next few weeks, Cousin Anna and Rich traveled all over Italy visiting historic spots and family in many towns across the country, including in Vatican City. (Rich's family were devout Catholics, like many Italians, and included clergy members—priests and nuns.) In every town they visited Rich's relatives there would host a dinner in his honor, and it was an insult to them if he declined to eat all of the delicious food piled high for him seated at the head of the table as the guest of honor and made to feel like royalty visiting from America. They also attended an Italian funeral which lasted all night until everyone dropped from dancing, drinking, and partying—not somber at all. He learned that the Italian culture was very gregarious and tactile—a lot of touching! He also learned that Italian culture had a few paradoxes. While the people were generally outgoing his cousin explained that they were also very sexually repressed, as the Catholic Church had a very strong and manipulative hold on them, mainly through fear and guilt and burdened with moral prohibitions which the Church leaders could not even follow. This resulted in the rampant sexual and other abuses the Church rained down on children which Church leaders, including the Pope, hid for decades if not centuries—really crimes against humanity in the name of religion by one of its most corrupt institutions in history! (However, millions of people there and in many other countries, including America, still blindly follow this distortion of Christianity—based on blind tradition---which shows the absurdity and danger of not independently investigating truth.)

On the positive side, Italians were not afraid of "socialism" (the boogeyman of America) and found ways to incorporate it into a democratic and capitalistic system (as much of Europe has done), so that all of the people, including and especially the poor and marginalized, are taken care of. This is a major lesson that America has yet to and desperately needs to learn— *we are **EQualized.**)*[13]

Rich left Italy with a richer understanding of his own familial culture, as well as a realization that every country and culture has something to teach Americans, and each other. ***We are EQualized.*** (Travel abroad is a great ***Equalizer!***)

Episode Five: The Death of Richie

Rich then returned home to New York after his European adventures and education.(After his many travels abroad, some highlighted throughout this narrative, and later, having lived abroad, not as a tourist but as a participant in and student of the cultures he experienced, Rich has always maintained that for an American to really know the world, not through the lens of the intense American delusional and supremacist propaganda and conditioning received here from birth, it is necessary to do what he did—travel, and if possible, live abroad, as it is eye-opening and transformative. The internet certainly helps, but there is nothing like experiencing it firsthand. *You will be **EQualized** .*)[14]

Soon after his arrival home, Rich learned that one of his close friends since elementary school, Richie Diener, a fellow nerd and later drug-using buddy, had been shot and killed by his own father in an alleged scuffle over his drug use. This shocked the entire community, as well as the fact that his father was not charged at all, alleging self-defense. This was also a dangerous precedent as more and more parents started saying that they would rather have their kids dead than on drugs as they viewed it as a major embarrassment

---

[13] For more on Italy's and Europe's progressive Democratic Socialism combined with Regenerative Capitalism, watch the movie, *"Where to Invade Next"* by Michael Moore https://en.wikipedia.org/wiki/Where_to_Invade_Next .

[14] A great guide to this type of immersive travel is Rick Steve's book and movie "Travel as a Political Act" at https://store.ricksteves.com/shop/p/travel-political-act and https://www.ricksteves.com/watch-read-listen/video/travel-talks/political-act

and false stigma of failed parenthood. Later, a book and tv movie were produced called *"The Death of Richie,"* in 1977, which helped launch Rich's counseling career as he and his family were briefly portrayed in it. Also, since he was directly acquainted with Richie and all of the details leading up to the tragedy, he was asked to speak on college campuses about the movie and those details. By then he was "clean" and sober, off drugs and alcohol, and had helped start peer-counseling groups at schools and colleges to help students struggling with addiction and other mental health maladies. (Later he would start walk-in/call-in crisis help centers and drug rehab and prevention programs and centers, both in America and abroad.) Richie's tragic death and story helped launch and cement Rich's recovery and first career--one of many. But first he had to hit rock bottom. (See Episode Seven.)

Episode Six: Cross-Country Hitchhiking Journey

Now that he had traveled across some of Europe, it was time for Rich to do the same in America, as up to this time he had only been up and down the East Coast and in New England. So, Rich, and best friend, fellow-hippie, and Italian-American, Mario, set out on foot for the West Coast with only a few belongings which could fit in their backpacks, and their thumbs ready to hitch rides. Everyone was hitchhiking rides in those days, and the biggest challenge for Rich and Mario was that when they arrived at a highway on-ramp, there was often a long line because there were so many young people, including females, already there waiting for rides.

It didn't take Rich and Mario long to get their first rides, which took them all the way to Indiana, and then another took them all the way cross country to Arizona. They often partied all the way, sharing and smoking pot with their drivers. Arriving in Arizona two days into their journey, they were dropped off in a very small town on the edge of the desert and were warned not to dally there as the townspeople were very conservative and didn't like hippies. Though hungry and thirsty, as soon as Rich and Mario exited their ride they stuck their thumbs out to not waste any time getting out of that town before dark. But, sure enough, after only a few minutes, they heard some voices shouting from the direction of the General Store behind them, "Hey, you fucking hippies"! Rich told Mario not to look around and to just ignore the taunts while they continued trying to hitch a ride. Just then, an old cowboy looking guy came near them and said "Hey, you hippies, some of your friends are calling you," and when they looked around they were shocked and surprised to see that it was fellow hippies playing with them and actually trying to get their attention to offer them a ride. Relieved, they accepted the invitation gladly and hopped into the vehicle which was a fully loaded RV. Turned out, they transported people's RVs coast to coast and were going straight to Los Angeles, which was Rich and Mario's destination too—plus there was a fridge on-board full of beers, and plenty of pot and other drugs, so it was a party all the way to L.A.!

When they reached the San Bernadino Mountain pass, overlooking Los Angeles in the valley below, all they could see was a faint outline of the city covered and blocked by clouds of smog—thick air pollution! (This was before emissions tests and similar environmental regulations which have definitely helped clean up our air, though there is still a long way to go with reducing carbon emissions and reversing global warming and related climate change, regardless of what anti-science naysayers claim. *They are **EQualized**).*

Rich and Mario arrived in Los Angeles and, after visiting some of the sites there, they resumed hitching rides up and down the California coast. During their travels, not only in California but nationwide, they kept running into young people who were on their way to "Children of God" farms to live, work, and dedicate their lives, including their money and savings, to "God." Rich and Mario were naturally skeptical and wondered who this "God" was. When they questioned the young converts, they became very defensive, so it sounded like a cult was manipulating those youth who were now disillusioned with both the corrupt system and the hippie/drugs lifestyle and needed something to fill their newly created void. The guys tried to talk them out of it by explaining the holes in their plans, however they would have none of that and appeared brainwashed already. Their suspicions were confirmed when they got a ride to San Diego from an Italian guy, Nick, who had just been released from prison due to his involvement in organized crime (which was code for "the Mafia"). He had a small yacht docked in the San Diego harbor and invited the guys to spend the night with him on the boat and then get back on the road in the morning, an invitation they thankfully accepted. The three partied all night, smoking and drinking, and Nick asked the guys if they had heard of or run into "the Children of God" farms. They told him they had run into many travelers who were on their way to those farms and that they had tried to talk some out of going. Nick, who was quite intoxicated by then, laughed and said, *"Can I trust you guys with a secret?"* He made them swear that they wouldn't tell anyone and then told them that those farms are founded and run by organized crime syndicates. These syndicates realized that after young people were finished using drugs in the record amounts they were consuming (and which the syndicates were also supplying and profiting from), and after the civil rights and peace movements waned, they would be turning to religion in their search for self and further meaning, so they got into the business of religion and founded Children of God, among other similar organizations![15] This revelation confirmed what Rich and Mario had thought, based on their interactions with the new devotees to this corrupt

---

[15] There is no mention of Children of God's ties to organized crime, however it was definitely a notorious cult which preyed on young people. https://en.wikipedia.org/wiki/The_Family_International

cult, however they were also worried that in the morning when Nick sobered up and realized he had spilled the beans to them that they might be in danger. So, bright and early, before Nick awakened, they slipped off the boat and got back on the road. (This is another lesson in having your own mind, and independently investigating anything which is presented to you as "truth" authoritatively by anyone, because no one has a corner on truth. I have my "truth", you have your "truth", they have their "truth", and then there is "the truth", which we all perceive, to a greater or lesser degree, through our own filters and lenses. So anytime anyone says, *"I know the truth,"* that is suspect as *"You know YOUR truth."* **They are EQualized !**)

Rich and Mario then got a ride traveling north to San Francisco with a modern day "Bonnie and Clyde" couple, who, while "Bonnie" flirted with and kept store clerks distracted, "Clyde" would steal gas and other items. So, though the guys were going further up the coast all the way to Seattle, Rich and Mario were fearful that the police may catch up with them and ditched that ride in Portland, Oregon.

At this point the guys were running low on money so they ate in a soup kitchen for the homeless and saw a help-wanted poster on the bulletin board there seeking farmworkers, berry pickers, on a raspberry farm just outside the city. They thought this could be both a fun new experience and also help replenish their funds, so they signed up. Upon arrival at the farm, they noticed that the other workers were migrants from south of the border and that they all would be staying in a barn together. The next day, when they got started working in the field at the break of dawn, they found the work excruciating, in the hot sun. Also, the raspberry bushes had thorns, so the picking was very slow and painful, and the pay was per bushel. It took a long time for inexperienced pickers like Rich and Mario to fill a bushel, even with some of the migrant farmworkers helping as they laughingly took pity on these crazy gringos. Their pay at the end of a long, hard day was under $10.00 each, and that was their first and last day as berry pickers. However, that night, they got to sit around the campfire with the migrant workers and enjoy their food, music, and company—men, women, and children—who were all very warm and welcoming. (It was a great, eye-opening glimpse into the back-breaking, slave-type labor which the migrants do in this country, day in and day out, to provide food for our tables. And the haters have the audacity to look down on them, especially when they try to emigrate and stay here, when all our ancestors---unless you are full-blooded Native American--- did the same and worked hard to earn their place here. Migrant bashing is therefore the height of hypocrisy, arrogance, and bullying. *The haters are* **EQualized**)

That episode concluded their West Coast adventures, and the long trip home to New York was relatively uneventful.

Episode Seven: Drug Dealer/Junkie/Addict/Spiritual Transformation

For most of his adolescence, Rich, like many of his peers, was high on and addicted to one drug or another nearly every day, while also dealing drugs, not only to school mates but also to their high school teachers. (They took the term "high" school to a new level. 😊) One of Rich's teachers took him and groups of fellow students on ski trips to the Vermont mountains, which were big parties. The teacher's wife, who disapproved, and eventually divorced him, was into spiritual practices, including TM --Transcendental Meditation. She always told Rich that when he was done with all the drug foolishness and was ready to discover his true self, she would be there to help teach and guide him. (Rich later realized, with feelings of extreme gratitude, that at every critical juncture in his life there was someone like her—a teacher, guide, mentor—who saw something in him that he didn't even see in myself and helped get him to the next level in his journey forward.)

After graduating high school in '72, Rich briefly moved upstate to the Adirondacks, in the NY "North Country," and dealt drugs there in the vast region between Albany and the Canadian border, earning the notorious distinction of being the first to introduce narcotics to this area on any significant scale. (Later, after he was clean and moved back to that region to open up faith-based, storefront, walk-in crisis counseling centers, the police thought that they were just fronts for continued drug dealing.)

During this period Rich also decided to enter the New York City police department so that he could continue his drug use and dealing under the cover of a badge and the "blue wall," as he had witnessed so many do before (but not his father, who was clean and straight as a whistle). He was partly influenced by the true Al Pacino movie, "Serpico." (Some thought he resembled Pacino, and when he had a security officer's job on the set of "The Godfather" movie filmed in New York's "Little Italy" neighborhood, he was even considered for a stand-in role as a second to Pacino for one scene.) Rich aced the police civil service exam and was getting ready for the next steps when everything came to a grinding halt as he was indicted for several felony counts of selling narcotics, facing a maximum of 60 years in prison. His parents helped him hire the best attorney, and they paid off whomever they could bribe in the D.A.'s and judicial offices in an attempt to avoid jail time and just get him probation. However, when they arrived in court his attorney stated that the best deal he could get was just a couple of years in jail. Rich was devastated to face losing his freedom, and, for the first time in his life he made a sincere prayer and "deal" with his God, saying, "*If you're real, and you help me get out of this, I will change my life for the better and serve you.*" He went before the judge, pled guilty to the lesser charges his attorney had negotiated, and was stunned—along with his attorney and parents—when the judge said, "*I have researched your background and discovered you graduated in the top 10 percent of your class even while engaged in this extensive drug abuse and dealing, so it looks like the good Lord gave you some brains. I am going to give you one more chance to use those brains to do good rather than harm, so I sentence you to five years' probation but if I see you in this or any court again, I will lock you away for many years."* Rich was extremely grateful and later realized that light sentence was due to his extreme white and blue privilege. There is no doubt in his mind, backed up by tons of experiences and statistics [16], that if he were Black, or any person of color, he would have suffered a much different fate and may still be languishing in prison decades later. (An entire book can be written about this unearned privilege which will be referenced throughout this book, but suffice it to say, that the "war on drugs", which had its start in the 70s but really took off in the 80s, has always been and still is a war on the poor and people of color, by the elite. Many of those elite are also drug abusers and dealers—and were Rich's suppliers-- but are protected. Most drug policy has also always been for economic purposes to make the rich richer, as they have benefited from both the sale and interdiction of illicit drugs, and the mass incarceration by law enforcement of the lower-level drug dealers to divert attention away from who and what is really behind both. ***They are EQualized.***)

They say in addiction counseling that an addict will not admit he is an addict and seek help until he hits rock bottom, and that was Rich's bottom—facing all of those years in jail—so he decided then and there to do whatever it took to stop using and selling drugs. Easier said than done, but it is half of the battle and the first step. (Incidentally, one of the surprises Rich experienced in the courtroom was learning that he had graduated at such an advanced level in high school as he had been so out of it that he wasn't even aware of that fact until the judge informed him.) So, the recovery period began.

Rich tried quitting narcotics "cold turkey" and through counseling and methadone treatment, but nothing worked until he set out, quite accidentally, on a spiritual path by taking Tae Kwon Do martial arts and TM (Transcendental Meditation) classes, one rooted in Buddhist and the other in Hindu philosophies. They taught him about his true self—body, mind, and spirit—and how to honor and develop the powers of each while attaining a "natural high" without the use of mind-altering drugs, which he was then able to stop using rather quickly and almost miraculously. (This holistic and spiritual education had never been taught to him before, in school, in church, or at home. In fact, the only times he had experienced it before was during use of hallucinogenic drug "trips" which produced visions of a new and different reality--somewhat akin to the use of the same during some Native American

---

[16] "Black men are six times as likely to be incarcerated as white men and Latinos are 2.5 times as likely."
"The United States is the world's leader in incarceration. There are two million people in the nation's prisons and jails—a 500% increase over the last 40 years."
"https://www.sentencingproject.org/criminal-justice-facts/

vision quest ceremonies.)

This transformation thrust Rich into the study of all spiritual paths, beliefs, and practices. He focused initially on Far Eastern ones and then back to the major Middle Eastern and western religions and philosophies of Christianity and Islam, as well as Native American and other Indigenous peoples' beliefs. (One day, when Rich was on a train subway platform bound for one of these spiritual workshops, it hit him like a ton of bricks that he had stood in that same spot countless other times high as a kite bound for a drug dealer to get supplies to support his habit and to resell. The impact of that realization that his life had experienced such a dizzying 360 degree turn around and transformation literally made his head spin and he almost fainted on the spot before regaining his composure. This is why throughout his life he has had hope for everyone's transformation, no matter how lost, and judges no one as beyond help.)

Rich's probation officer was so impressed with his apparent transformation that he allowed him to move back upstate to the Adirondack Mountains and to only periodically check in remotely. So, he moved to Saranac Lake, near Lake Placid, enrolled in the community college there (which gave him credits for life experience since he helped start a peer counseling program on campus for students with drug and other problems.)

Rich continued his spiritual search and studies there and befriended two other guys who were on similar spiritual searches, Rob & Frank, and they all moved in together to search and study as a group. Frank was an Olympic bobsledder, a former Green Beret, and a black belt martial artist, so they all trained with him (which was quite grueling and often outside in 30 below zero temperatures). They spent days of intensive study and practice of all the spiritual philosophies they could find information on, including many metaphysical ones relating to "mind control," "the third eye," "clairvoyance," "astral projection," among others. They had many mystical experiences, including learning to communicate, at times, telepathically.

Episode Eight: The Big Deal-European Pilgrimage Two

Eventually, when Rich, Rob, and Frank had exhausted all of the spiritual books and resources they could find, the trio decided it was time to find their spiritual guide, their Guru, or indigenous Shaman, so they decided to travel to either India or the American southwest. To do this, and to sustain their spiritual search, they needed money. So, in a hypocritical paradox, they decided to do one final big hashish drug deal—an international one. (They still used marijuana in various forms, including hashish, at times, to enhance their spiritual experiences, but didn't sell it any longer to avoid criminal consequences. They rationalized that one bigger deal to end all deals and set them firmly on their spiritual paths was worth it. Rich later learned, in Narcotics

Anonymous, that this rationalization was called the "stinking thinking" of addicts.)

Going forward, they became like a "mission impossible" team, in between spiritual training and studies, training, and planning for this mission. It was decided that since the Olympic bobsled trials were later that year in Europe, and Frank was participating, he could easily cross borders and customs without scrutiny traveling with the team. We learned that the best source of hashish was the country of Morocco, so all we had to do was get the hash from Morocco to Italy or Greece, where Frank would be practicing. To do this most efficiently and practically, we decided to get hash oil, another form of hashish, and to transport it in specially made bobsled equipment. Each of the mission team had a special role: Frank--the means of transport across borders; Rob—the money to finance the operation; Rich—the dealer connections in the States to purchase the product from us, and the Moroccan connections to supply us.

Finally, the day came, and Rob and Rich left a couple of weeks before Frank and his team to get and ship the product. They flew to Paris to have some fun and see some sights on their trip to Malaga on the Mediterranean coast of Spain where the boat for Morocco would depart from. Ironically, everyone they met on that trip was also on similar spiritual searches, so they shared notes and learning (but never disclosing the nature of this particular trip and mission). Upon arrival in Spain, they had a couple of days wait for the boat to Morocco so decided to hang out in the nearby town of Torremolinos, as it was a mecca and party spot for youth from around the world (which they had read about in the popular book of the time by Michener, *"The Drifters"*).

At this point in their journey, Rich was having second thoughts about the whole mission and deal because if anything went wrong, especially in Morocco, they could get shot or imprisoned for decades. But he didn't want to be the spoil sport and kept his misgivings to himself while secretly praying that something would disrupt their plans.

In Torremolinos, on the Mediterranean beaches, there were young people known at the time as "Jesus freaks," proselytizing and recruiting other young visitors for their "Christian communes" and organizations and inviting them to become "born again Christians." Some approached Rich and Rob and invited them to their hacienda in the hills, overlooking the Mediterranean, to stay and study with them while they waited for the boat to Morocco. Rob, who was raised Jewish, was really into the Bible and Christian mysticism, and Rich, who was more into the Eastern religions, was wary of any Christian cults (partly based on his past interactions with "The Children of God"). Rob accepted their invitation, so Rich had to tag along. But Rich's silent prayer was being answered as Rob fell for the group, becoming a "born-again Christian," and decided to stay with the "Jesus freaks" commune and ditch the whole drug deal. Since his money was financing it, the deal was dead. Rich breathed a sigh of relief, though he didn't know how Frank was going to take it. Rob gave him enough money to return to New York, but the "Jesus freaks" and their pastor wanted Rich to stay and convert to their religion as he was a challenge because of his firm belief that all religions were equal and teaching the same spiritual truths. But that belief, in their eyes, was blasphemy, and of the devil (since they believed in "Christian supremacy" and the falsity of all other religions and spiritual paths.) So, they asked Rich if they could pray over him, lay hands on him, and speak in tongues. Rich didn't know exactly what that meant however he felt that their prayers couldn't do any harm, especially since he needed some spiritual guidance and a vision as to what he should do next because the continuation of his spiritual search had been conditioned on the successful completion of the now defunct hashish deal. So, they took him to their church, surrounded him, and performed their prayers. Rich just closed his eyes and asked the God of his understanding and the Universe for guidance or a vision on what he should do with his life, while their prayers and speaking in tongues became rhythmic, as in a meditation mantra repetition, And the vision came in clear as day--- since he had come to believe that all religions and spiritual paths are essentially one and lead to the same sources of enlightenment, that he should go back to New York and open a center of spiritual study where people could be exposed to and learn about all the paths and decide for themselves the religion, philosophy, and spiritual path they choose to follow.

He immediately arose from his prayerful meditation, thanked the congregation for their hospitality and prayers, and set out to return home. (They asked Rich if God spoke to him, and he told them yes and shared his vision, which they hated as they were still wrapped up in the false religious doctrine of Christian supremacy. His parting words to the "Jesus freak" congregation were, *"Whenever you say that this is what I believe, and nothing else, you have put yourselves in a box and begin to die."* **They were EQualized.***)*

Episode Nine: Spiritual Oneness—Set in Motion

Rich flew back to New York, broke the news via phone to Frank that the deal was off and mission aborted, moved back in with his parents, and got a motel job so he could start saving for his "Spiritual Oneness Center". To learn more about every faith community and spiritual path, and to invite them to his Center when opened, he spent his free time attending meetings, services, meditations at any and all temples, mosques, churches, and ashrams he could, and read and studied the scriptures and writings of them all, continuing his own life-long practices of meditation, yoga, and martial arts.

One such meeting he saw advertised, called a "fireside," was for the Bahai Faith, which he had not heard of before (or perhaps, he had, but only in passing and didn't pay attention, as a popular rock group, Seals & Crofts, were members and their music reflected the Baha'i principles). So, with some apprehension, he attended the Bahai fireside meeting in the home of an older and fairly wealthy Persian couple in an affluent section of Long Island, all of which made him suspicious as he had learned not to trust most anyone over thirty, and especially those with money. He rode his motorcycle there, dressed in his "hippie uniform"(patched jeans and a t-shirt, with long hair) feeling a bit out of place. But he was welcomed warmly by the hosts upon entering a large living room filled with a remarkably diverse group of people---old and young, American and foreign-born, Black and white. (In fact, it was the most diverse group he had seen during his spiritual search and attendance at many religious and spiritual gatherings.) There were no clergy, and everyone shared roles. The speaker was young, Rich's age, and shared some wonderful quotes and commentary from the Bahai scriptures regarding Oneness-- the Oneness of God, the Oneness of Religions, and the Oneness of Humankind. These teachings and beliefs were the same as those Rich had already discovered and held as a result of his own search and study of all religions and spiritual paths. When he told those gathered about his vision in Spain and his goal to open up a spiritual center teaching all the paths to encourage seekers to independently investigate which path is for them, they told him that is exactly what they are already doing in thousands of localities around the country and world. Rich was excited to learn that but told them, somewhat arrogantly (he later realized), that no one wanted to have to learn a whole new religion, with foreign sounding Arabic and Persian names, and that they should all join an existing religion and reform it from within bringing their new teachings of oneness-- since that was the foundation of all religions at their beginnings before people corrupted them for power. They patiently replied that they understood his concern and gave Rich some of the Bahai Writings to study on his own.

Upon further investigation, including reading some of those Baha'i Writings (which are extensive, with over one hundred volumes), and attending another fireside meeting, Rich realized the need for a new religion since there was so much disunity and strife in and between the existing ones. He contemplated and asked himself why to reinvent the wheel and open his own spiritual oneness center when it's already being done. So, in 1975, he joined the Bahai Faith community in that mission to teach and spread Oneness. When the Bahai friends discovered he had lived in and had connections in the upstate New York north country, they encouraged him to move back there and start a Bahai spiritual center in that region, since that had not been done before.

So, at the age of 21, he packed what few belongings he had on his motorcycle, bid has parents, grandparents, and siblings farewell—once again—and headed up to the majestic Adirondack Mountain "north country", back to the Saranac Lake/Lake Placid area where he had resided briefly before—then as a notorious drug dealer, but now, to open a spiritual oneness study center. (This concluded his transformational first five-year period of the 70's; the next five years, and really the next decades, would serve to deepen his knowledge, awakening or "awokening" transformation and application of everything learned to be used in service to community and humanity.)

Some of the basic principles Rich learned from the Bahai Faith (and later taught to thousands around this country and overseas), some of which he had learned from his previous religious and spiritual studies but were now confirmed in this newest and most modern world religion, include:

1. The independent search after truth, unfettered by superstition or tradition;
2. The oneness of the entire human race, the pivotal principle and fundamental doctrine of the Faith;
3. The equality of men and women, the two wings on which the bird of humankind is able to soar;
4. The basic unity of all religions;
5. The condemnation of all forms of prejudice, whether religious, racial, class or national;
6. The harmony which must exist between religion and science;
7. The abolition of the extremes of wealth and poverty;
8. The glorification of justice as the ruling principle in human society, and the institution of a world tribunal for the adjudication of disputes between nations;
9. The establishment of a permanent and universal peace as the supreme goal of all humankind.

He also learned about the progressive advancement of civilization, just as the human goes through various stages of progressive development, from the fetus to infancy, to toddler, to childhood, to adolescence, to adulthood, so has humanity developed from the single cell of the individual to the family, to the tribe, to the nation state, to the nation, and now to the one world neighborhood. And we are now entering the stage of the adulthood of humanity (with all the accompanying turmoil of transitioning from adolescence), which is characterized by oneness and one world unity. (Anyone, or any group, or any nation, who is against these progressive characteristics of universal oneness, or "wokefulness," is still stuck in relative adolescence, or worse, childhood. And all the previous religions, philosophies, prophecies, and scientific discoveries have prepared us for this transition and this glorious day.)

Episode Ten: The North Country

What is referred to as the "North Country" is in upstate New York, above the state capitol, Albany, and extending to the Canadian border. This region is as rural and "country" as is any other region of America, with very little diversity—mostly white. Some people born there had never traveled to the next town thirty miles away, or had never seen a Black person, except on television.

So, to bring a new religion, and especially one which emphasizes unity in diversity and promotes not only interracial amity but interracial marriage and many other progressive ideas, was a real challenge, but one Rich was up for. (One of his mottos has always been: *"Will the people who say it can't be done please get out of the way of the people doing it."* And another: *"Whether you say you can or can't, you are right."* Of course, it helps when you have both self-esteem plus faith in a higher power which guides you. And that higher power, or the God of your understanding, doesn't have to be a religious one—it can simply be a support group, or nature, or anything beyond you. Rich liked the Bahai concept of God, described as *"an unknown essence"*, the Star Wars movie concept, *"the force be with you.,"* and the AA/NA concept, *"the God of your understanding."*)

Upon arrival in Saranac Lake, Rich landed a hotel job as a desk clerk/night auditor on the graveyard shift—the person who both checks in latecomers and balances the day's books. That position would serve to sustain him many times, in his future travels, as there were almost always night audit openings in motels or hotels, and sometimes they provided both lodging (or an opportunity to get some sleep on the job overnight) and meals, as well as a modest salary. So initially, instead of renting a room or apartment, Rich rented a small storefront shop on Main Street (for $75/month, or about $400 in todays' dollars--but still a great bargain) and converted it into a combination walk-in/call-in Crisis Center and Bahai Spiritual Center. He couldn't afford a phone so he had a payphone installed which could receive calls for free. This caused quite a stir in this small town---a long-haired hippie opening up a strange center. The police thought it was a front for selling drugs, but one by one townspeople trickled in to check it out, including pastors, off-duty police, business owners, organization leaders. Some, though wary, welcomed it as a good and needed community service.

Then Rich became somewhat of a small-town celebrity and hero in the local newspaper as one night the hotel was held up by masked robbers and Rich tricked them out of getting into the safe, so they only made off with a few dollars from the register. They were dubbed the "gentlemen bandits" since one of the thieves emptied Rich's pockets of the few dollars he had, but their ringleader told him to put it back. (Of course, this made the police become suspicious that it was an inside job which Rich was involved in.)

Now everyone in town had something to talk with Rich about so he and his center's acceptance and popularity grew quickly. This inspired him to open similar centers in other small towns with the help of volunteers and Bahai friends he trained. The local community college gave him life and experience credits leading to an Associate Degree in Community Mental Health for the work he was doing in both the community and on campus. They also allowed him to teach an adult education class in Comparative Religions since he was knowledgeable in and often a public speaker on that subject due to his extensive search and study of all religions and spiritual paths.

Sometimes fundamentalist and fanatic Christians (who really are not Christian at all, based on how Christ acted and what he taught) would come into the Center to tell him he was going to hell because he didn't follow their version of Christianity, which was blasphemy to them. Rather than get into arguments with them he learned to gently interrupt their tirade and say, "*Excuse me, but please don't use your interpretation of your religion to tell me what you really want to say, and that is, that you think you are better than me.*" That usually shut them up. The sincere ones, who didn't realize they were sounding holier than thou, stopped, apologized and then were open for a mutual dialogue on the scriptures rather than spewing diatribes, while the others realized that they were caught and sped out of the Center never to return, but likely cursing and consigning Rich to the devil under their breaths. *They were* **EQualized!**

There were only a few people of color in the whole town and region, and each of them found their way to Rich and the Bahai/Help Centers, attracted there because of the Bahai teachings of oneness elevating all cultures and religions to equality and emphasizing the unique but interrelated contributions of each to enable humankind to *"carry forward an ever advancing civilization."*[17] One of these new friends was Glory, a Black female prison guard at Dannemora State Prison. She arranged for Rich to become the NAACP representative for the prison, enabling him to meet with prisoners of color to hear their grievances and needs. (That was when he was introduced to the whole mass incarceration/prison industrial complex and culture for the first time, firsthand, later to learn that it was a continuation of slavery which was abolished in the 13th Amendment except as a punishment for a crime. So, slavery was continued, and still is, with a new name.[18])

Another new friend was Muna, from Nigeria, who taught Rich about his experiences in the Nigerian civil war, and his country's history, along with the rest of West Africa's---stories of European colonizers who set tribe against

---

[17] From the Bahai Scripture book "Gleanings from the Writings of Baha'u"llah" https://reference.bahai.org/en/t/b/GWB/gwb-109.html

[18] So, to reinstate slavery, particularly in the southern states, they criminalized Blacks and other people of color and made almost anything they did a crime; to learn how slavery was never really abolished see the movies "13th" by Ava DuVernay and "Slavery by Another Name" (book and movie), by Douglas A. Blackmon.

tribe and community against community to divide and conquer. He was a general in the Nigerian civil war, on the losing side, and fled the country with his mother and sister escaping to France when his father was murdered in that conflict.

Another new friend was Kara, a single mother of three who had lived in spiritual communes. She became enamored of the Bahai teachings, and of Rich. They dated and were soon married. Kara, who was always attracted to Native American culture, suggested that they relocate to the nearby Akwe-sasne (Mohawk) Indian reservation to serve the Native Americans who were experiencing difficulties with alcohol and drugs there, and to share our Faith's teachings of oneness with them (since there were many prophecies in the Bahai scriptures regarding the spiritual leadership which the Indigenous peoples were destined to resume.)

Before they moved, Rich's parents came to visit him and his Center, and were proud of what he had become even though he was not a carbon copy of them or what they had envisioned. (This was an important reconciliation for Rich, which lasted for the remainder of their lives together—and eventually they learned from and rubbed off on each other, as Rich became a bit more conservative as a family man, and his parents a bit more liberal, overcoming their biases. **We were EQualized!**)

Episode Eleven: Warriors of the Rainbow/Native American Journey

While living in the mountain communities, Rich had become a student and friend of the Faddens, historians of the Iroquois nation and curators of their Six Nations Iroquois Cultural Center, where Rich was a frequent visitor. There he learned many things including the true history of the initial founding of America, especially in relation to the Indigenous original inhabitants and many facts regarding their culture, none of which are taught in schools.

For example, he learned that the Iroquois had one of the world's first democracies (long before the Greeks), and one of the first confederations, of six nations, which was also matriarchal in nature. They also had their own religion and culture, both of which were more advanced than those of the European settlers in many ways. One of the artifacts in the museum attesting to this is a document which British spies sent to the King in England indicating that these "Indians" elect their own leaders and, if they are not serving the people adequately, they can be removed from office. It then warned that this is dangerous as the colonial settlers are getting ideas from the "Indians" about freedom from British and monarchial rule. *They were* **EQualized!**

Rich also witnessed how the Native peoples communicated directly with wild animals, including bears. When hunters would come from the city to kill wildlife for sport, Ray, the elder Fadden, would try to protect the animals by tracking the hunters and offering for them to hunt each other and leave the animals alone. That would scare the hunters sufficiently to make them dash to their vehicles and high tail out of that area. *They were* **EQualized!**

Though Rich still had some of his ingrained white arrogance and superiority complex, the Faddens saw a sincerity in him and willingness to learn, so they overlooked his "paleface" shortcomings and taught him. And when he moved to the nearby Reservation, which they didn't think was a smart move due to the turmoil there, they had his back and were a source of constant support.

Rich and his brand new, ready-made family of five, were blessed to find a farmhouse (complete with barn and acres of farmland) to rent, right on the border of the Reservation. Soon after arrival, he learned that they-- he and his family-- were not welcome there and were to be treated with suspicion. Another white man speaking with forked tongue to "help" the Indians and also teach them a new religion--that's all they needed after being abused, tortured, raped, and murdered by white men preaching religion for centuries. So, Rich realized he would have to work hard to earn their trust, mainly by listening and learning at first.

Another thing he noticed immediately was how divided they were---the Reservation was cut in half by the U.S./Canadian border, with Reservation land on both sides. Each of those halves were further divided into two counties on the American side and two provinces on the Canadian side. Then there were the Catholics, the Protestants, and the traditional Iroquois religions---all competing for the allegiance of the native population. So here come the Bahais trying to unite them all.

Also, it is important to note that this tribe—really nation—the Mohawks (or Akwesasne people, in their language) were not a docile or passive people but very rugged and aggressive. They are the steelworkers who built many of the skyscrapers in New York, Canada and beyond, fearlessly walking the beams high in the sky without any rope harnesses. So, the more militant among them got together and decided that they didn't want any more outside interference, and, to send that message, they set Rich's barn on fire to scare him away, not aware that one of their own Chiefs had asked and received Rich's permission to store his farm's hay in that very barn only a couple of days earlier. (Karma is real, and they were *EQualized!*)

After this, and similar incidents, Bahai friends from around the country, including other Native Americans, came to visit, protect, and support Rich and his family. Eventually, Rich and the Bahais were accepted, even by the most militant Mohawks, because their sincerity was recognized and the fact that the Bahai teachings both praise and highly value Native American cultures and religions, which should not be abandoned or suppressed in any way. In fact, Bahai was only adding, not subtracting---much different than the Christian missionaries from the beginning of America who beat, tortured, and sometimes murdered Native Americans, including children, into submission and acceptance of their form of Christianity, not only centuries ago but in the 1900s. A Mohawk woman who befriended Rich and family showed them the scars on her back which the Catholic nuns inflicted on them when they attempted to speak their native language in schools. (So, who were the real savages? *They are* **EQualized!** The fact is that this country was founded and settled, and then sustained, through genocide, a fact not taught in schools.)

Once Rich and his family were accepted, they were able to help. Rich started NA (Narcotics Anonymous) and AA (Alcoholics Anonymous) groups to help with the addiction problems. And he started to build a foundation of oneness and unity among the different factions there. Above all, he went there to help and teach but also had one of the greatest learning and eye-opening experiences of his life. (One funny story: Some people in the North Country were afraid to attend N.A.—Narcotics Anonymous—meetings, because they believed the mafia, which they knew mostly from tv shows, controlled the drug trade and would come and shoot up the meeting to scare away participants. So, when I introduced myself as Rich Pellegrino from New York City—forgetting to omit my last name due to anonymity-- many jumped up and ran out of the room, fearing that I, an Italian from NYC, was sent by the mafia.)

Due to his successful experience on the Mohawk Reservation, the Bahais asked Rich to go on the road to other Native reservations around the country to bring the same message of oneness and unity there, and to help fulfill the prophecies regarding the Native nations and tribes uniting. So he gathered some young Native Americans and one Asian youth, and they formed a musical and performance group, "Warriors of the Rainbow" (named after and presenting skits from a book of the same name about the end-times prophecies when all of the tribes and nations would unite) [19] They traveled around the country in Rich's old, three-speed, Dodge Valiant (whose gears sometimes got stuck when stopped at a traffic light, and he would have to pop the hood, jump out, and unstick them), performing on Cherokee, Seminole, Iroquois, Choctaw, and other Native reservations.

During this journey, Rich learned and experienced more about the true history of the founding of this country, and how many of the early presidents and "Founding Fathers" were not only slave owners but purveyors of mass genocide of the Native Americans. One example of this was Andrew Jackson, who was not only an elite plantation slave owner against abolition but who brutally removed Native Americans from their ancestral homelands and forcefully marched them to Indian Territory (now Oklahoma), known as

---

[19] https://en.wikipedia.org/wiki/Legend_of_the_Rainbow_Warriors

"The Trail of Tears"[20], during which thousands died. Rich and his band of "Warriors of the Rainbow" traversed that trail beginning on the Cherokee Reservation in the mountains of North Carolina and culminating in Oklahoma, performing along the way, and participating in the dedication ceremony of a statue of famous Cherokee leader Sequoia, carved from a single California Sequoia Redwood tree, in Tahlequah, Oklahoma.

Rich and his band learned that the early history of this country was replete with an ongoing series of murderous treachery, broken treaties and lies toward the Native Americans. (He has also learned that, even in this day, centuries later, they are treated similarly, without ever receiving due compensation and reparations for these travesties. America will never reach its true destiny of oneness until that is fully acknowledged and remedied. It is a Bahai teaching and belief that the indigenous people of every land have a special role as spiritual leaders of the coming new world order, based on oneness, justice, and equity. Rich is a collector and wearer of t-shirts with slogans and one of his favorites pictures a Native American woman with the caption: "No One is Illegal on Stolen Land." Another one pictures a few Native American chiefs with the caption: "The True Founding Fathers.")

This trip and Rich's time on the Akwesasne Mohawk Reservation, which lasted only a year, was one of the highlights and most profound educational experiences of his life. He learned from the Native Americans a profound respect and reverence for all life forms, which their prophets and spiritual leaders taught them, and which formed the basis of their religion. (This was deliberately misunderstood and twisted by the Christian missionaries, who labeled the natives as heathens who worshiped nature, the moon, the stars, when theirs was a religion of thankfulness—giving thanks to their Creator, Great Spirit for all those gifts. The missionaries, who suffered from delusional white and Christian supremacy and who obviously knew nothing about their own religion or Christ—just like the "Christian right" today, said they must be converted or killed. In a museum Rich saw Bibles bound with baby Indian's skin. Who were the savages? ***They are EQualized.***)

Upon returning from his travels, Rich's fledgling marriage did not survive all the turmoil on the Reservation, combined with his lack of attentiveness to his new family. Kara took her kids and ran off. Rich decided to leave the Reservation as well, and moved to Plattsburgh, New York, on the borders of

---

[20] "The **Trail of Tears** was a series of forced displacements of approximately 60,000 American Indians of the "Five Civilized Tribes" between 1830 and 1850 by the United States government. Part of the Indian removal, the ethnic cleansing was gradual, occurring over a period of nearly two decades…The relocated peoples suffered from exposure, disease, and starvation while en- route to their newly designated Indian reserve. Thousands died from disease before reaching their destinations or shortly after. According to Native American activist Suzan Shown Harjo of the Smithsonian's National Museum of the American Indian, the event constituted a genocide," https://en.wikipedia.org/wiki/Trail_of_Tears

Canada and Vermont, to attend the State University of NY (SUNY) and finish his bachelor's degree. While there, he visited both Montreal and Vermont often, finding both beautiful and unique in their own ways. Montreal was a very international city, much like European cities. He attended a Bahai meeting there attended by fifty people who were from forty different countries. And after being used to the very dirty U.S. subways and train stations, he witnessed in Montreal almost spotless trains and stations, with the latter decorated like museums with paintings and artifacts, seldom vandalized and with no graffiti. (He had witnessed the same in Paris during his earlier European travels.) And he would take the ferry across Lake Champlain (site of the legendary Champy monster) to the beautiful mountains of Vermont, where he had skied in his high school years.

But Rich's stay and studies in Plattsburgh were cut short when he was invited to a Bahai conference in Greenwood, South Carolina. While attending, he met and fell for a Black southern belle, Ginger, who had a young son and was studying at Tuskegee University. He had always wanted to move to the American South to learn about the Black culture in the aftermath of Jim Crow, recently, and slavery and reconstruction in the past. Also, the Bahai teachings of oneness, justice and racial solidarity were spreading like wildfire in the Black townships there. He also found there, just as in South Africa, a system of American apartheid with the remnants of Jim Crow and the plantation mentality still widespread.

The people of color in the South were ready for oneness, equality, and equity. American hero Dr. Martin Luther King Jr (MLK) had prepared them but was cut down before he could fulfill his total mission which was to bring economic empowerment to lift the masses out of poverty, and end war and violence, not just for Black people but for all peoples. (Most know about his civil rights victories however he stated, and Rich believed, that the "Triple Evils" holding us back from "the beloved community" are "Racism, Poverty, and Militarism".[21])

Also, Rich wanted an interracial family since that was encouraged by the Bahai teachings and it made sense as one sure way to bring the so-called races together. ("So-called" because the whole concept of the different races was an economic and social construct, with no basis in science, invented by Europeans to justify the colonization of Africa and enslavement of Africans. Thus, the whole idea of "Black and White" was a European elitist invention which was adopted by the elitist American founding fathers for their economic benefit. This also had the residual effect of robbing Europeans of their distinctive cultures—Irish, Italian, Spanish, French, etc.—by lumping them

---

[21] "The Triple Evils of POVERTY, RACISM and MILITARISM are forms of violence that exist in a vicious cycle. They are interrelated, all-inclusive, and stand as barriers to our living in the Beloved Community. When we work to remedy one evil, we affect all evils." –The King Center on the MLK Philosophy of Non-Violence https://thekingcenter.org/about-tkc/the-king-philosophy/

all together as "White" Americans.)[22] ***They have been EQualized.***

70's Musical Soundtrack

While there were many musical artists who provided the "woke" soundtrack for the 70's, some of the standouts include: Elton John; Bee Gees; Fleetwood Mac; David Bowie, Led Zeppelin; Pink Floyd; Eagles; Gladys Knight & Pips: Three Dog Night; The Fifth Dimension; Stylistics.

---

[22] Read the book "How to Be an Antiracist" by Ibram X. Kendi, especially in Chapter 3, where he writes: *"THE FIRST GLOBAL power to construct race* happened to be the first racist power and the first exclusive slave trader of the constructed race of African people. The individual who orchestrated this trading of an *invented people was nicknamed the "Navigator," though he did not leave Portugal in the fifteenth century. The only thing he navigated was Europe's political-economic seas, to create the first transatlantic slave-trading policies."*

4 **EXCELLENCE & EXIT 80's**

From Wikipedia: "The decade, known as the Excellence Eighties and the Moderation Decade, saw a dominance of conservatism and free market economics, and a socioeconomic change due to advances in technology and a worldwide move away from planned economies and towards laissez-faire capitalism compared to the 1970s. As economics and politics shifted to the right, multi-national companies moved into countries around the world, exploiting the masses on a global scale never seen before, giving rise to economic globalization." "The AIDS epidemic became recognized in the 1980s and has since killed an estimated 39 million people (as of 2013).Global warming became well known to the scientific and political community in the 1980s." "Developing countries across the world faced economic and social difficulties as they suffered from multiple debt crises in the 1980s, requiring many of these countries to apply for financial assistance from the International Monetary Fund (IMF) and the World Bank" (which was a continuation of economic colonialism and even slavery, as the U.S. and Europe control those institutions and therefore control the economies of those countries borrowing from them.[23]) The "cold war" between the US. And Russia wound down with the dissolution of the Soviet Union (U.S.S.R.), as Russia granted independence to many of the member countries."

At home, Ronald Reagan was elected president in 1981, and started "The Reagan Revolution" which rolled back most of the progressive strides of the previous two decades. (As Ibram X. Kendi wrote in *"How to Become an Anti-racist"*: *"The Reagan Revolution was just that: a radical revolution for the benefit of the already powerful. It further enriched high-income Americans by cutting their taxes and*

---

[23] For a full discussion of this continued economic slavery a must read is the book *"The Sovereign Psyche: Systems of Chattel Freedom Vs. Self-Authentic Freedom"* by Ezrah Aharone , who writes:*" The Sovereign Psyche is not just the title of the book. More importantly The Sovereign Psyche is the motivating consciousness, intellect, and will-power that is necessary to materialize what the book defines as "Self-Authentic Freedom" as opposed to "Chattel Freedom." Chattel freedom is when the value of a people is predicated upon the extent to which they serve the interests and institutions of others." http://ezrahspeaks.com/current-books/*

government regulations, installing a Christmas-tree military budget, and arresting the power of unions. Seventy percent of middle-income Blacks said they saw "a great deal of racial discrimination" in 1979, before Reagan revolutionaries rolled back enforcement of civil-rights laws and affirmative-action regulations, before they rolled back funding to state and local governments whose contracts and jobs had become safe avenues into the single-family urban home of the Black middle class. In the same month that Reagan announced his war on drugs… in 1982, he cut the safety net of federal welfare programs and Medicaid, sending more low-income Blacks into poverty. His "stronger law enforcement" sent more Black people into the clutches of violent cops, who killed twenty-two Black people for every White person in the early 1980s. Black youth were four times more likely to be unemployed in 1985 than in 1954. But few connected the increase in unemployment to the increase in violent crime. Americans have long been trained to see the deficiencies of people rather than policy. It's an easy mistake to make: People are in our faces. Policies are distant. We are particularly poor at seeing the policies lurking behind the struggles of people."[24]

And so began the explosion of the war on drugs (which has always really been a war on people of color and the poor), the *"New Jim Crow"*[25] of mass incarceration, and the re-institution of slavery (since the 13th amendment didn't abolish slavery as punishment for a crime).[26]

Episode One: A Yankee Goes South to Tuskegee

During the nation's conservative "Reagan Revolution" (which we have never really recovered from), and his own personal recovery and spiritual path, Rich packed up and moved south to Tuskegee, Alabama. Located there is one of the most famous Black universities, founded by Dr. Booker T. Washington and attended, at the time, by Lionel Ritchie—who was born and reared there---and his band, The Commodores. This was the immersion in the American Black culture which Rich had sought, and he was often one of the only white men walking the campus and attending events there. One of those memorable events was a speech by Nikki Giovanni Jr., a Black American poet, writer, commentator, activist, and educator, who was invited to speak there in the aftermath of the Reagan election as the Black community was extremely worried and complaining about what that would mean for them, their families, and the poor of all backgrounds. She opened her speech by saying: *"Well, Reagan has been elected President,"* and then paused while the crowd booed, and then she stunned everyone by saying, *"And I am glad!"* Everyone's jaws dropped in surprise, they looked at each other in disbelief, and then she continued, *"I'm glad because it will teach you, us, my people, not to*

---

[24] Read the full text in Chapter Two: Dueling Consciousness, in "How To Be An Antiracist" by Ibram X. Kendi

[25] Title of the book by Michelle Alexander: ***The New Jim Crow: Mass Incarceration in the Age of Colorblindness*** *https://en.wikipedia.org/wiki/The_New_Jim_Crow*

[26] See the movie by Ava DuVernay "13th " https://en.wikipedia.org/wiki/13th_(film)

depend on the white man and his government and his institutions because they have always failed us. It is time for us to unite and do for ourselves." And then everyone understood and shook their heads in affirmation.[27]

Rich and Ginger, as an interracial couple, traveled throughout the deep South—Carolinas, Georgia, Alabama, Mississippi-- teaching the Bahai principles of oneness, racial unity, justice, and equality, and enduring many instances of racism, including sometimes refusing to be served by stores and restaurants, repeated stops and harassment by racist and corrupt sheriffs and other law enforcement, and threats of violence. The Bahais were the first faith community to have interracial meetings in the South, and sometimes they were disrupted by the KKK and/or law enforcement. Rich and Ginger were present when this happened and were taught by the Bahais to respond non-violently, which helped diffuse the situations. When white Bahais visited the Black townships in the rural South, the local police would stop and detain them for some trumped up charges, like a broken taillight, so that they would miss their meetings. So, to not be detected as white, they began blackening their faces with make-up so that while driving and from a distance they looked Black, which Rich did at times as well. ***They were EQualized.*** When Rich and Ginger, and other Bahais, visited people in their homes and left Bahai literature, the police would go to the same houses telling the people not to listen to them, that they were troublemakers and would get them in trouble, and then confiscated the literature they had given them. (This is in the eighties, post-Jim Crow, and not in some far distant past.)

Episode Two: Albany, Georgia

The small city of Albany in southwest Georgia was an epicenter of the Southern "story" and civil rights history, and another turning point for Rich. He and Ginger had difficulty getting her parents' consent to marry (required in the Bahai community, for the purpose of unity in the family), so in Albany, where her father resided, they decided to put their relationship on hold for a while, separate, and work on her parents from a distance. But, before that, they were invited to attend a church service in a church with one of the few mixed congregations they had encountered. After the service, as the white pastor was greeting the guest attendees as they left the church, he took Rich and Ginger aside and in the nicest manner possible, said, *"Thank you for coming however if it were not against the law of the land I would have taken out my shotgun and shot both of you because interracial relationships are an abomination and blasphemy against the law of God."* Rich and Ginger were shocked but not surprised, as they had

[27] Read the book "Sovereign Psyche: Systems of Chattel Freedom vs. Self-Authentic Freedom" by Ezrah Aharone, to understand how to achieve this sovereign and independent state of mind, and then strive for interdependence, skipping dependence.

found many so-called Christians to be among the most racist folks---and Dr. King had said that Sunday mornings were the most segregated times in America. (This church had decided Blacks and Whites could mix in the same building for the service, sitting separately of course, and everything would be rosy if the Blacks just stayed in their place. Poor Jesus, to have these people bear his name, just like the so-called "Christian-right" today—major hypocrites! *They are EQualized!*)

Ginger's father and his family wanted to rent a nice house they saw advertised for rent on a big yard sign in a slightly upscale Albany neighborhood. When they called the number, the realtor told them that it was still available and invited them to her office downtown to put in an application. They went straight there however once she saw them the house was suddenly off the market. This sounded fishy to Rich and Ginger so Rich went to the office and said he was interested in the same house, and, confirming their suspicion, it was magically still on the market for a white man. Rich told the realtor that he was going to rent it for his extended family, who were outside in the car. He summoned them to the office and when the realtor saw who they were she knew she had been caught red-handed in racial discrimination, and she turned red in both embarrassment and anger. *She was EQualized* ! Rich explained to her that they are Bahais and believe in forgiveness, self-correction, and reconciliation, so they would not report her to the state board to jeopardize her realtor's license if she would rent the house to Ginger's family, which she readily did--and they enjoyed many years in that home. (Rich enjoyed that experience so much that in later years he became a HUD Fair Housing undercover investigator in Georgia, having many similar experiences and *EQualizing* some discriminatory leasing companies.)

Ginger went back to Tuskegee and since Rich had no concrete plans anywhere else, decided to stay in Albany for a while and took a job at the local Job Corps Center as a Counselor (which was his first paid counseling job since getting his degree, as he had continued to work at hotels and motels everywhere while moving around the South.) He rented a room in a downtown hotel and one night as he was just out for a joy walk downtown after hours when everything was closed, he noticed people going in and out of one storefront, which had its windows painted dark so no one could see inside. He walked up to one person who was about to enter the mystery storefront and asked him what it was all about. The gentleman explained, and Rich was shocked to learn, that it was a crisis center and suicide help-line—the same type of store-front center which he had opened and operated in upstate New York. Rich tried to enter but the gentleman, a volunteer, said only volunteers were allowed inside as they did not take walk-ins. As Rich was enthusiastically explaining his background and experience with these types of centers, another volunteer—an older gentleman, overheard some of what he was saying and invited Rich in to sit with him on his shift to see if he would like to sign up to volunteer since he was already so experienced. Rich eagerly accepted both invitations, and the older gentleman, Bob, and he spent the whole night there together, discovering that they had a lot in common and becoming fast friends. Bob, twice Rich's age, was an Italian American from New York, just like Rich, and he now resided with his wife and teenage children in south Florida. His work as an industrial engineer brought him to Albany periodically and since he had his evenings free, and no friends or family there, he spent his free time volunteering at the crisis center. He told Rich that he was also attending special classes some evenings at the courthouse preparing to be an Emotional Maturity Instructor for those arrested and awaiting pre-trial who could opt to enroll in an EMI (Emotional Maturity Instruction)[28] class as an alternative sentence. This intrigued Rich as he had come to believe in "restorative justice" as opposed to the norm of "punitive justice," and EMI sounded like a great alternative to more punitive sentencing. Bob further explained that the source of the EMI curriculum was the most recent Aramaic translation of the Bible New Testament (gleaned from recently translated scrolls discovered by archeologists in the Holy Land)[29] In other words, it contained what Christ really said and taught, in his own language and context, and was alleged to be more accurate than Greek translations. This knowledge was combined with ground-breaking scientific, neurological research on how we form and maintain our emotions and spiritual values to produce EMI.

It was amazing to Rich that in this small, Bible-belt, Southern city, such an amazing and progressive strategy was launched and being used to both punish and prevent crime, but he was becoming used to such strange and small miracles guiding his path and learning. Rich said eagerly to Bob, "Sign me up for that class and training". (That course, EMI, would be a significant milestone in Rich's evolution and preparation for his role as the *"Woke EQualizer"* as it further and exponentially opened his eyes to the brainwashing of the American people, by both corrupt government and corrupted religion—how they did in the past and continue to do so today.) So, Rich took the EMI course, and it was the most profoundly transforming course he took in his life (and still is). While in Albany, he taught the course to pre-trial detainees and witnessed how it helped transform their thinking and lives. He learned that everywhere it was being taught---in Georgia, the Carolinas, Florida-- crime, alcoholism and drug abuse were decreasing—it was working! And then, suddenly, funding and support for it by the local, state, and federal politicians ended (as it was cutting into their profits and plans.) Rich later learned that whenever and wherever programs like EMI worked, they were somehow sabotaged by those in office---Chicago, Philadelphia, New York,

---

[28] For more about EMI (Emotional Maturity Instruction). from the US Dept of Justice website: https://www.ojp.gov/ncjrs/virtual-library/abstracts/emi-emotional-maturity-instruction-new-approach-social-education
[29] For more on the Aramaic scrolls and Bible: https://en.wikipedia.org/wiki/Khaboris_Codex

Los Angeles. Why? Crime pays—it pays the police departments, the prison-industrial complex, the white collar, organized crime drug and gun dealers (which includes many politicians) and provides free, slave labor for the corporations. So, it is a disincentive for them to reduce crime; especially when the victims of it are people of color.

What were some of Rich's takeaways from EMI? It confirmed that how Christ taught and lived was not how so-called Christianity, which Rich called "Churchianity," in the West is taught and lived. Jesus' teachings were non-judgmental, forgiving, loving, welcoming. There was no "fire and brimstone" or hell-fire damnation, and even sin was just an archery term which meant missing the mark—no burden to carry, when you err you simply try and try again until you get it right. In fact, most or all his teachings were parables, analogies, symbolic—not to be taken literally, which is the opposite of the Christian fundamentalism taught and practiced in many churches today. (Fundamentalism, in every religion, is a violent distortion of the spiritual truths contained in that faith, and often fundamentalist fanatics justify violence toward those whom they consider non-believers, which is why these false religions have been the cause of more wars than anything else, and have been used to fuel colonialism, slavery and other forms of oppression.) Rich had learned these spiritual truths from his past studies of religions and spiritual paths but now these learnings were confirmed in Christ's own words and actions, in his language and culture. He also learned from EMI's research into how we learn, and how the human mind can be conditioned and brainwashed, that Americans are among the most brainwashed people in the world, and, as prisoners of war in the world wars, were the weakest and easiest to crack and reveal military secrets, among all other captors, according to independent research.

With the demise of EMI, Rich decided to leave Albany (however he would carry the EMI materials to use in other places and settings for years). When Bob heard that Rich was leaving, he invited him to his home in South Florida to see if he would like to relocate to that area and manage a new fast-food franchise which Bob was purchasing there. It was an offer Rich couldn't refuse since his marriage and other plans were up in the air. So, he said good-bye to Albany and moved south to Florida, near West Palm Beach.

Before moving on from Albany though, it was nearly thirty years later that Rich would learn the true significance and history of that small southern city, where he had learned so much. It had many firsts and has been called the "birthplace of the civil rights movement" as the Albany Movement was among the first organized protests in the 1960s against racist Jim Crow laws and for the right of African Americans to vote. Martin Luther King Jr., Ralph Abernathy and many other civil rights leaders were among the organizers and were jailed more than once there. One of the country's first "Community Land Trusts" or land cooperatives was established by the Black community there, giving Black Americans over five thousand acres of land—the largest Black owned land tract in the country. This progress was fought by every government institution, as well as the KKK and other white supremacist terrorist groups, just as "Black Wall Street" in Tulsa, OK, and every other significant economic and social advancement which Black Americans achieved were sabotaged by the white establishment.[30] (It must be asked, if whites thought they were so superior, how come anytime and every time Blacks start to get ahead, building family, community and business according to the very principles of the so-called "American dream"---opportunity, personal responsibility, liberty, and family values—that white folks organize to try and sabotage that progress, sometimes violently, not only in the past but today as well. They also try every tactic to try and suppress the Black vote--which people died to achieve and protect. There are thousands of examples of this in both past and modern history. Do white people really suffer from such an inferiority complex—which we know is the basis of all superiority complexes-- that they cannot compete, or cooperate, on a level playing field? White folks suffer from mass mental health and identity issues, which have never been adequately addressed due to denial and delusional white supremacy issues. *They are EQualized!*)

Episode Three: Exit the U.S. and Enter a Whole New World of Fulfillment

While visiting Bob in South Florida and scoping out the area's opportunities, including Bob's generous offer, Rich attended a Bahai gathering in which the presenters, from British Guyana in South America and St. Lucia in the West Indies, were recruiting "pioneers" (the Bahai term for missionaries) to come to their countries to help spread the Bahai teachings of oneness. (The Bahai Faith has no professional or paid clergy, or missionaries, as everyone can investigate and discern truth for themselves in this age of the maturation of humanity, and everyone can be a minister or teacher who can teach and learn from each other. They believe that no longer, in this era of the maturing of humanity, is there a need for one person to lead or pastor a flock, and for others to blindly follow. So, in that spirit, Bahai "pioneers" must be self-supporting and bring value to wherever they go, rather than extracting it from the people they serve, and must live among the people they are teaching and serving and endure the struggles which they are suffering. *They are EQualized.*) This appeal caught Rich's interest as most of his previous travels overseas, including in the Caribbean, were as a tourist. But to live in another country among the grassroots people was another enticing prospect.

---

[30] For more on the Albany Movement, and its revival today in the "New Communities" initiative, read https://cltroots.org/the-guide/early-hybrids-breeding-and-seeding-the-clt-model/georgia-seedbed and https://www.newcommunitiesinc.com/

So, he consulted with Bob, and Ginger (since they were still hoping to reconnect), and both told him to go for it. Bob thought that he should go for an exploratory trip and get it out of his system, because he believed that when Rich experienced the realities of the poor "third world" countries he would come running back to "exceptional" America, and Ginger said, *"If we are still meant to be, we will be."*

So, in early 1982, Rich set out on an exploratory trip to St. Lucia, part of the Windward chain of islands in the Eastern Caribbean, formerly a colony of both England and France but independent since 1979. It was a longshot for Rich to be able to stay there long-term because typically one would need either a professional skill and advanced degree which the country was in short supply of, or money to invest in a business with a local partner—neither of which Rich had. But he put his faith in his higher power and the Universe with the knowledge that if it was meant to be the path and means would be provided. (This is one of the secrets of the "power of attraction" he was unknowingly practicing at the time, and which had guided him throughout his life's changes. He would later learn more about this power from the book and movie *"The Secret."* In that movie, author Jack Canfield states *"Life is like driving in the dark. Your headlights show you the two hundred feet in front of you and as you move forward, the next two hundred feet are shown to you. You don't need to see the entire path to reach your destination. In other words, you don't necessarily have to see how to get to your end goal, you just need to decide what you want and take the step that is directly in front of you. The next steps will be revealed to you as you go."* [31])

Rich immediately fell in love with the people, culture, and terrain of St. Lucia. It was like a whole new world opening up to him, a different reality. He had traveled throughout Europe before, but this was a totally different culture, composed almost entirely of Black African and indigenous peoples, with some mixture of European and East Indian/Asian-- very exotic, and diverse. (And no, he wasn't another lost Italian claiming to discover anything ☺ except himself and the fact that another whole world exists outside of America and Europe, and its propaganda of exceptionalism and superiority.) This island, like the others in the Windward chain, was among those least visited by tourists though it has a pair of dramatically tapered mountains, the Pitons, on its West Coast, and its entire coast is home to volcanic beaches, reef-diving sites, and fishing villages. Trails in the interior rainforest led to waterfalls like the 15-mile high Toraille, which pours over a cliff into a garden. Soufrière, the former capitol town, is located within the immediate vicinity of the dormant Qualibou volcano, which you can drive through, and the area is geothermally active, with numerous hot Sulphur springs. The people opened their arms and hearts to Rich, partly due to his white and American unearned privilege, but it became quickly apparent to Rich that the St. Lucian

---

[31] From the book and movie by Rhonda Byrne *"The Secret"* : *https://www.thesecret.tv/*

people genuinely appreciated people, and each other, over material things.

One thing he also immediately noticed was that the Eastern Caribbean (EC) currency dollar was worth about one third of the U.S. dollar, rendering Rich's money triple in value there. Since he had dealt with currency differences and exchanges in Europe, he wondered who had devalued the EC dollar to make life more of a struggle for St. Lucians than Americans---certainly, their value as humans was not one third of Americans. (He then quickly understood the Bahai teaching of the need for one universal currency; if we really believe in the oneness of humanity, then that's a no-brainer. Later he would learn about the role of the World Bank and International Monetary Fund in controlling this and keeping poor countries poor--institutions controlled by the U.S. and Europe. Just as American institutions are designed to keep poor people poor and a permanent underclass in America, these international institutions do so worldwide—the "Triple Evils" in full play.)

Together with the local Bahais, Rich took a side trip to a Bahai conference and teaching project in the island nation of Grenada, known as the "Spice Island," located in the same Eastern Caribbean, Windward Island chain. There he met and befriended a man who would become his future father-in-law, Luther Thomas, who was visiting from St. Vincent & the Grenadines (SVG) and invited Rich to visit his island country too. Rich felt immediately at home in this "new world" of warm and welcoming souls who put people before things, and he wanted to stay. Back in St. Lucia, he found a potential St. Lucian business partner in the Bahai community there and they decided to open a West Indian/Italian restaurant together, which would enable Rich to live there since he would be investing in a 51% St. Lucian owned business. They put together a budget for the enterprise and Rich headed back to the States to raise the necessary funds in their goal timeline of three months. Back in Florida, he resided with his grandmother (who had recently returned to America from Italy) and worked three jobs, around the clock, catching bits of sleep, when possible, in order to save the money to reach his goal.

In the summer of 1982, having reached his monetary goal, Rich returned to St. Lucia with just a few personal belongings that he could fit into a small suitcase and a backpack. Since music had always played an important part in his life and journeys, and is a universal language, he also packed a few recorders (flute-like musical instruments).

Rich and his new St. Lucian business partner, Tim, started making plans to open their restaurant when some members of the St. Lucian Bahai community invited them to travel to the neighboring island-country, St. Vincent & the Grenadines (SVG), for a Bahai summer school camp on the beach there. Tim told Rich to go and they would reconvene upon his return, not knowing that Rich would not return until some months later, but for his honeymoon.

Rich and Ginger had about given up on getting consent to get married, so they gave each other their blessings to find other spouses, and Rich made it known to everyone that he was seeking a wife. When he traveled to St. Vincent and reconnected with Luther (whom he had met previously in Grenada and who had mentioned, at the time, that he had several daughters available for marriage), he met and married one of Luther's daughters, V, after a whirlwind courtship of only three months.

Rich and V spent their honeymoon in neighboring St. Lucia. He became a citizen of St. Vincent, through marriage, and then had dual citizenship (well on his way to becoming a "world citizen.") He and his new bride got right to work building a family with their first child, a daughter, born one year later, and second child, a son, born two years after that. They rented a small cottage in a seaside town. Rich quickly found that a whole new world of business and work opportunities opened up for him, as employers and business partners didn't care about "paper qualifications" as much as practical qualifications— asking only *"can you do it?"* Of course, he benefited from both white and American privilege because the attitude there at the time was if it comes from America, it must be good. (This is no longer the case in most countries because Americans abused that privilege so often, producing the "ugly American" syndrome, and people worldwide are seeing through the American propaganda.) Rich was accepted by some local businessmen and friends as a partner into their business, and he opened a counseling practice, taught high school briefly, and served as a purchasing manager for one of the off-islands, Mustique, home of the rich and famous (and had movie stars and royalty in his office regularly). In these positions he would travel the entire island and fly around the Caribbean to nearby islands, often in small planes, sitting in the co-pilot's seat to learn the ropes. He also traveled the seas, between the islands, in boats of all sizes which were tossed like match boxes by the rough tides, often sitting at the controls near the captains, again, to learn (and to be comforted by their relative calmness when the seas were rough).

When Rich's small American dollar savings was exhausted and he had to live on the Eastern Caribbean (EC) wages he earned, which were significantly less than American wages, reality set in, and he became a "local." Learning to survive like all his new fellow countrymen, he worked several jobs simultaneously while V minded the kids. Even though they were "cash poor," there was always an abundance of food since it grew so readily.

Rich and V lived in St. Vincent for almost six years, in the eighties, having three children along with many adventures which could fill another book, and a lifetime of learning. One thing he learned there about the power of attraction and faith is that when you focus on what you want to achieve, rather than on what you don't want, you will likely attract what you want and fulfill your goals. However, before (or, at least, while) doing that you have to also learn about and love your holistic self---your body, mind, emotions, and spirit. And you can't be afraid of making mistakes; you must make mistakes to learn. (One of Rich's mentors, a motivational speaker and award-winning salesperson, J. Richard Hoff, used to say, *"If you aren't making mistakes then you aren't doing anything; you're already dead."*) Also, he learned there is a difference between striving for "excellence" rather than "perfection." In the former you make mistakes, learn from them, and keep trying until you get it right; in the latter, because you are human and no one is perfect, you make mistakes and try to hide them so people think you are progressing but you waste so much energy on being fake that you likely will not advance, or, if you do, it will be at a high cost and sacrifice of moral and human values. (That is the problem with America—it tries to be perfect, or "exceptional," projecting an image of perfection while hiding and denying its mistakes so it cannot learn from them and move on to fulfill its true destiny. This translates to a lack of true self-love and self-esteem, manifesting itself in violence towards itself and others and becoming the ultimate bully. Americans wonder why there is so much violence within its borders and towards each other. Frederick Douglass, the great American social reformer, abolitionist, orator, writer, and statesman, warned: *"The American people have this to learn: that where justice is denied, where poverty is enforced, where ignorance prevails, and where any one class is made to feel that society is an organized conspiracy to oppress, rob, and degrade them, neither person nor property is safe."*[32])

Episode Four: Goals Fulfilled

Rich had made many mistakes in his young life, some dangerous and near fatal, however somehow, through the grace of God or the Universe, he had learned from them, learning to know and love his true reality. Based upon that true reality he made goals which he felt were in alignment with the Universe and the universal Bahai principles helping to guide his quest for oneness and for personal and societal progress, through service to others. The fulfillment of his goals reached hyper-speed once he ventured out of his American bubble and comfort zone and was able to see the world in a whole new light. In just a couple of years and in his late twenties, while in St. Vincent, he was able to fulfill most of his long-term life goals:

--Married and had a family, especially an interracial one. (Not only did he marry a Black woman but she, like many West Indians, has East Indian, African, Amerindian, and European ancestry, rendering their children true world citizens with all the "races" represented.)

--Started and operated businesses, which provided value to both customers and staff rather than only extracting profits.

---

[32] For more on Frederick Douglass, the great American social reformer, abolitionist, orator, writer, and statesman, https://en.wikipedia.org/wiki/Frederick_Douglass

--Started and operated his own counseling practice, and related non-profit institutions, helping those with addictions and other maladies. (He became the only "psychologist" on the island, getting referrals from the only psychiatrist.)

--Became a world citizen, partly accomplished with his dual citizenship, obtaining a British commonwealth passport enabling easier travel worldwide

-- Learned the optimum civics lesson, as in these small countries he was to have easy access to all levels of government allowing him to influence positive changes, with less bureaucracy and "red-tape" than in America.

--Began teaching others what he had learned, and was still learning, both formally as a high school teacher and informally as a spiritual teacher, motivator, and author, through the written word, public forums, and tv and radio (as he had his own programs in St. Vincent, and this was before the internet and social media).

--Became a servant leader and advocate for the oppressed, as he was able to begin addressing injustices in his newly adopted country.

--Began learning many new skills, including how to be a minimalist and survive without running water, electricity, and other amenities, at times.

Most importantly, he was learning, once again, to see through the eyes of people from a completely different culture, just as he had learned before from the Native Americans and African Americans. Now the West Indians were teaching him, in a so-called "third world," lesser developed country, and he was also seeing America, with the West Indians' help and insights, from a whole new perspective. (You know the saying *"too close to the forest to see the trees;"* well, that is exactly what we Americans are, especially with all the false conditioning, propaganda, and mind control.)

Here are some of the lessons learned and Rich's take-aways from these lessons:

--He noticed how eager everyone he met in St. Vincent was to learn, and when engaged in such learning how focused and thoughtful they were. For example, he met Gregory, a self-taught refrigeration technician who, based on his reading and writing skills, would be considered functionally illiterate here. However, Gregory was a great thinker and philosopher (really a prophet because a philosopher visualizes and writes lofty thoughts and ideals but doesn't necessarily act upon them, while a prophet has both the vision and the action). Gregory, like many Vincentians, would sit and listen to the BBC world news and other programs aired over their radios, and then would have the deepest analytical conversations about what he heard. Rich remembers sitting under the mango tree with Gregory, and sometimes others, debating world news topics in more depth than he had ever done with Americans back home. (Gregory, like many less formally educated West Indians, appeared smarter about the world, even in his relative functional illiteracy, than most highly educated PhD's Rich was acquainted with back home. ***They are EQualized!)*** Even school-aged children had such a thirst for knowledge and books and Rich and V had such an extensive library of books that they had to make office hours for kids in the village to visit and check out books from their homemade library—otherwise they would've been inundated with kids 24/7. (Because of this thirst for learning, West Indian children who emigrate to the U.S. generally do better than American children in schools here, as do those from many other areas of the world. ***We are EQualized.***)

--The Vincentians' (people of SVG) eagerness to learn, study, and debate secular subjects was only matched or surpassed by their desire to do the same with religious, especially Biblical and Christian, subjects. St. Vincent was a so-called "Christian" country, though split by many major denominations and small churches. Before the proliferation of so many churches, many of which were imported from America or England, the people used to work together to help each other build homes and other cooperative endeavors, however religion or what is called "Churchianity" split them apart into different factions which then only assisted each other within their respective congregations. This was a pattern observed worldwide, including America. Wherever "Churchianity" spread it divided the people, and that is how they were kept in control. (So false religion was, and is, used to divide and control, while "true religion" unites and frees. Rich often used to say that "*true religion has selfless prophets and false religion has selfish profits.*")

In the evenings there were only two places to go in the St. Vincent towns---churches or rum shops. The few times Rich entered the rum shops he found patrons discussing and debating the Bible, over mugs of beer or rum. This was another great opportunity for Rich to teach and learn. He had studied all the world's religions and even taught a comparative religions course at a college previously and was there to help spread the Bahai message of oneness and unity. However, he was not as versed in the Bible as he felt he needed to be to converse intelligently with the Vincentians, so he undertook an intensive study of it, especially the New Testament, including all of the prophecies regarding the end days and awaited return of Christ. He also wrote tracts with his understanding of what certain principles and parables were illustrative of in the Bible teachings, partly based on the Aramaic scrolls which formed the basis of Emotional Maturity Instruction and were supposed to be the original teachings of Christ—much more loving and forgiving than some of the other harsher translations that most churches used. Rich's new friend Gregory, who had similar understandings of the Bible, joined him in setting out to share those with the people. This was a major threat to the pastors who feared losing control of their congregations to Rich's, Gregory's, and the Bahais' encouragement for people to think for

51

themselves, independently investigate these new perspectives, and decide for themselves the truths contained therein. Before, they were supposed to rely only on the pastor's interpretations of truths. (And their interpretations were largely based on traditions handed down from their former colonial masters, which is one way the pastors continued to enslave and colonize the minds of the people, all based on power and control. This was no different than the role of 'Churchianity" in America.) Some of the pastors got together and, on the only tv station in the country, denounced Rich, Gregory and the Bahais as being false teachers and demons. This backfired, however, as more and more people wanted to find out what they were teaching (the "forbidden fruit.") Rich and Gregory traveled the island holding tent-style public meetings to share their glad tidings, and the meetings were packed. Also, around this time, the Bahais began to get organized, and started asking members to serve in various ways, including serving on administrative bodies called Local Spiritual Assemblies in positions of 'servant leadership". (The Bahai Faith is a "do it yourself" religion, without any clergy—it is about self-determination and empowerment---and the Bahais are organized by a system of self-governance which includes electing nine members in every town to serve as their administrative body, called a "Local Spiritual Assembly" It is a consultative body which conducts the business of the Bahais in their respective localities, as a pastor and board of deacons would in a church. And, in every country, the Bahais elect a similar nine-member body called a National Spiritual Assembly. The elections of both are done without anyone campaigning and in a secret ballot, which removes all the corruption of other electoral systems. This Bahai system, which has been called the most democratic system in the world, has been studied by think tanks, including the prestigious Club of Rome, and the U.S. government election reform task forces.[33])

Rich realized that if they are asking people to take roles of "servant leadership", and to sacrifice their time and energy in the promotion of this cause of oneness and unity, then first they must be given the opportunity to learn about and develop their own intrinsic and unique capacities. How can you ask people to sacrifice when they don't even know what they must contribute, or may already be struggling to survive? So, the first step was to teach people about their true selves. Everywhere in the world there is a true hunger for that type of teaching and learning because it is not taught in schools or other institutions, especially religious ones. (Rich had experienced that void when he set out to find his own true self and capacities as a youth and young adult, so his self-knowledge education and training took place in non-traditional settings such as meditation temples, yoga ashrams, marital arts studios, Emotional Maturity Instruction classes, and Native American sweat lodges and

---

[33] More about the Bahai electoral process and administrative order can be found at https://bahai-library.com/pdf/p/poirier_bahai_electoral_process.pdf and https://www.bahai.org/library/authoritative-texts/compilations/sanctity-nature-bahai-elections/sanctity-nature-bahai-elections.pdf?cd07923f

ceremonies. Since there were none of those alternative types of learning centers in St. Vincent, he decided to start one.) Rich developed a holistic, self-empowerment workshop and course, called *"Total Human Development,"* based on all he had learned in those settings and incorporating some elements of the Emotional Maturity Instruction. (He had to type the curriculum and learning materials on an old-fashioned manual typewriter and then make mimeograph copies, as this was before computers, word processors, photocopy machines, and electric typewriters had entered St. Vincent.)

Rich and Gregory, with the assistance of a few other Bahai and like-minded friends, traveled the island holding these "Total Human Development" classes and workshops. They attracted many people from all walks of life, including police chiefs, elected representatives, health professionals, community leaders, and the common people (who were mostly farmers). The class was rapidly gaining in popularity nationwide. This further angered the corrupt pastors and those whom they had influence over, so they employed fear tactics and threats of violence to attempt to shut this movement down from empowering the people for spiritual, emotional, and intellectual self-determination. That was a threat (and always is) for those, at all levels, who want control over the people. The intimidation worked and both the Bahais and some other supporters withdrew their participation and support out of fear. (This was Rich's first major lesson in organized opposition to grass-roots progress relating to spiritual and personal development. He had experienced brutal and organized resistance by government and law enforcement to the anti-war and anti-racist movements in the U.S., but this was the first similarly organized religious-based resistance he had encountered. He was aware, though, from his studies of religion historically, that every major religion has a period of a few centuries where it helps produce societal advancements based on the founders' principles, but then corrupt clergy take over and pervert the religion for their own selfish purposes, mainly power and control. Christianity has been in this corrupted stage for centuries now and more people have been murdered, oppressed, and manipulated in the name of corrupted Christianity than all the other religions combined. It is important to note that there are still remnants of uncorrupted or less corrupted Christianity, just like in any other world religion, and there are certainly Christ-like people, or true Christians, who have helped many in their personal development and in the development of the "Beloved Community.") In St. Vincent, the opposition to Rich's and the Bahais' program of growth and self-determination came from both small and mega churches founded by those trained in America. While, on the other hand, the home-grown African-inspired Spiritual Baptist churches welcomed Rich to speak from their pulpits, and even the long-established Anglican and Roman Catholic churches, by far the most powerful in terms of wealth and influence, stayed out of the fray since their strongholds were relatively secure. A few other important lessons learned by

Rich in St. Vincent:

--Though the colonies, like St. Vincent, gained political independence, which did not include economic independence as they were still dependent on England and Europe for trade. That is why the West Indian nations were sometimes described as *"Banana Republics"* ---because their main crop was bananas, and they were dependent on England and other European countries to buy their bananas. If these countries stopped buying their bananas, the island countries' economies would collapse. (This is another aspect of colonial control, which happens in Africa and all over the world, and is what author Aharone, in his book *"Sovereign Psyche"* calls *"chattel freedom vs. self-authentic freedom"* and shows how Europe and America have transitioned from land conquest to intellectual, technological, and financial conquest—trying to keep other countries colonized and dependent. [34]) One of Rich's many jobs while in SVG was to help farmers diversify the crops they grew so they would no longer be dependent on bananas as their main export, which they have done successfully, to some extent. (But they are still dependent on Europe and America economically, and don't have to be. If they formed an effective union of Caribbean countries, like the European Union and the United States, then they could trade with each other and reduce their dependence on their colonial masters. Again, unity is the answer. They have a similar union called "Caricom," however it rendered weak and ineffective by American and European interference and control.)

--Bribery is openly part of the economic system there. For example, you must bribe customs workers to avoid paying exorbitant duties and tariffs on imported goods, and, at election time, candidates may come to your door asking what you need to vote for them (e.g.," Do you need your roof repaired, or some lumber for your addition or repairs?") However, though bribery in America is supposedly "illegal" it is a huge part of the way business and politics is conducted here ("pay to play" lobbying as a prime example) with so many government workers in every agency on the take, trying to hide it with terms like "lobbying," "gifts," "incentives." America has many layers of bureaucracy and red tape, and many games one must play to get anything done, especially if one is poor. Little is based on merit, equity, or equality but on who you know, while in St. Vincent and many other countries life is much simpler and more honest, with less games to play. In other words, not only life but corruption is much simpler outside America, which is among the most corrupt countries and systems in history but spends inordinate time and energy trying to hide and deny it. ***They have been EQualized.***)

--Most of the Americans and Brits Rich met in St. Vincent, including

---

[34] Read "Sovereign Psyche: Systems of Chattel Freedom vs. Self-Authentic Freedom," by Ezrah Aharone.

those residing or visiting there to "help" the people and country, wanted to dictate how the local people should be helped, rather than sufficiently asking, surveying, and listening to them—a symptom of a deeply ingrained and delusional superiority complex. (This, Rich found, is rampant in non-profit and NGOs in the U.S. as well as abroad, attempting to "help" disadvantaged communities through a top-down approach rather than a bottom-up or "grass roots" one, and therefore not really helping at all, at least not on a sustainable basis. He liked and adopted the motto of leftist groups who were more experienced in effective mutual aid*:" Not Charity, but Solidarity."*)

--All U.S. foreign aid had strings attached, and sometimes chains, primarily helping local elites and wealthy families in these countries, rather than the poor.[35] (That is the result of the top-down, superiority complex approach.) On the other hand, Canadian aid had none of that nonsense and actually reached those who needed it.

--Toxic and carcinogenic substances, including foods and pesticides, while banned in the U.S. and UK, were still manufactured and shipped to poor countries, often sent as aid paid for by U.S. tax dollars, spreading poisons around the world--the result of corporate greed!

--The same for toxic practices, like corporeal punishment of children in schools, while banned in the U.S. and UK but still used in the former colonies. (Rich would come to learn later that this was due to "internalized racism" and "internalized oppression."[36]) Also, there were literally no consumer or worker protections, so both were routinely mistreated. Rich would not stand for that and was the first person to report companies, mostly foreign run, to the government's labor department. He also forced a retail chain to provide basic consumer protection by offering a refund for or replacement of a defective product. (In this incident, he had purchased a pair of defective sandals from the local outlet of a European based shoe store chain. When he immediately returned them for an exchange or refund, the manager, while not denying his product was defective, said they had a no refund or exchange policy. Rich told him that from this day on they must change that policy and that, until he did so, Rich would go into his office and put his defective sandal-clad feet on his desk until he agreed to replace the sandals—which he did finally. ***They were Equalized.*** Another time he had to do the same at an insurance agency which was not honoring its health insurance contract to provide airfare to a specialist in neighboring Barbados when a local doctor referred Rich's young son for advanced tests there to rule out leukemia. Rich

---

[35] Read *"Confessions of an Economic Hit Man"* by John Perkins https://en.wikipedia.org/wiki/Confessions_of_an_Economic_Hit_Man

[36] "Internalized racism is a form of internalized oppression, defined by sociologist Karen D. Pyke as the "internalization of racial oppression by the racially subordinated."[11] In her study *The Psychology of Racism,* Robin Nicole Johnson emphasizes that internalized racism involves both "conscious and unconscious acceptance of a racial hierarchy in which whites are consistently ranked above people of color." https://en.wikipedia.org/wiki/Internalized_racism

took over the manager's office, sitting at his desk and computer and refusing to move until he agreed to honor the referral. The police were called, and he vacated while they contacted the home office in Trinidad to see what could be worked out. However, in the meantime, a doctor friend in the U.S. reviewed the lab tests and said no further tests were warranted as he was sure it was not cancer but a mild infection which could be successfully treated there—and thankfully, it was.)

--The image of the U.S. portrayed to the world through its media and other propaganda is as a "land of milk and honey" where no one is poor, homeless, or oppressed. This is why everyone wants to come to the U.S., in addition to the fact that the U.S. foreign economic policies impoverish their countries. (If America really wanted to stem the tide of undocumented immigration it would need to stop raping their countries and producing economic refugees. *It is EQualized !*) But when many immigrants get here-- especially from the island nations where people may be cash poor but are food and housing rich (as all have adequate home-grown and raised food, and own a small piece of land and a home, however modest, in a beautiful environment and tropical paradise), they are in for a rude awakening---often in a polluted, dirty, concrete jungle American city, and a struggle to eat and live. Also, many foreigners, especially in developing countries, view the U.S. and Americans with great suspicion, since they hear American politicians beating their chests boasting of all the foreign aid they give, however the people who really need it in these countries never see or receive any of it.

--On the more humorous side, it appeared that upper class Brits were a bit stuffy. At an initial management staff meeting at one of Rich's jobs on Mustique Island (home of the rich and famous, and run by Brits), when they went around the room and introduced themselves Rich heard that all the British executives had titles such as "Lord" this or "Duchess" that. So, when it was his turn, he jokingly introduced himself as "King Richard." There was dead silence and not a laugh in the room. (He didn't last too long at that job.)

--In 1983, neighboring island-nation Grenada had a revolution, which started much the same as Cuba's revolution in the fifties. A local group led by Grenadian Maurice Bishop decided to rid the nation of an American-backed dictator, Eric Gairy, who used violence to silence his opponents. Since Cuba supported the new revolutionary leaders, the U.S., under President Reagan, viewed them as enemies. In violation of international law and nations' rights to sovereignty (which the U.S. never honors), the U.S. invaded militarily to reinstall its puppet regime. [37] (The U.S. rarely honors international law, so the notion that this is a law-abiding country which reveres the

---

[37] Read more about the Grenadian revolution and America's invasion of Grenada at https://en.wikipedia.org/wiki/United_States_invasion_of_Grenada

rule of law is pure rubbish. *It is EQualized.*) [38]Rich, who had been traveling back and forth to Grenada for business and Bahai purposes, continued to travel there during this revolutionary period, meeting some of its new, young leaders and finding them to have the peoples' best interests at heart. However, he noticed that there was disunity within their ranks in the revolutionary party, which ultimately led to violence and Maurice Bishop's death. Also, a war of propaganda between Cuba and America about what was actually taking place in Grenada, placed the Grenadian people in the middle while their economy suffered. The U.S. invasion ended that, with some lives lost and a U.S. friendly government installed. (Rich learned that misleading propaganda, from both the left and right in this instance, hurt everyone, which is why it is vitally important to independently investigate and verify truth for yourselves and not trust the vested-interest information dispensed by governments and corporations.)

--Relating to America's hyper-gun violence, Rich experienced an important "before and after" learning experience in St. Vincent. When he arrived there, St. Vincent was a country with virtually no guns; even law enforcement didn't routinely carry them. And there was little violent crime. However, a few short years later, with the addition of guns to that country, violence dramatically increased. (So, for those who say that guns are not the problem, Rich experienced it firsthand—a whole country before and after guns. And many other countries have experienced the exact same result—more guns equating to more violence! In America, the bought-and-paid-for corrupt and greedy politicians and gun-lobbyists peddle their lies but the truth is, and research proves, that more guns produce more violence, less guns produces less violence---period. It is not rocket-science. And the U.S. Constitution's 2nd amendment did not authorize the proliferation of guns we have today, so judges at all levels who interpret it otherwise are similarly corrupt, period. *They are Equalized!*)

Rich and V were expecting their third child (in six years). Since Rich's colleagues had been intimidated through fear to pull back on his spiritual teaching and empowerment work, Rich decided that V, who was an excellent mother and wife, needed a break to begin focusing on her own personal and educational development (since she had never even had the opportunity to finish high school there). Influenced by the Bahai teaching of the equality of men and women, and the fact that the women, as mothers, are the first educators of the children, it was time for her to start pursuing her goals. Since there weren't many opportunities for women to do that in St. Vincent, they decided to move to the U.S., at least temporarily. When V got her education and Rich worked and saved some money, they would return to St. Vincent

---

[38] To read about America's lawlessness in the world read William Blum's "Rogue State" and "Killing Hope" books https://en.wikipedia.org/wiki/Rogue_State:_A_Guide_to_the_World%27s_Only_Superpower https://en.wikipedia.org/wiki/Killing_Hope

to live a bit more comfortably with a growing family and in their own home built there—that was the goal.

They also started thinking about and researching other parts of the English-speaking Caribbean which were larger and more developed to possibly relocate to after this hiatus, including the countries of Guyana and Belize. They found that Guyana, as part of its new economic redevelopment phase, was offering free land for homesteading in its interior, and Belize had opportunities to own farms supplying oranges to major American juice companies. But first, back to America, and a new chapter.

Episode Five: Robin "Rich" Hood, the born-again EQualizer: Coming to America

Coming back to America with two young children and one on the way, and an immigrant spouse, was easier said than done. Just because V was married to an American citizen didn't mean that she could easily emigrate there, even with citizen children. For her to apply for entry at the U.S. embassy in Barbados and comply with the standard procedure the process could take years. So, Rich, never one for restrictive and unjust laws and red tape, planned another route. He made sure his children had birth certificates as citizens born abroad, and that V had her St. Vincent passport with their names added, and a visitor's visa. (They had decided to reside in south Florida, at least initially, since the climate and proximity to the islands were right and Rich's grandmother who lived there offered some assistance. So, Rich went there in advance, in 1986, a month ahead of V and the kids, and prepared the way, getting a vehicle, job, and apartment.) When it was time for V and the kids to arrive, Rich went to meet them at the immigration checkpoint at Miami airport, and he told V, if necessary, to have the young kids act up a bit as a distraction when she was being processed for entry. (It was a bit of a harrowing moment because they believed there was a possibility the children could have been admitted and V sent back to St. Vincent since she only had a temporary visitor's visa.) However, since it was plain for the immigration agents to see that she was the mother of U.S. citizen children, who were in her arms, and that Rich, their American father, was there to meet them, they were quickly processed and let through, granting V a temporary, 90-day visitor's stay, stamped in her passport. (This was a blessing as Rich knew that with her "foot in the door" he could now work to get V permanent residence. Little did he know the nightmare and lengths they would have to go to dealing with a corrupt and dysfunctional immigration system. And this was before 9/11, after which it was a thousand times worse. So, Rich laughs heartily at the ignorance of people when they say, *"why can't they just come here legally, through the system set up to facilitate that,"* especially when most of their ancestors circumvented it, a fact many either don't know or choose to forget. **They are**

EQualized.)

Rich and his growing family settled in West Palm Beach. He landed a job with a substance abuse counseling agency because of his degree and experience in that field, plus a huge and growing crack cocaine problem in the area. (The city had removed most of the traffic lights in downtown West Palm Beach because when motorists stopped at a traffic light crack addicts would swarm the cars to beg for money and clean their windshields for donations. Also, some addicts were going over the bridge to affluent Palm Beach and robbing the rich people there.) In his resume and application for that job, Rich listed all the drugs he had used and abused and included some of his drug adventure history and experiences, which the hiring manager said was totally unprofessional but admitted that it caught his attention and he had to meet Rich. (That's all Rich would ever need—a foot in the door and an interview, for any job, as he was good at selling himself and convincing hiring managers that they needed him. Later he would start a marketing and human resource agency, assisting businesses to market their products and individuals seeking positions to market themselves. And the strategy was always producing creative ways to capture the targets' attention, which Rich became an expert at. Even in his advocacy work today, Rich is still doing that with a car full of bumper stickers and even periodic slogans drawn on the windows ☺.)

The counseling job was good but not great pay, and Rich had a growing family with three young children, so he was on the lookout for a better paying job. He applied for a dispatcher position with a trucking and road paving company, with zero experience, and was hired because of his drug counseling experience, as the company wanted someone who could spot and help (or so they said) drivers with alcohol and drug problems— a huge liability for them. That was Rich's first entrance into corporate America (though it was a relatively small, family owned, corporation. Later he would work for some of the largest corporations in America and the world). It was also his first experience of many dealing with racism and corruption in the corporate workplace. Rich quickly realized that he was actually hired to find and fire anyone with a drug or alcohol habit, especially the drivers of color, as the white drivers were given many chances and much more leeway (which is *always* the case in America—land of extreme, unearned, white privilege). Rich could not tolerate that racism and became an informant and whistleblower (the first of many times in his career and life, earning him the nickname "*undercover brother*"). He secretly warned the drivers targeted to watch their backs, and eventually reported the company to the government equal opportunity agencies (though they were largely ineffective in Florida and most southern states). ***This company was EQualized.***

Outside of work, Rich, and especially V, as a mother of three small chil-

dren, had a difficult time finding like-minded friends in the fast-paced, ur-
banized, South Florida communities. (They had just come from a relatively
slow paced, laid back, environment where people mattered, to a fast-paced,
stressful, place where things mattered more than people—so it was quite an
adjustment for V and readjustment for Rich.)

They had heard of the plight of some imported West Indian sugar cane
workers slaving on the sugar plantations in the swamps of the nearby Ever-
glades, so they visited the Bahais in that area of the Florida interior, near Lake
Okeechobee, to learn more. There they learned that sugar corporations imported the immigrants to work as slave labor for low pay and in dangerous
and substandard conditions. So, they helped shine the light on these abuses
through the media, aid agencies, and labor unions. (When Rich was living in
the islands, he learned from the Cubans and their supporters that before the
Cuban revolution led by Fidel Castro in the 1950's, these same American
sugar companies had their plantations in that country, enslaving the local
people with the cooperation of the local dictator and American puppet, President Batista. That is why there was no choice but to overthrow him, to end
that slavery and abuse. Because America and its corrupt corporations tried to
reinstall him, there was no choice but for Cuba to seek military aid from
Russia, hence the long-standing "cold war" between the U.S. and Cuba. You
will not learn this in American schools.[39] **They are EQualized.** America still
supports and utilizes slave labor, not only in this country as punishment for
a crime and for migrants, but around the world, including on and around our
military bases where we contract with corrupt human trafficking companies.[40])

To find a home and community more like the pace and environment of
the islands, Rich & V considered moving to the Lake Okeechobee area. However, after a visit to South Carolina where Rich had lived before and had
established many contacts, they decided upon Rock Hill, SC, a small city and
suburb of Charlotte, NC.

Two significant historical facts about South Carolina which heavily influenced Rich's journey to wokefulness and EQualizing: 1) South Carolina and
the West Indies have close "blood" and historical ties since many of the slave
ships delivered some of their "human cargo" to the island of Barbados, and
then sailed on to the port of Charleston, SC, to deliver the rest. So, many of
the Black people along the SC coast are distant cousins to those in Barbados,
and some even retained their Afro-Caribbean accent and culture and are

[39] Fulgencio Batista y Zaldívar was a Cuban military officer and politician who served as the elected
president of Cuba from 1940 to 1944 and as its U.S.-backed military dictator from 1952 to 1959, when
he was overthrown by the Cuban Revolution. https://en.wikipedia.org/wiki/Fulgencio_Batista
[40] EXCLUSIVE: Conditions for foreign workers at U.S. military bases overseas likened to 'modern day
slavery' https://www.washingtonpost.com/world/2022/10/27/defense-contractors-persian-gulf-
trafficking/

known as the Gullah/Geechee people.[41] (You can visit the preserved Charleston slave market, and the Gullah/Geechee cultural centers in the Charleston area, both of which Rich and the local Bahais helped preserve and promote. They also helped preserve, in Charleston, the birthplace home of Louis Gregory, who became one of the earliest Black attorneys working for the government in Washington, DC, and was a pioneer and champion of interracial unity in the early 1900s.[42] Rich and V named their first son, Louis Gregory, after him.) 2) Rock Hill, SC, was at the center of the civil rights struggle to overthrow Jim Crow laws as it was the first town where an organized group of Black civil disobedience protestors sat and refused to move at an all-white lunch counter. Once arrested, they refused to be released on bail pending their hearing, also a first. Both of these actions drew national and international attention and visits from MLK,Jr., John Lewis, and other freedom fighters, including the Freedom Riders.[43] (Once again, an "invisible hand" seemed to be guiding Rich to places of historic significance in the battle for oneness, equality, equity, and justice. on his journey to becoming a *"Woke EQualizer"* warrior and peacemaker. Rock Hill became his family's early home base in America as they moved back there four times in the next two decades and birthed two children while there.)

Rich hated being back in the States after having escaped "the American propaganda and brainwashing matrix" and being reborn in a whole new environment in other countries, while realizing how entrenched "the triple evils" (racism, poverty, and militarism) are in America. His goal quickly became to re-escape as soon as possible back to his "new world." V was enjoying what was a whole new world for her, as her whole world previously had been a 140 square mile island. And it was fun for Rich to vicariously experience everything anew together with and through her, many of the things Americans take for granted.

However, there was the issue of immigration and Rich's first real encoun-

---

[41] "The **Gullah-Geechee Cultural Heritage Corridor** extends along the coast of the southeastern United States through North Carolina, South Carolina, Georgia and Florida in recognition of the Gullah-Geechee people and culture. Gullah-Geechee are direct descendants of West African slaves brought into the United States around the 1700s. They were forced to work in rice paddies, cotton fields and indigo plantations along the South Carolina-Georgia seaboard where the warm and moist climate conditions helped them to preserve many African traditions. After the abolition of slavery, Gullah-Geechee people settled in remote villages around the coastal swath, where, thanks to their relative isolation, they formed strong communal ties and a unique culture that has endured for centuries". https://en.wikipedia.org/wiki/Gullah/Geechee_Cultural_Heritage_Corridor

[42] Louis George Gregory was among the elite group of highly educated African Americans whom W.E.B. Du Bois called the "talented tenth." As an attorney at the U.S. Treasury Department, Mr. Gregory became active in political and cultural life in the nation's capital...In 1905 the *Washington Bee*, a local black newspaper with a national reach, lauded him as "one of the most gifted writers and speakers in this country." https://www.louisgregorymuseum.org/louis-g-gregory

[43] Read more about the "Jail-No Bail" Rock Hill sit-ins at https://www.zinnedproject.org/news/tdih/jail-no-bail/ and https://snccdigital.org/events/rock-hill-sit-ins-and-jail-no-bail/

ter with the dysfunctional, condescending, and racist U.S. immigration system and agents as he was trying to secure V's work authorization and permanent residence (otherwise known as a "Green Card"). They had started the paperwork and application in the Miami immigration office and when they moved from Florida to South Carolina, and reported to the closest office in Charlotte, NC, immigration had lost or misplaced V's paperwork, so they suggested starting the process from scratch, again. However, that would have set the timetable back a couple of years during which time V would not be legally present in America and could not leave to visit her country. On top of that, the immigration agents were rude, condescending, and unprofessional, as if Rich and V did something wrong (e.g., typical American superiority complex arrogance). Rich noticed that is how they treated most immigrants, especially those of color, as if they were less than human.

He would have none of that, and, when visiting the immigration office periodically, he would stand up in the front of the waiting room and speak to those immigrants waiting to be seen, telling them, in a voice loud enough so that all the immigration agents working at their desks behind him could hear, that they are human beings, equal to Americans in every way, and must demand to be treated with dignity and respect. Rich told them that the immigrant agents are public servants supported by the taxes of both American citizens and immigrant workers, so they must treat everyone equally and courteously. *They were Equalized!* (The immigration agents hated to hear that, and the office manager/chief agent would sometimes call the police or security to try and shut Rich up however he told them that it was within his first amendment rights to speak the truth, especially in a public, government office. *They were EQualized, again!*) From that point on, only the supervisory Immigration Officers would deal with Rich and V, because they didn't want any trouble. and they said they were trying hard to find V's paperwork which had been lost.

Rich contacted the media, elected officials, and anyone who would listen to speak about their bungled case and the incompetence, disrespect, and racism of those immigration agents. Finally, Rich, who had learned how to do some investigative work through his marketing research job, found the number of the head of the Miami immigration office. Using the name of the chief immigration officer in Charlotte, he called the Miami chief officer, impersonating the Charlotte officer, asking him to personally find V Pellegrino's paperwork and to expedite sending it the Charlotte office. This apparently worked as her paperwork was found and processed quickly, and V got her "Green Card". (No human beings should be mistreated like new immigrants are in this country. It is inhumane and barbaric! It is no fault of theirs that they were born elsewhere and that, in most cases, America abused and oppressed their country so that they had to flee it. Because of that and the fact that America has space and resources to accommodate millions of economic and other refugees, America must take responsibility and allow them to emigrate. Anything less is barbaric! *We are EQualized!)*

To support his growing family (as child number four, which was daughter number three, was born in 1988), and to save for their planned return to St. Vincent, Rich switched professions from human services (which he still did part time as a counselor in psychiatric and substance abuse hospitals) to corporate marketing, working for Fortune 100 companies such as AT&T, and IBM. (With no experience and not even a bachelor's degree, one or both of which were normally required for those positions, Rich's white privilege combined with a quick mind and tongue enabled him to convince recruiters that he could learn on the job, so he was given opportunities to prove himself. Also, they utilized personality screening and role play tests, which, due to his counseling and psychology training and experience, he aced.)

This entrance into corporate America was eye-opening for Rich and was another needed experience on his path to becoming a Woke Equalizer. Beyond all the glitter and imagery, he found these huge private companies to be as or even more corrupt than government, and their workplaces were throwbacks to the plantation. For example, in the sales and marketing departments where Rich worked, they put the staff through some world class training however still emphasizing that the main goal was to win at all costs over competitors, even if they had to lie and cheat.

One thing Rich was constantly learning and experiencing is that lying and cheating to get ahead or beat the competition seemed to be an American practice at all levels of society and in all American institutions, since the founding of America had been built on those practices, and still is. Whenever property and profit come before people and principle, the system will be totally corrupt. *They are Equalized.* And there was rampant racism; just like on the plantation, Black workers were sometimes given supervisory roles but only if they would control and manipulate the people below them, sometimes brutally. And everyone was incentivized to snitch on other workers, while surveillance was widespread. It wasn't long before Rich was refusing to play by their rules and was whistleblowing to both unions and government agencies. For that reason, he didn't last long with any company.

In Rich's new "Robin Hood mentality," he was determined to **EQualize** America and its economic institutions, which, as he had witnessed overseas, rose to economic dominance by stealing from the poor and giving to the rich. To level the playing field (and because he believed the Bahai teaching that there should be one world currency), whenever he owed a debt, he offered to pay it in Eastern Caribbean dollars (worth only a third of American dollars). His creditors thought he was crazy, but Rich was serious. (One such debt was to the Charlotte, NC, hospital where his daughter and fourth child was born. When they wouldn't accept his offer to pay their exorbitant hospital fees with E.C. dollars, and kept harassing him with debt collection calls, he told them that if they didn't stop bothering him, he would return the merchandise 😊—and they stopped!) He bought as much as he could on credit-- mostly electronics, books, and household goods to ship to St. Vincent for his family there and his imminent return. And if the creditors didn't accept his terms of payment in E.C. dollars, they didn't get paid a cent. Eventually the sheriff came to his home to repossess some of the goods, but it was too late---they were already shipped.

Rich's side jobs were in private psychiatric and substance abuse hospitals, where he learned about the corrupt "insurance cure"—that is, if you had 30 days insurance coverage you were "cured" in 30 days, and 90 days coverage was a 90-day "cure". He also found that some patients were involuntarily committed by corrupt psychiatrists just to get their money. He exposed all of this to the media, and received threats of violence from the corrupt, organized crime syndicate that owned one of the hospital chains.

Due to his awareness of American corruption, which he saw and found everywhere and in almost everything American, he could not stand it any longer, so he, V, and their four young children (while pregnant with their fifth) packed up and, in 1990, escaped America and moved back to St. Vincent and the Grenadines.

Before leaving the 80s, some of the "woke" soundtrack of that period was provided by: various West Indian Reggae/Soca artists; Queen; Michael Jackson; Paul McCartney; George Michael; Public Enemy; Twisted Sisters; Hall & Oates; Run-D.M.C.; Tupac Shakur; Seals & Croft; Luther VanDross; Notorious B.I.G., Biggie Smalls.

5 THE CLOSING DECADE OF THE TWENTIETH CENTURY: 1990's

The 1990's was characterized by an explosion in technology and communications--the rise of the internet, world-wide-web, personal computers, mobile phones—bringing the entire world closer together as one global neighborhood (as poets, philosophers and prophets had predicted for thousands of years). While the world increasingly began embracing their multiculturalism, America also struggled with reactionary forces mounted against that progress, as evidenced by the white supremacist, Oklahoma City bombing of the federal government building there in 1995 (which killed at least 168 people, injured more than 680 others, destroyed more than one-third of the building, destroyed or damaged 324 other buildings within a 16-block radius, shattered glass in 258 nearby buildings, and destroyed or burned 86 cars, causing an estimated $652 million worth of damage.[44]) Also, the acquittal of white police officers in the 1992 beating of Rodney King in Los Angeles, caught on camera and watched by millions worldwide, sparked the "Los Angeles Uprising" and race riots by thousands resulting in 63 people killed, 2,383 injured, more than 12,000 arrested, and estimates of property damage of over $1 billion.[45] Gun violence and mass shootings, even at schools, were on the rise, due, in part, to the American "gun culture", and the decade ended with the deadliest school mass shooting (at that time) in 1999 at Columbine High School in Colorado, with 12 students and one teacher murdered, and 21 injured.

Bill Clinton served as President from 1993 to 2001, and though he championed some progressive policies and reforms, his tough stance on crime and

---

[44] Read more about the Oklahoma City bombing at https://en.wikipedia.org/wiki/Oklahoma_City_bombing
[45] Read more about the Los Angeles Uprising at https://en.wikipedia.org/wiki/1992_Los_Angeles_riots

drugs increased mass incarceration exponentially, propelling America to the most incarcerated nation in the history of the world, with people of color disproportionately represented.[46]

On the international front, the first Iraqi war, Desert Storm, took place in 1991, setting the stage for the later illegal and unjust U.S. war and invasion of Iraq after the 9/11 terrorist attacks. And there were mass genocides in Rwanda and Bosnia which America watched and did nothing about. In South Africa, Nelson Mandela was released from prison and was elected President in 1994, the country's first Black head of state and the first elected in a fully representative democratic election, ending the system of apartheid. (Apartheid ended politically and legally, however economically it remained, and remains to this day, with white money and power dominating still, to a significant extent, just as in America. This is another example of the necessity to tackle the triple evils of racism, poverty, and militarism together, as they are all interrelated and one cannot be eliminated without eliminating the others.) Also, scientists worldwide began raising the alarm regarding the potential deadly effects of global warming and climate change largely due to greenhouse gas emissions from human activities.

Rich and family began this decade with a return to St. Vincent & the Grenadines (SVG) in 1990, where their fifth child (and fourth daughter) was born. Rich and V found that in the few years they had been gone SVG had become much more materialistic, corrupt, and violent (with the advent of guns, which had been absent before), patterning itself after America (which exports its corruption worldwide).

While in the States, Rich had begun to study international economics to see how he could help his newly adopted country and other similar countries in the region become more self-sustaining and independent of America, Europe, and other empire-building nations' influence, or, at least, to begin reducing their dependence. A major part of that study were the books and teachings of professor and economist Dr. Ravi Batra, author of *"The Great Depression of 1990: Regular Cycles of Money, Inflation, Regulation and Depressions "and "Surviving the Great Depression of 1990".*[47] Rich was so impressed with his works that he reached out to Dr. Batra and connected on both intellectual and spiritual planes as they were both members of the same international Hindu meditation and social service organization. (Though Dr. Batra's exact prediction did not materialize, America and the world have teetered on the edge of economic depression several times since, and most of what he wrote was in harmony with the Bahai teachings and Rich's belief that economic

---

[46] For more on mass incarceration watch the movie "13th https://en.wikipedia.org/wiki/13th_(film)

[47] "The book was frequently criticized by economists after it became a best-seller, as it focused on a darker side of capitalistic development, notably Batra's main claim that excessive inequality in capitalist societies can lead to financial crises and economic depressions" https://en.wikipedia.org/wiki/The_Great_Depression_of_1990

crisis and disaster must come to bring balance and equity to the global economic system—a great "economic correction." Dr. Batra's advice, though, on how to prepare for and survive economic crisis was and is still invaluable.) Rich bought many copies of Dr. Batra's books to give to heads of State in the islands, encouraging them to divest of attachments to the American economy and become more connected to and interdependent with other nations in the region. These leaders politely accepted the books and advice however didn't heed it much. Though they continued to be connected to and dependent on the American dollar, their attitudes gradually changed decrying American manipulation and oppression, as have most countries worldwide (though they still are forced, sometimes violently, by America and its allies to conform and bow down to American corporate capitalism, all of which is economic terrorism well documented in the books by General Smedley Butler, *"War is a Racket",* John Perkins, *"Confessions of an Economic Hit Man,*" and William Blum, *"Rogue State"* and *"Killing Hope".*) Because of this American interference in their countries, America's reputation continually plummeted in the ensuing years, especially among the younger generations worldwide who, thanks to advances in communications and technology, have much more accurate information about America's corrupt motives and practices. (A constant theme of Rich's work and beliefs is that America must experience some radical changes to fulfill its' true destiny and world servant leadership role as opposed to its traditionally pursued world ruler role.) Regarding these so-called underdeveloped, poor countries, noted American political scientist, academic historian and cultural critic Michael Parenti says it best: *"There are very few poor countries in this world. Most countries are rich! The Philippines are rich, Brazil is rich, Mexico is rich, Chile is rich…only the people are poor. But there's billions to be made there to be carved out and be taken. There's been billions for 400 years, capitalist European and North American powers have carved out and taken the timber, the flax, the hemp, the cocoa, the rum, the copper, the iron, the rubber, the bauxite, the slaves, and the cheap labor, they have taken out of these countries. These countries aren't poor. These countries are rich! Only the people are poor!* **They're not underdeveloped, they're overexploited!"**

This time, due to the rising costs and materialism in SVG, and continued opposition to change by religious and other leaders there, Rich and family only lasted a year before their money and patience were depleted. They realized they had returned too soon, unprepared to survive and thrive in the worsening conditions with their large and growing family. So, they returned to their new home base in Rock Hill, SC, and resumed teaching oneness and unity throughout the Bahai communities around the southern U.S. In 1992, they had their sixth child (and second son). Rich resumed his corporate and small business marketing and sales work, including starting his own marketing and human resource consulting business on the side. Having a large family of eight now and desiring to spend adequate time with his children while still having time leftover for traveling and teaching spirituality and social justice advocacy, he had to be creative in finding ways to earn enough for basic needs by working forty hours or less per week.

V, who was (and still is) an incredible mother, sometimes even homeschooling the kids when the local schools were deficient, helped a great deal by running a thrifty household making do with whatever was provided, using her skills learned growing up in SVG to clothe and feed the children for a fraction of what most Americans spend. Rich coined the term *"voluntary poverty"* to describe their lifestyle, since they could certainly have made much more money and lived a more comfortable lifestyle but would have had to sacrifice valuable time spent both building the family and the community. (Rich's training as a seventies hippie provided a good foundation for detachment from material things beyond necessities, and for V, who was not raised as a materialistic American, thriftiness also came naturally. One of Rich's mottos has always been to *"live simply so that others may simply live."* It is not hard to see how insidious American materialism is, like a disease or addiction whose excesses cause most of this society's and the world's problems---war, bullying, crime, mental illness, addictions, sickness, inequities, injustices, oppression, climate change. Therefore Dr. King labeled materialism--under the heading of poverty--as one of the triple evils, along with racism and militarism, since they are all closely related. And he said *"I am convinced that if we are to get on the right side of the world revolution, we as a nation must undergo a radical revolution of values. We must rapidly begin the shift from a thing-oriented society to a person-oriented society."* [48] Sadly, we have still hardly begun undergoing that radical revolution, fifty years later.)

What had attracted Rich initially to the Bahai Faith was its emphasis on self-determination and advancement for all peoples, especially those who had been marginalized in the past, which, in the U.S., was mainly communities of color but also poor white rural communities. So, Rich, V, and family spent most of this decade traveling to such marginalized communities to help teach spiritual and equitable, social and economic development in many states, including but not limited to FL, GA, NC, SC, AL, MS, TX, OK, TN, NY, NJ, PA, KY, IL, IN, KS, MO,VA,WVA, DC.

Since both Rich and V's extended family support systems were far away (Rich's in NY and V's in SVG), they were always seeking the proverbial village of mutual support to help raise their children. They also had a dream of opening their own school based on the universal spiritual and practical principles they had learned and were also interested in starting or joining an "intentional community" (the new term for a "commune") composed of members of their faith community and/or like-minded and spirited friends. So,

---

[48] **"A Radical Revolution of Values"** *Remembering Dr. King's speech that the power elite want us to forget.*
https://www.levernews.com/a-radical-revolution-of-values/

almost every two years, like clockwork, they moved to new communities they had discovered in their many travels, in SC, NC, GA and FL. All these travels and moves brought many adventures, especially with a large multi-racial family of ten (ultimately) in the deep South and elsewhere (a few of which are shared in the following episodes).

Episode One: PeeDee Region, South Carolina

The PeeDee region of South Carolina is the northeastern section of the state, including Myrtle Beach which is one of the most visited tourist destinations on the East Coast. Inland is comprised of rural small towns and villages, some of which could be characterized as Black townships. Since Rich had traveled and briefly lived in this area when single in the 70s, he was familiar with the area and still had some contacts there. V was interested in organic agriculture---specifically permaculture---and the Bahai's owned acreage, an Institute (for summer and winter camps), and an FM radio station near the village of Hemingway in this region, where they were interested in hosting a demonstration permaculture garden and farm. (Many Black families in that region and throughout the South were losing their farms and lands to big agribusiness and developers through the racist, corrupt practices of local and state government, so the Bahais wanted to help them retain their land and grow marketable organic crops, the demand for which was increasing.) So, Rich and family moved near to the Bahai Institute so that V and the kids could help on the demonstration garden/farm and in the radio station while Rich commuted to work in Myrtle Beach. In their quest for building an intentional community, Rich and friends found some acreage near the Bahai institute and started planning to purchase and subdivide it for those friends from around the country who might be interested in living or investing there to form a cooperative, intentional eco-village, including a credit union. However, the project fell apart when some outsiders (who were white and thought they knew better what the local people of color needed) felt it would be competing with the Bahai demonstration farm project, which could ultimately benefit the Black families and farmers there. (Rich had witnessed this top-down, liberal, and religious "white savior mentality" ruin many social and economic development projects, both in the Caribbean and in the U.S., often coming from those who were highly educated and arrogantly looking down on those without as much formal education. He could not tolerate such intellectual snobbery---just another form of bigotry which seemed endemic in the U.S., along with race, class, and gender bigotries and could write a whole book entitled "*Golden Opportunities Lost*" about the loss of Beloved Community opportunities due to this bigotry.) So, Rich and family packed up once again and moved back to the Rock Hill/Charlotte area.

Episode Two: Lynchburg, SC

On one of their many trips crisscrossing South Carolina, Rich, V, & family were driving through the town of Lynchburg. (Even the town's name gives you the chills.) Rich was aware that many of these small towns were speed traps which is how they fattened the town's coffers, so he was sure to slow down when entering them. Also, it happened to be one of the first times V was sitting in the front passenger seat because she often had a young baby or child in the back with her, nursing or otherwise. So here they were, Black and White, clearly visible sitting together when suddenly and appearing out of nowhere were blue flashing lights and sirens behind them—several police cars worth. Rich immediately pulled over and the local Sheriff, a white "Boss Hogg" type (if one recalls the "Dukes of Hazzard" tv show) strutted up to the driver's window while several deputies, all white, stood back and surrounded the car. The Sheriff asked Rich if he was from the nearby military base (likely because only soldiers had interracial relationships and were bold enough to display them in that area) and told him he was speeding. He also said he was training a group of new deputies, so that was the reason for the group presence and asked if that was ok. Rich, wanting to avoid any trouble, consented, but stated that he was not speeding. Nevertheless, one of the deputies in training wrote up a speeding ticket and the Sheriff gave it to Rich as if he was doing him a favor. (Maybe in a town named "Lynchburg" he might have been.) Rich wasted no time in getting out of that town. Rich, V, and family were a bit shaken by this encounter and while happy to only get a traffic citation they decided it was bogus revenue collecting, whether racist or not, and decided to fight back. While in Rock Hill they had learned about an anti-government group, mostly white and right wing but including some diversity, called the U.S. Patriots Movement. That group assisted citizens to place liens on the homes and property of any corrupt government officials, including law enforcement. (Sheriffs in the South had a history of corruption and lawlessness, and they used to make you go to jail or pay fines on the spot—which, of course, went into their pockets. The Patriots took credit for putting a stop to that practice by targeting sheriffs' personal property with liens.) So, Rich put a lien on the Lynchburg Sheriff's property. (He would have given anything to see that Sheriff's face when he learned that his personal property was tied up in court over one of his bogus speed-trap charges. **He was Equalized.**) But Rich didn't have the time to drive hours on multiple visits to fight the citation in court so eventually he just paid the fine and removed the lien---however the feeling of empowerment that an ordinary citizen could hold a corrupt official accountable was immeasurable. (Eventually some of the Patriot Movement leaders were jailed for refusing to pay taxes and other more violent crimes, and they morphed into mainly white supremacist militias.)

Episode Three: Indian Land, SC

Rich and family also had tried living in an intentional community with some Bahai friends in Indian Land, SC, a rural area near Rock Hill, Charlotte, and the Catawba Indian Reservation. He invested what savings they had, along with his marketing expertise and "sweat equity," in a few businesses with that group, however because they were organized as traditional corporations (LLC's and partnerships), rather than as cooperatives, they failed and broke up due to greed, internal competition, and personality clashes. Rich learned the lesson that these traditional business structures and models set the stage for and actually enable those problems, even among friends and family—which is one reason so many small and start-up businesses fail. So, he studied and adopted the cooperative model for future endeavors, more in line with his spiritual principles. (Even though he had lost a few thousand dollars and a few friends in that endeavor, he gained a "million-dollar education" on what not to do and what to do in business.)

Episode Four: Kokomo, Indiana (not the Beach Boys' "Kokomo")

During their many travels teaching spiritual, social, and economic development principles and strategies, Rich and family were invited by some Bahai friends to Kokomo, IN, where the friends had established a relationship with the local courts and jail to assist in the rehabilitation of those incarcerated. They had recently received custody of papers and a course based on both science and the spiritual principles found in all religious scriptures, entitled "Successful Self Direction (SSD)." This was very similar to the "Emotional Maturity Instruction" program that Rich had learned and taught in Albany, GA, some years earlier, so he wanted to help get the SSD program adopted as both a pre-sentencing option and a training class for inmates already incarcerated. Because it was based on all the world religions and not just Christianity, they encountered fierce opposition from local chaplains and clergy, however eventually succeeded in getting SSD classes started in the jail, but not to the extent that they wished due to the religious bigotry and opposition. (Again, "Churchianity," which is pseudo-Christianity that has little to do with Christ's teachings, reared its ugly head in opposition to true religion and spirituality, and blocked justice and progress. ***They are Equalized!)*** Despite the haters' opposition, the jail-based SSD program has helped many people through the years.

Episode Five: Oklahoma/Indian Territory:

The significance of Oklahoma as the former "Indian Territory" ---basically the colony where all southern Native tribes were forcibly removed to, hence called "Indian Territory", and eventually becoming the state of Oklahoma, drew Rich and family there many times, especially considering the Bahai and Native prophecies that the indigenous peoples would eventually spiritually lead the world. Plus, Tulsa, OK, was the site of the historic and horrific 1921 Black Wall Street massacre, where state-sponsored white mobs mass murdered and burned an affluent Black community.[49] Sadly, in 1995, Oklahoma City suffered a new mass murder in the bombing of the Federal building there, again by white supremacists. Rich and family, in dealing with the repercussions of that tragedy, traveled to these communities to bring the healing message of unity and oneness, often walking the streets in the neighborhoods of both the Native and Black communities to meet and greet them as one human family and to find out what their needs and wishes were. They found that these peoples, who had relied on their Higher Powers, spiritual powers, and ancestors for generations, did not need more spiritual teachings or guidance but wanted more equitable social and economic development opportunities. In one rural town near Oklahoma City, some of the Bahais had purchased a farm with over a hundred acres containing some sacred Native sites (which they were determined to turn over to local Native Americans for their use) and were seeking a family to live on and caretake that property. They offered the opportunity to Rich and family, who seriously considered it, but the location was   too isolated and rustic for their needs. (Plus, Oklahoma was not an easy place to live due to much racial strife and racism, and bad weather and tornadoes. It was no accident that the government forced the eastern Native tribes to relocate there, far from their lush lands, and when oil was discovered in some parts of the state, they forced the Natives off that land and into other more barren areas. More broken promises and treaties. That is the story of America—everything, including the cherished Constitution, was designed and reserved for the elite few wealthy landowners, including the right to vote, which was not extended to the general white male population until nearly a century after the country's founding, and to Black men a century after that, and to women of all colors after another hundred years. The Founding Fathers wanted only large property owners to vote but left it up to the states to decide.[50] *They are Equalized.*)

---

[49] Read about the Tulsa Race Massacre at https://en.wikipedia.org/wiki/Tulsa_race_massacre
[50] " In the 18th-century Thirteen Colonies, suffrage was restricted to European men with certain property qualifications.": Read about U.S. voting rights at https://en.wikipedia.org/wiki/Voting_rights_in_the_United_States

Episode Six: Texas

Rich and family crisscrossed the vast state of Texas several times visiting diverse communities which included many Mexican and other immigrants from south of the border—a rich, Tex-Mex culture many of whom were also of mixed Native American heritage. White Texans also had a history of extreme racism towards peoples of color and immigrants and were notorious for being the last state to free slaves, two years after the Emancipation Proclamation and ending of the Civil War, now celebrated as the Juneteenth holiday. In this setting, those traditionally marginalized communities of color were very receptive to Rich's and the Bahais' message of unity and oneness.

While there, Rich befriended and learned from one of their own prominent native sons, Bransford Watson (also known as Brande, pronounced 'Brandy')—a civil rights advocate, Olympic sprinter, pilot, and champion of racial oneness and unity (who, in earlier years, was pictured with his plane on the front cover of an Ebony magazine as one of America's most eligible Black bachelors). Brande grew up in Marshall, Texas, home to Wiley College in northeastern Texas, a historically Black college where his father was a professor and colleague of Professor Melvin B. Tolson of "Great Debaters" fame (memorialized first by Brande and then by Denzel Washington in the film of the same name in which Tolson led Wiley's all-Black debate team to historically defeat all-white teams in the 1930s, risking their lives to do so in the segregated South and beyond.)[51] Later Brande wrote screenplays about other little-known American Black community leaders and game changers, and about his experiences in the deep, segregated South as a long, tall Texas Black man who didn't back down from racist police and other white supremacist encounters. Rich and Brande became good friends, close as brothers, and would travel together as a team-teaching oneness and unity for the next twenty years, experiencing many adventures throughout the Deep South.

Episode Seven: North Carolina

North Carolina was another stomping ground for Rich & family, from Asheville in the western Blue Ridge mountains, to the Greensboro/Raleigh/Durham tri-cities area, to Lumberton (home of the Lumbee Native American tribe), to Fayetteville and Fort Bragg U.S. Army base, to Jacksonville and U.S. Marine base Camp LeJeune, to the coastal Wilmington areas— a state rich in Native American and Black American history of resistance to oppression, and, like Texas, communities of color ready for and receptive to the Bahai message of oneness, unity, and justice. In Cherokee, NC, home of

---

[51] For more on the Wiley Debate team and "The Great Debaters" https://en.wikipedia.org/wiki/The_Great_Debaters

the Eastern Band of the Cherokee nation (where Rich had visited before he had a family), local Cherokees performed a reenactment of the "Trail of Tears" tragedy, which showed the resistance they put up to President Andrew Jackson and the American military when they violently tried to remove them. While many were removed, some hid in the mountains and fought the removal, eventually succeeding in staying while many of their fellow Cherokees were brutally removed to Oklahoma and thousands died along the way (which is why today, there is an Eastern Band and a Western Band of Cherokees, with separate leadership; some years earlier the Bahais and Rich had participated in a successful project to reunite the two Bands). The NC Cherokees also held a stagecoach and horseback trip each year to Oklahoma organized in memory of and following that infamous trail of tears. Rich and family considered joining the stagecoach trip however declined since there was so much work to do right there in North Carolina. From the mountains, they traveled past Charlotte (where they were residing at the time) to the Greensboro/Raleigh/Durham area, rich in historical Black resistance and home to the early lunch counter sit-ins (and violent repression), as well as the first Black owned insurance company in the state and largest in the nation, North Carolina Mutual, in Durham. (Durham was once called "the Capital of the Black Middle Class" and the "City on the Hill for Blacks." It was home to more Black millionaires per capita than any other place in America.) Then on to Lumberton and Robeson County, home of the Lumbee Indian Nation and famous for the "Battle of Hayes Pond" in which a band of Lumbee Indians supported by Black residents routed the KKK who were holding a rally and cross burning, chasing them into the woods.[52] In Fayetteville and Jacksonville, NC, home of the Army and Marine bases, Rich and family noticed that there were a large number of interracial families, like his, who were very receptive to their teaching of oneness and unity. This was due to the early integration of the armed forces (one of the few positive outcomes of the American military Rich witnessed in his lifetime). In the coastal town of Wilmington, the wounds were still open nearly a hundred years after the Wilmington Insurrection of 1898--the violent overthrow of a duly elected government by a group of white supremacists. (It is the only such incident in the history of the United States,[53] which later a defeated President Trump would try to copy and repeat.)

---

[52] Read the" Battle of Hayes Pond: Routing of the KKK" at https://www.uncp.edu/resources/museum-southeast-american-indian/museum-exhibits/battle-hayes-pond-routing-kkk and https://en.wikipedia.org/wiki/Battle_of_Hayes_Pond

[53] Read the " Wilmington insurrection of 1898 at https://en.wikipedia.org/wiki/Wilmington_insurrection_of_1898 and https://www.ncdcr.gov/learn/history-and-archives-education/1898-wilmington-race-riot-commission

Episode Eight: Metro Atlanta/Decatur/Bahai Unity Center/Retreat to Loganville

In the closing years of the nineties, Rich and family moved to the metro Atlanta area at the invitation of the Bahais of Decatur and Dekalb County. They had just purchased a church property with a school and other buildings, including a residential house on-site, and needed a caretaker and property manager, roles which Rich and V gladly agreed to undertake. They had always wanted to start their own cooperative school based on Bahai and universal spiritual principles of oneness and unity, and this appeared to be the perfect opportunity to do so. Plus, they had visited Atlanta on their spiritual teaching trips, especially to participate in the renown Atlanta MLK Day march and parade—co-hosted and co-organized by Coretta Scott King, the King Center, and the Bahais, and one of the largest in the nation. After getting settled into their new community and role, Rich and family worked hard to promote the new Bahai Unity Center in the surrounding areas, and it was attracting a diverse crowd from around metro Atlanta to attend its children, youth, and adult programs, including the formation of a choir.

They, together with community members, began laying the groundwork for a cooperative school, including recruiting schoolteachers and a principal, and setting a start date, when disunity, fears and intellectual bigotry disrupted their plans--another failure at getting Americans to cooperate due to so much divisive conditioning.

Disappointed, again, they literally "retreated to the wilderness," buying a mini farm with acreage in the small town of Loganville in the Georgia countryside, between Atlanta and Athens, GA, to form their own "intentional community."

This was the first time they had considered buying a home because they moved around so often, and it wasn't easy getting credit for such a large family with a very modest income. But this was during the housing mortgage boom, before the bubble burst, and banks were giving mortgages out so easy and even fudging the qualifications—another American Ponzi scheme and scam. When Rich studied economics in earlier years, he learned how the whole capitalist system is based on a very weak foundation for everyone except the wealthy, on an "invisible hand" protecting the profits of the very rich and corporations and putting everyone else's money and property at risk through a series of recessions and near depressions causing most Americans to never get ahead, with limited resources that can last only a few months. Rich and family were riding the wave on an upswing due to a lot of relatively easy money and easy credit flowing, but, like many others, were not preparing for the imminent downturn and crash. He learned that the American economic system is dependent on there being many losers for every winner, and only those too big to fail get taken care of, proven time and time again. (One wealthy entrepreneur who Rich worked for in one of his many jobs told him *"Rich, whether you owe a million dollars or have a million dollars in the bank, you are still viewed as a millionaire and will be lent and even given more money to dig out of debt."*) The only people who are viewed as debtors are the poor and middle classes, and they are badgered and pressured to pay up or are threatened with every possible consequence. And the U.S. is the largest debtor nation in the history of the world. Once he realized all of this is a con game and Ponzi scheme, Rich also learned how to play the game and get around the system, not to amass wealth but to survive without pressure. He knew that anyone who has amassed wealth in this system, no matter how nice and righteous, has played this con game, broken laws, and likely cheated workers, customers, suppliers, or others—however unintentionally. After working in dozens of industries, in marketing, sales, and operations, at both staff and management levels, and for employers of all sizes, from Fortune 100 corporations to small mom and pop businesses, he saw how they were all corrupt to a greater or lesser degree, because they operate in a corrupt system and environment.

Rich's family already numbered eight, and in 1998, grew to nine with the birth of their seventh child and fifth daughter, so they had enough for an intentional community on their own. But their idea was to attract like-minded folks from the city to enjoy their idyllic property in the country, with botanic gardens, fruit trees, its own soccer/football field, a stream, and woods. V's father came from SVG for a long stay to help plant organic gardens, and to help tend to the property. He even built a bench in the gardens so he could nap and eat his dinner out there. It was a good time for family growth and bonding with each other and nature. Rich was also able to overcome one of his biases towards his many white neighbors who were characterized as work-ing class "rednecks"—a term that could also mean they are backwards or racist. Rich found his "redneck" neighbors to be very welcoming to his multi-racial family, and so his bias toward working-class whites gradually dissolved. He found that they wanted to live their rural lives enjoying family and friends without too much government interference, which Rich could relate to and understand. However, like most white folks, they lived in their own bubble totally unaware of the struggles of American people of color or of their roles in either helping to lessen or worsen those struggles. (Rich also realized that they were often manipulated through the fear tactics of conservative politi-cians to be afraid of the "other" ---Blacks, immigrants, LGBTQ, Muslims, liberals, etc.---whichever boogeymen the corrupt politicians could dig up dur-ing election season to keep white working-class folks in fear. ***They are, and will continue to be, Equalized.***)

During this two-year period in their idyllic intentional community and mini farm, there were many adventures in learning and growth, but one stands out.

Episode Nine: Loganville/Walton County, GA/Moore's Ford Lynching

It seemed that even when Rich and family tried to retreat from the direct social justice action arena in order to build family and community, the Universe had other ideas. In the nearby Walton County seat of Monroe, he saw a meeting advertised of the Moore's Ford Memorial Committee to commemorate what was called "the last mass lynching in America" and attended just to learn local history. There he learned that on July 14, 1946, four African American sharecroppers, including a World War II veteran and his pregnant wife, were lynched by a white mob at Moore's Ford, a local bridge. The killers were never brought to justice despite multiple GBI and FBI investigations, due to the silence of the townspeople who knew the perpetrators. This was a turning point in civil rights history as it caused President Truman for the first time to push for both anti-lynching legislation and laws to fully integrate the military.[54] When one of the white men who witnessed the event as a child while hiding in the bushes was now on his death bed, he wanted to confess. A committee was formed to accept his confession as well as to bring healing to the community and closure to the victims' families. When the committee organizers learned of Rich's social justice background and experience, they invited him to serve on the committee, an invitation he accepted, participating in the healing process of truth and reconciliation which followed. (That is a process which needs to happen in every community of America—truth and reconciliation, and then reparations for the victims of racism, before America will ever heal and fulfill its true destiny.)

Episode Ten: Conference of Badasht Births the "Eagles"

The original "Conference of Badasht," held in 1848 Persia (now Iran), signaled a turning point in the replacement of Islamic sharia law with a more progressive Bahai law which, among other reforms, uplifted the station of women.[55] Almost simultaneously, in America, the Seneca Falls Convention was held in New York—the first women's rights conference in American history. At that time, many men and women from diverse cultures around the world realized that they were entering a new history-making era—a focus on the rights of women.

Fast forward to 1998, on the 150th anniversary of these two epic events, some of the Bahais organized a new Badasht Conference in North Carolina bringing together some of the most audacious teachers of oneness, unity, and

---

[54] To read more about the Moore's Ford lynching and its aftermath : https://www.blackpast.org/african-american-history/moore-s-ford-lynching-july-1946/   and https://en.wikipedia.org/wiki/Moore's_Ford_lynchings
[55] Read more about the Conference of Badasht: https://en.wikipedia.org/wiki/Conference_of_Badasht

equality in the country. As one who had made his mark through years of traveling the country teaching the message of oneness, racial unity and justice, Rich was invited to attend as one of the speakers and workshop leaders, which he did, accompanied by some of his family members. It was here that Rich met some of the most fearless teachers of oneness that he had ever known, each in their senior twilight years—Howard (successful entrepreneur who had lived in Africa), Richard (number one in sales in the world for his company, and a renowned motivational speaker and trainer) Brande (Black Olympian world record holder and fearless civil rights advocate, from Texas), Fuad (Persian/Muslim engineer, businessman and racial amity organizer), and others (including their wives, whose shoulders they stood upon and who were fearless warriors for truth and justice in their own right). They forged a friendship which grew into a traveling teaching team called *"The Eagles"* (really *"Gnats into Eagles"* taken from a Bahai prayer, but eventually shortened to just the *"Eagles"*). Rich was the youngest of the group, at age 45, and his personal mission became to share these talented and audacious gems—our elders-- with people of all ages, but especially youth nationwide while they were still with us—as they were all in their sixties. (Later, many others around the country joined the "Eagles" teaching group, one of whom was Alice, a prayer and forgiveness warrior, who taught us how to rely on both and had forgiven the men who killed one of her sons years earlier in Detroit.) The Eagles believed and acted upon their belief that we are all one human family, so everywhere they went together—restaurants, gas stations, Walmart, parks, neighborhoods, churches, synagogues, etc., they wanted to meet and greet and share the good news of oneness with everyone they encountered and spend time getting to know their newfound "family members." (Their rationale and belief were that if you go into a restaurant or store and bump into a cousin you haven't seen in a long time are you going to just brush past quickly, say hi, and go about your business? No, you are going to stop, chat, and find out how they are and what has been going on in their lives and share what's going on in yours—that's what family does. So, if you really believe we are all one human family, then everyone you encounter is a long-lost cousin. When the "Eagles" went into a restaurant, before leaving, often hours later, they met and knew every worker, the manager, and many of the patrons. This was a normal occurrence. For how would or could we build the beloved community if we don't even know our neighbors?)

During the next few years, Rich and the Eagles, together with their families, would travel much of the country, spreading the teachings of oneness and unity and training others to do the same and not to be afraid to reach out and talk to people, especially people who look different than them. They had many adventures; however, one stands out.

In Oklahoma, a very racist state, they met a man who liked everything they told him about oneness and unity, and especially their friendliness. However, when they asked him to join their movement, he politely declined stating that he was very biased against Blacks and had to work through that before he could be part of such a welcoming movement. When they dug deeper, they discovered he was the KKK Grand Dragon in those parts. He later admitted that to them and said he wanted to learn how not to be a racist. They spent time praying and meditating with him and educating him on the principles of oneness and unity, as well as the history and origins of the false doctrines of racism and white supremacy. They were hopeful for his eventual transformation but realized that his years of conditioning would be difficult to overcome. However, surprisingly, soon after their initial encounters and in a speech before his KKK followers he denounced racism and said he was learning to be an antiracist and better person. He resigned from the KKK and later joined the Eagles teaching team when they were in Oklahoma again. (The "Eagles" witnessed hundreds if not thousands of similar spiritual transformations, including some miraculous ones like that of "Papa John," the nickname he went by.)

Episode Eleven: Business Ethics, Amway, Dignified Marketing & Materialism

With his growing family, Rich had to be creative in order to earn a living and still have time for his large family and beloved community-building endeavors. While still living in South Carolina, Rich had learned about the new phenomena of multi-level marketing businesses, and he joined on the ground floor of one of the first and biggest —Amway. He was always seeking ways to not only economically empower his family but also Black and other marginalized families as well, and these low cost and low barrier of entry, multi-level business concepts seemed a perfect way to do so. So, Rich dove in headfirst, being a natural salesman, recruiter, and marketer. He rolled out Amway in the Black churches in Rock Hill. His up-line and founders of that Charlotte area Amway chapter were so-called Christians from the nearby PTL (Praise the Lord) Club, including founders Jim and Tammy Faye Bakker (televangelists eventually convicted of fraud), headquartered at their Heritage USA Christian community and theme park in nearby Fort Mill, SC.[56] Rich found them just as fanatical about Amway as they were about their religion, and just as fraudulent as in their other business dealings. When he realized that the Amway products were way overpriced compared to other cleaning products and tried to find ways to reduce the prices so people from marginalized communities could participate, he received anonymous death threats and was expelled from the organization. He still liked the concept, though, so joined

---

[56] For more on PTL Club, Jim Bakker, and Heritage USA; https://en.wikipedia.org/wiki/Jim_Bakker

other multi-level distribution businesses, like nutritional company Shaklee. He also found those products to be overpriced when compared with similar products in retail stores. After a few more false starts, he realized that in order to pay distributors bonuses for selling products and recruiting others all of these companies employing multi-level marketing had to artificially inflate the product prices and basically rip-off consumers. They were all also run like cults with intense pressure on members to recruit others and not to quit, or else they and their families would be told that there was something wrong with them—that they were not "prosperity-oriented," which, to some pseudo-Christians, was a sin. These were typical cult brainwashing and pressure tactics. Just as in corporate America, only a few members made good money while most lost money, including their start up or entry fees.

In Atlanta, Rich met and befriended two Black entrepreneurs and joined them in a business start-up as a partner of a third-party marketing company for new electricity and natural gas providers. The industry had just become open, competitive, and deregulated and the consumer could, for the first time ever, choose their own utility providers in many areas of the country. Rich and his new business partners put together teams of door-to-door marketers in the inner cities on the whole East Coast, from Miami to New York, to sign up customers in the "hoods," where no other company would go. They hired young people from the neighborhoods who were not afraid of their own area and people. The promise was that customers would see a savings on their next electric and gas bills, so they easily signed up thousands and were making and paying their workers good money. (One interesting sidenote: There were no mobile phones then, only pagers and pay-phones, and they had no trouble staying connected with their teams in every state.) But when their customers' first new utility bills came, they were actually paying more. Rich and partners had been lied to by the companies they were representing and performing contract marketing and sales for, and, unknowingly, in turn had lied to the customers, many of whom were poor. They immediately decided to cease operations though they could have made millions because they were breaking records in acquiring new customers. The utility companies they had contracted with offered them much more money to stay on board and continue, but it was against their ethics and shut it down, exposing the lies to the media and warning customers to beware.(Rich witnessed, in his many years of sales and marketing experience, that similar dishonest practices were the norm rather than the exception, in most companies, large and small, though he refused to participate in them and had to quit and whistle blow often.)

After that, Rich retreated to what he had known and been trained for by ATT, IBM, and others: telemarketing, inside sales, lead generation, and appointment setting. In that field he found a wide-open niche because there were very few legitimate business-to-business telemarketing professionals or firms at the time. That was because it had a rotten reputation as a boiler room, high pressure, discourteous method of marketing, usually barging in and bothering people at home, during dinner or other inappropriate times. Rich simply applied the spiritual principles and ethics he had learned and been teaching others-- the golden rule to treat others like you wish to be treated—and he changed how it was done by not calling people at dinner or inappropriate times at home, and, while calling both homes and businesses, by asking people if they had time and getting permission to speak rather than just barging in and assuming they had to listen. This strategy of employing common courtesy worked and soon Rich and his firm, *Dignified Marketing*, had many clients, from Fortune 500 to small businesses, desiring his services. (It was "dignified" because of the courtesy and ethics practiced, and because he would only market products and services which he felt were not harmful and were a value to the customers.) He added a division with the name *"Dignified Telemarketing,"* and that attracted even more attention as, to many, it was an oxymoron because company CEOs and most people believed it could not be done in a "dignified" manner. When they finished laughing after hearing the business name, Rich simply told them *"Let me prove to you that we can do telemarketing in a both dignified and profitable manner for you."* Many said, *"yes, show me."* Often Rich produced so many leads and new prospects for his clients that they had to put his marketing campaigns on hold just to catch up and be able to service the new customers. The majority of times his contracts ended prematurely because they were too successful and exceeded all expectations and demands, literally working themselves out of jobs. Often, he had too much work to handle himself, so he farmed it out to trusted colleagues in the same field who shared his values. Later, he would recruit friends and his own grown children on some contracts. This business has sustained Rich and family to this day, allowing him to work remotely, way before the Covid pandemic, and to have quality time with his family and pursue his pro-bono spiritual and social justice advocacy work. (Rich believes sales and marketing is a profession and business he would never have chosen, and it pretty much chose him, as his passion was always in counseling and addiction treatment and prevention--which he still does on a volunteer basis. But it helped sustain his large family with time left over for building family and beloved community.)

Speaking of riches and wealth, Rich often said they cannot be measured in dollars and cents. As this book outlines, not only his name but his life has been "rich" in experiences: travel, adventure, love, learning, family, service to others, recovery, redemption, transformation, friendship, mentorship. Even measured in material wealth and dollars, he, and most Americans, including those beneath the poverty line, are richer than more than half of the world. At times Rich earned enough—at not even six figures-- to be in the world's top 10% richest.[57] So, it is all relative. Once one's basic physical needs are met, Rich believes, the rest is unnecessary luxury though we have been brainwashed to judge our "success" by the material luxuries we have amassed. That is the disease of materialism—one of the "triple evils" (relating to poverty) and couldn't be further from the truth. Everything he accomplished, his true "richness," was with only basic and minimal material needs fulfilled—nothing more or less. Without planning it, he became a minimalist. Having worked with and for multi-millionaires, and, having become intimately acquainted with their lives, Rich found they were among the most miserable and insecure people he has known, for many reasons. But the main reason was that they worried about their money and material things all the time-- who was trying to get it, including and especially family and friends, and who really liked them or really only liked their money—a sad way to live.

A basic Bahai principle that Rich wholeheartedly supports and promotes is the elimination of the extremes of wealth and poverty. This does not mean absolute equality as there can be levels based on many factors such as capacity and achievement, but absolute equity, meaning a level playing field with everyone's basic needs met, especially those marginalized communities that have been oppressed for centuries. Not only is that possible but it is already happening in some countries, which America needs to learn from. No one needs inordinate material wealth, and just like any excess, it is detrimental to their well-being and to the well-being of the world, as greed and material excesses have caused most of the world's problems. ***They are EQualized.***

Remember Dr. King's definition of "beloved community" and "revolution of values": "*I am convinced that if we are to get on the right side of the world revolution, we as a nation must undergo a radical revolution of values. We must rapidly begin the shift from a thing-oriented society to a person-oriented society.*" This cannot be emphasized enough as it is the main obstacle holding us back—the attachment to material things. And poverty and materialism—which are directly related—are considered together as one of MLK's "Triple Evils".

After two years living in the "wilderness," Rich and family decided that the "village" they were seeking was not to be there and, just when they had given up the idea of opening their own school in Georgia, they learned about a fairly new phenomena called "charter schools" forming in different areas of the country. Charter schools could be formed by teachers and parents around a central theme or common principles, including spiritual ones, and are funded by public education dollars. At the turn of the century, Florida and Arizona were leading the nation with such experimental schools, so Rich researched the ones in Florida and found one to his and V's liking in Tallahassee, the Florida capital on the northern Gulf coast (only four hours from

---

[57] https://www.cnbc.com/2018/11/01/how-much-money-you-need-to-be-part-of-the-1-percent-worldwide.html

Atlanta). So, in the new century, 2000, they packed up once again and moved to Tallahassee to help start a charter school.

Before leaving the nineties, here are some of the artists providing this decade's woke soundtrack: Mariah Carey; Backstreet Boys; Spice Girls, Tupac; Biggie Smalls; Green Day; U2; TLC; Rage Against the Machine; Celine Dion; Jay-Z; Snoop Dog; Michael Jackson; NYSNC; Aaliyah; En Vogue; Destiny's Child; OutKast; England Dan Seals.

6 THE 2000's: FIRST DECADE OF THE NEW MIL-LENIUM (2000 – 2010)

Technically, the new millennium started on January 1, 2001, however for our purposes, and that of much of the world at the time, we begin in the year 2000. The main event leading up to the year 2000 was the Y2K millennium bug scare—referring to *"potential computer errors related to the formatting and storage of calendar data for dates in and after the year 2000. Many programs represented four-digit years with only the final two digits, making the year 2000 indistinguishable from 1900. Computer systems' inability to distinguish dates correctly had the potential to bring down worldwide infrastructures for industries ranging from banking to air travel."*[58] Some people thought this could signal the end of the world, as we knew it. In fact, due to the remedial efforts to correct this, plus the belief that the problem was overstated, nothing significant or damaging occurred.

The next world-changing event in this new century, which would catapult America's empire-building efforts abroad, and police-state, military-industrial complex, and bigotry at home to new and unprecedented levels was the "terrorist" attack on America, on September 11, 2001.(The word *"terrorist"*, though aptly applied to those who carried out the 9/11 attack, could also aptly be applied to thousands of American actions against peoples and countries worldwide for at least the last sixty years, as well as the state-sponsored terrorist attacks against Black Americans and Native Americans for centuries. All this makes the 9/11 attacks, which some say were retaliation against American terrorism abroad, pale in significance.) In fact, because that attack was used to justify wars which America had been wanting to undertake against Iraq and Afghanistan for years, for economic reasons, some claim it was a false flag attack either staged by the U.S. or allowed to take place despite warnings which could have prevented it. (So, before you make a big deal about 9/11, or any acts of foreign terrorism against America, look in the mirror and work to stop American global gangsterism worldwide, which is more

---

[58] https://en.wikipedia.org/wiki/Year_2000_problem

terroristic and deadly than anything Al-Qaeda or ISIS could ever do. **_They are Equalized!_**) Thus began America's and its allies' endless _"war on terror"_, targeting mainly Iraq, Afghanistan, and radical, fundamentalist Muslim organizations like Al-Qaeda, which was based mainly on lies (e.g., non-existent weapons of mass destruction), killing thousands of combatants on both sides and tens of thousands of innocent civilians, including children, totaling approximately 900,000 lives lost, at a cost of trillions of dollars. [59]

At home in America, the police state surveillance and arrest powers were extremely broadened with the Patriot Act and other draconian legislation enacted on a bi-partisan basis. And extreme bigotry and violence toward Muslims in America and worldwide grew exponentially. (That bigotry was already latent and simmering among so-called Christians--an ignorant, religious bigotry based on their false assumptions and beliefs that Christianity was the "only true religion. The same fundamentalism which fuels Muslim fanaticism and violence has fueled Christian fanaticism and violence for centuries. Most Americans and Christians still don't realize the profound positive impact Islam had on both America and Europe, in the fulfillment of their own Biblical prophesies. **_They are Equalized._**)

Later in this decade, that vitriol would be extended to immigrants of all backgrounds, especially undocumented immigrants from south of the border (even though most levels of government and many corporations and industries imported them for cheap and highly productive labor, and no "terrorists" have ever entered the U.S. from its southern border, contrary to what lying politicians say).

Globally, in the early part of the decade, China and India saw economic booms, however the economic developments in the latter third of the decade were dominated by a worldwide economic downturn that started with the crisis in housing and credit in the United States in late 2007 and led to the bankruptcy of major banks and other financial institutions. (This is when we learned the concept of _"too big to fail"_[60] which means when wealthy individuals or companies owe or control large amounts of money they will always be bailed out by government—the ultimate welfare system for corporations and the wealthy and example of crony capitalism and not a free market economy at all. Only the small guy is forced to be fiscally responsible. That is why one of his former bosses, Rich recalled, told him that whether you have a million dollars in the bank, or owe a million dollars, you are still considered a millionaire and will be protected. So, it is ludicrous for anyone in America to complain about any funds spent on a social safety net for the poor when the rich routinely have billions of dollars of government welfare. **_They are_**

---

[59] A report from the Costs of War project at Brown University revealed that 20 years of post-9/11 wars have cost the U.S. an estimated $8 trillion and have killed more than 900,000 people.
https://www.brown.edu/news/2021-09-01/costsofwar
[60] Too big to fail: https://en.wikipedia.org/wiki/Too_big_to_fail

EQualized.) The outbreak of this global financial crisis sparked a global recession, beginning in the United States and affecting most of the industrialized world.

The growth of the Internet contributed to globalization during the decade, which allowed faster communication among people around the world; social networking sites like Myspace and Facebook arose as a new way for people to stay in touch from distant locations. And in 2008, Barak Hussein Obama was elected 44th President, a symbol of hope and change, the first African American to hold that office. He inherited an extremely divided country and the worst economy and recession, bordering on collapse, in nearly a hundred years. (Ironically, decades earlier when comedian Richard Pryor was asked if he would like to become the first Black president, he replied *"Hell no, they will only put us at the helm of a ship when it's sinking and already half sunk"*—how prophetic he was!)

Episode One: Tallahassee 9/11/2001: "War is a Racket"

For Rich and family, the new millennia started with a bang, -- the move to Tallahassee, Florida, to start a charter school, and the birth of their eighth and final child (and sixth daughter). And then the world, as they knew it, changed—on September 11, 2001, while Rich was at work selling cars at a Toyota car dealer (as there weren't many other good paying jobs in the area), he was taking a coffee break and watched in horror on the waiting room television, together with all of the other staff and customers huddled together also watching in disbelief and horror, the World Trade Center towers, which he had worked in years earlier, crumbling live on TV. (After watching that unfold, Rich immediately left the dealership to be with his family and to call his family in New York to make sure they were safe. That day he quit the job and never returned to the dealership as the nonsense they were peddling on how to pressure sell and rip off customers was not something he wanted to engage in, ever, but especially when the entire world was reeling from and processing what had happened—the first foreign attack on American soil in his lifetime.)

To put it in perspective, the last time the U.S. was attacked on its own soil causing mass casualties was at Pearl Harbor, Hawaii, in 1941, sixty years earlier, causing the U.S. to enter World War II against Japan, Germany, and Italy. That attack killed 2403 Americans, mostly soldiers, while the 9/11 attack killed nearly 3000, mostly civilians. So, the question in many people's minds, was what will be America's response, and would this lead to another World War? In the days that followed, many spoke of revenge and retaliation, including most elected representatives from both parties. However, Rich, who in Atlanta had begun learning more deeply about the non-violent tactics and teachings of Dr. King and Gandhi, wondered if America would instead exercise moral leadership and try to discover why those who orchestrated and supported this deadly attack hated America that much, and then try to reduce or transform that hate by means other than war. This was to be a major test of America's moral character and leadership.

America failed that test and opportunity miserably using the tragedy to not only retaliate against the attack's alleged organizers but to dishonestly justify a war against countries it had wanted to invade and control for years—just a repeat of the same corrupt and terroristic, colonial-minded, empire building of the past. So, Rich found himself at massive anti-war demonstrations once again, as he had in the 70's except this time there were global demonstrations against U.S. aggression. The anti-war coalitions were broader, including leftists, pacificists, Muslims, and their supporters.[61] (Rich's thoughts and actions in this regard are summed up in the following two statements. One is from Congresswoman Barbara Lee, D-California, who cast the only dissenting vote in all of Congress against the immediate use of force against "terrorists", when asked why she voted against it Lee pointed to her professional training as a social worker and remarked, "*Right now, we're dealing with recovery, and we're dealing with mourning, and there's no way... [we should]... deal with decisions that could escalate violence and spiral out of control.*"[62] Her words were prophetic as that is exactly what happened—retaliatory violence and war "spiraled out of control" for over twenty years. And the other statement came from British journalist Martin Woollacott, writing in *The Guardian*, who called the attacks, "*above all a stupendous crime*", but also wrote, "*America's best defense against terrorism originating from abroad remains the existence of governments and societies more or less satisfied with American even-handedness on issues which are important to them. Plainly, this is furthest from the case in the Muslim world.*"[63]) Still, America is not "even-handed" in the Muslim world, causing continued hatred and only increasing the threat of terrorism. Imagine you are a young Muslim man or women, and the U.S. considers you and your family as collateral in their war on terror, so they kill one of your innocent parents or siblings. Will you not grow up with a hatred for America and a thirst for revenge against its terrorism? Now multiply that by the thousands or millions. Everywhere we go in the world we create enemies through our violence and terrorism, just as we create crime and gangs in America through our inequitable and racist policing and police-state system of mass incarceration, which increased exponentially after 9/11, and our system of punitive rather than restorative justice. ***They are EQualized.***

---

[61] For more on the Post–September 11 anti-war movement read https://en.wikipedia.org/wiki/Post%E2%80%93September_11_anti-war_movement

[62] http://www.daveyd.com/barbaraleevotepolitics.html

[63] https://www.theguardian.com/politics/2001/sep/12/september11.britainand9111

Despite all of the public opposition to and outcry against the invasions of Afghanistan and Iraq, and the predictable endless "war against terror, "when the U.S. government would not listen and had their own agenda, the power and influence of the military-industrial complex became much clearer and apparent to Rich and to millions of others. Now that he was more mature and experienced than when he had protested the Vietnam War as a youth, it opened his eyes wider, and, after studying the issue more thoroughly, he became much more anti-military and anti-militarism—one of MLK's triple evils.

One major influence were the writings of the retired and late Marine Major General Smedley Butler, who, at the time of his death, was the most decorated Marine in U.S. history, and especially his book *"War is a Racket"* in which he says, *"I spent 33 years and four months in active military service and during that period I spent most of my time as a high class muscle man for Big Business, for Wall Street and the bankers. In short, I was a racketeer, a gangster for capitalism. I helped make Mexico…safe for American oil interests…. I helped make Haiti and Cuba a decent place for the National City Bank boys to collect revenues in. I helped in the raping of half a dozen Central American republics for the benefit of Wall Street. I helped purify Nicaragua for the International Banking House of Brown Brothers…. I brought light to the Dominican Republic for the American sugar interests in … I helped make Honduras right for the American fruit companies... In China…I helped see to it that Standard Oil went on its way unmolested. Looking back on it, I might have given Al Capone a few hints. The best he could do was to operate his racket in three districts. I operated on three continents."*

And, *"War is a racket. It always has been. It is possibly the oldest, easily the most profitable, surely the most vicious. It is the only one international in scope. It is the only one in which the profits are reckoned in dollars and the losses in lives. A racket is best described, I believe, as something that is not what it seems to the majority of the people. Only a small 'inside' group knows what it is about. It is conducted for the benefit of the very few, at the expense of the very many. Out of war a few people make huge fortunes."* And here are his recommended three steps to disrupt the war racket:

1. Make war unprofitable. Butler suggests that the means for war should be "conscripted" before those who would fight the war: It can be smashed effectively only by taking the profit out of war. The only way to smash this racket is to conscript capital and industry and labor before the nation's manhood can be conscripted… "Let the officers and the directors and the high-powered executives of our armament factories and our steel companies and our munitions makers and our shipbuilders and our airplane builders and the manufacturers of all other things that provide profit in war time as well as the bankers and the speculators, be conscripted — to get $30 a month, the same wage as the lads in the trenches get. In other words, draft the elitists to fight the wars and you will see how quickly they end

wars."

2. Acts of war to be decided by those who fight it. He also suggests a limited referendum to determine if the war is to be fought. Eligible to vote would be those who risk death on the front lines.

3. Limitation of militaries to self-defense. For the United States, Butler recommends that the Navy be limited, by law, to operating within 200 miles of the coastline, and the Army restricted to the territorial limits of the country, ensuring that war, if fought, can never be one of aggression.[64]

Rich also learned of the many hundreds of other racketeering interventions conducted by our military and CIA, in the works of William Blum: *"Rogue State"* and *"Killing Hope: U.S. Military and CIA Interventions since World War II."* In *"Rogue State,"* Blum writes: *"If I were president, I could stop terrorist attacks against the United States in a few days. Permanently. I would first apologize - very publicly and sincerely - to all the widows and orphans, the impoverished and the tortured, and the many millions of other victims of American imperialism. Then I would announce to every corner of the world that America's global military interventions have come to an end."*[65]

The United States spends more on national defense than China, India, Russia, United Kingdom, Saudi Arabia, Germany, France, Japan, and South Korea combined. Were it not for this, the U.S. could adequately take care of its poor, its veterans, its homeless, and solve most of its domestic social inequity issues.

Rich realized then, and continues to realize now, that the U.S. military-industrial complex and its enforcement arms of the U.S. armed forces and CIA is and has been the most destructive force in the world and at home since at least the early 1900's, causing many if not most of the world's and this country's problems. This is why Dr. King included militarism as one of the Triple Evils, along with racism and poverty; they are all closely interrelated.

As to those who volunteer to serve in the military, most may have good motives though they are unwitting pawns being used to further American terrorism, gangsterism, and empire building, and are sacrificial lambs to the gods of materialism and capitalism (which is why Rich and V blocked any and all military recruiters, who often lie about the benefits of service to entice youth, especially targeting minority communities, from even speaking with their children and youth in their schools.) We pay lip service in thanking military veterans for their service when we do not provide them with adequate

---

[64] Read more about Smedley Butler and War is a Racket at https://en.wikipedia.org/wiki/War_Is_a_Racket and https://en.wikipedia.org/wiki/Smedley_Butler

[65] Read more about Blum's works at https://en.wikipedia.org/wiki/Rogue_State:_A_Guide_to_the_World%27s_Only_Superpower and https://en.wikipedia.org/wiki/Killing_Hope

healthcare, and especially mental health care, so they become homeless and suicidal in record numbers. Thank you for your service---really? Hollow words of hypocrisy. (So, Rich vehemently dissuades any young folks, especially young people of color who are disproportionately targeted, recruited, and lied to by military recruiters, from joining, and he fights against military recruitment in our high schools.) However, it is a sad fact that many poor Americans, again disproportionately people of color, see entering the military as their only possible way out of poverty—which is another set up by the elites who have always used the poor as fodder for their wars, greed, and follies.

As Major General Butler said, make the elites send their kids to war and these wars will cease. The importance of this subject cannot be over-emphasized because, in this century, militarism channeled through the military-industrial complex pervades our society and is the root cause of poverty, racism, police brutality, the police state, mass incarceration, homelessness, and inequities in healthcare, education, and employment. If we don't cut off the head of that beast, which is the ultimate bully, by drastically cutting back its funding and operations, it will continue to devour us and the world. Dr. King and others spoke emphatically about this decades ago, and the same is even more true today. ***They are EQualized!***

Episode Two: Defending Muslims in America

Rich then focused his efforts on defending the Muslims in America and Islam in general since he found most Americans were and still are completely ignorant about the true nature of the faith of "true Islam" (as opposed to "political Islam" or "jihadist Islam", its gross distortions, just as "political Christianity", or the "Christian conservatives", or the "Christian right", in America, are gross distortions of true Christianity; ***they are EQualized***).

He found that most Americans didn't have a clue that Islam contributed the first concepts and practices of nationhood of universities, and of mathematics (which form the basis of computer algorithms today), and that while Christian Europe was in the Dark Ages only after the Europeans came in contact with and learned from the more advanced Muslim empire did Europe's rebirth and Renaissance take place. (You can even learn that fact from school world history textbooks.) In typical European fashion, the so-called Christians started a war, the Crusades, to forcefully invade and acquire Muslim controlled lands, including the Holy Land (which now is divided between the countries of Israel and Palestine).Today this continues in the endless war between the corrupt American and European backed Israeli government and the Palestinians, whose lands were stolen by the Europeans based on the two main causes of war: religious bigotry and material greed. Can you believe that a European coalition, led by England, gave Palestinian lands to Israel? How can you right the wrongs against the Jews by doing the same to another people? How can England give anyone land which is not theirs to give? That unbelievable arrogance of the Europeans is what has infected America and what America adopted and continues in that tradition. (Ironically, the Europeans seem to learn from their mistakes more quickly than do Americans. Why are we behind and backwards? Read on. *We are EQualized.*)

It appeared that Americans, especially white Americans, always need a boogeyman to be afraid of in order to be controlled by fear, so this time American corrupt politicians, aided and abetted by business and religious leaders, chose Muslims as that target and scapegoat, and, as always, fear turned into hate and violence towards them. Rich, proudly and publicly, proclaimed to his community that he was a Muslim (because as a Bahai one is a Christian, Jew, Muslim, Buddhist, Hindu, etc.), and that any threats of violence toward or bullying of Muslims would be considered as violence toward him, his family, and his faith community, and would be dealt with. (As Rich proclaimed and taught many times before, and cannot repeat enough, bigotry toward any one religion is bigotry and betrayal of all religions, since they are so interconnected, like progressive grades in a school, building on and fulfilling past learning and preparing us for the next level.[66] And whether one is a believer or not, all are impacted by the world religions, both positively and negatively, as most major progressive and spiritual ideas are first pronounced and proclaimed by the religious prophets long before they become accepted beliefs and practices in secular society.)[67] On the down-side, religious fundamentalism and bigotry is the cause of more wars than any other factors, except for materialism-- the quest for land, property, and economic domination—and they often go hand in hand. *They are EQualized.* That is why one must distinguish between false religion and true religion. The former is used to oppress, dominate, control, and limit, while the latter uplifts, empowers, enables self-determination, and is the source of limitless spiritual power, happiness, fulfillment, and goodness. However, the bottom line is that no one should be forced to believe, and the lack of belief in any part of it is no cause for any judgement because ultimately when it comes to one's spirit and spiritual beliefs that is a personal and private decision. (In his travels Rich met many humanists and self-declared atheists who were more spiritual or "Christian" in their acts toward others than the so-called Christian believers. He found that when many people say they are atheistic in their beliefs, when he drilled down and questioned them further, they really have objected to and rejected the concept of religion and "God" that has been forced down

---

[66] Read more about this Bahai concept of "Progressive Revelation" at https://bahaiteachings.org/bahai-concept-progressive-revelation/

[67] This was the view expressed and outlined by eminent historian, Arnold Toynbee, in his 12-volume seminal work *"A Study of History"*, that the advent of each true world religion, and the spiritual, social, and scientific principles each brought, caused civilization to progress , progressively. Read more at: http://nobsword.blogspot.com/1993_10_17_nobsword_archive.html#universal%20churches

their and others' throats—the false religion as described above—and they often do have their own spiritual concepts and beliefs, though perhaps different than those of mainstream religions. It doesn't matter because all true spiritual paths reach the same ultimate positive goals and values.) Also, just as it's important to distinguish between true and false religion, we need to distinguish between a true prophet and a false prophet. The former sacrifices for and serves the cause of oneness while the latter is self-serving, accumulating wealth and power in the name of spirituality or religion. Also, the difference between prophets and philosophers is the philosopher has great ideas and visions but cannot live by or demonstrate them in the field of action, while the prophet shares great ideas, wisdom and visions and demonstrates them in practical action, even in the face of violent opposition. MLK Jr. is a great example of a modern-day American prophet, and there are many others throughout history: Ella Baker, Harriet Tubman, Sojourner Truth, Frederick Douglass and many whose names are not well known. Some of the American founding fathers were great philosophers however they did not practice the ideals they wrote about, for example, the Declaration of Independence statement that "all men are created equal," while they owned slaves. Ask yourself: would you want to be known as a prophet or a philosopher? (More about that in the Epilogue and how we can help each other fulfill our life purposes.)

Episode Three: Quincy, Gadsden County, Florida: A Throwback

Back on the ground in Tallahassee, the charter school experiments Rich and family engaged in had their ups and downs and were definitely a learning experience in cooperative education. Meanwhile, their racial justice, spiritual oneness, and beloved community development work continued as Rich learned from local friends of a struggle taking place in a neighboring town, Quincy in Gadsden County, where the majority Blacks were fighting for self-determination wrested from a few wealthy white families whose money and power controlled the county politics and economics. Those white families had allowed some Blacks to be elected to positions there, as long as those Blacks jumped when their white masters said jump and dance to their tune—a throwback to plantation politics (which was and is still practiced widely, not only in the South but around the country). Rich and family visited the town regularly, teaching oneness and unity classes in the neighborhoods and gaining the trust of the Black community leaders who wanted change and more self-determination.

One qualified Black man ran for mayor, was elected, and decided it was time for change and that he was not going to dance only to the white elite's tunes any longer. That upset the whole plantation applecart, so the white moneyed families hired a private detective to follow the new Mayor daily and record his every move to find some dirt in order to oust him from office.

Eventually, they did, on a minor charge. (If we did the same, tailing anyone including all public figures, there will always be dirt or something minor but illegal found. **We are all EQualized.** In fact, as Equalizers, that may be a tactic to use on bullies, and with the advent of the internet and social media it is ever easier to track the words and actions of haters.) But that did not deter another independent and change-agent Black man to run for county Sheriff, and he eventually won and was not ousted. So, change was coming, and Rich and family, while playing a small part in helping to transform that town, learned a lot about plantation politics there. (One important lesson Rich learned was that though electing and appointing diverse representatives and officials is important, we must look past their skin color to determine if they are independent change-agents or controlled by the plantation house. One of Rich's closest, community activist brothers, the late Haroun Shahid Wakil, used to say" *Just because you're white doesn't mean you're right, and just because you're Black doesn't mean you have my back!")*

Tallahassee, being the state capitol, afforded Rich opportunities to participate in and support protests for various issues. One of the issues in question at the time was "affirmative action"—should it be ended? That was the position of GOP Governor Jeb Bush aided by Walter Williams, a conservative Black economist and professor (and likely beneficiary of affirmative action programs himself), who jointly held a public hearing and forum on the issue. It appears that Mr. Williams had "forgotten where he came from". At the forum, he stated that it was time to end "race-based privilege", so Rich asked him and the Governor one simple question, "How will you get rid of mine—that is, my white, race-based unearned privilege which I and my ancestors have had for generations in this country?" They had no answers for that, and abruptly changed the subject. (Rich had learned in the past that a few carefully placed questioners in any audience, with simple but confounding questions, often worked to change the dynamics of any gathering and expose any hidden or overt superiority complexes. In this case Mr. Williams' bigotry appeared to be educational or intellectual bigotry. In another, involving religious bigotry, when Rich was living in the Caribbean, he had attended a convention of "Christians," led by pastors who wanted to start a "Christian political party." When given the opportunity to speak he simply asked, "If elected, will you treat non-Christians as equals?" That threw their whole discussion into disarray because they did not want their Christian superiority complex exposed by answering "no," and they didn't want to admit that non-Christians were equals, since they didn't really believe they are, by answering "yes." 😊 **They were EQualized!)**

Episode Four: "Count on Being Busted": Cobb County, GA--2002

As Rich and the Pellegrino family's two-year charter school experiment in Tallahassee was coming to an end, they decided that while there were a lot of both good and learning (a nice way to say "bad") experiences there, it was not the "village" or "beloved community" they were seeking to help them raise and grow the family. They decided to move back to the Atlanta area in Georgia mainly for economic reasons since there had been few good paying jobs in Tallahassee.

However, their two eldest children decided to stay and attend college in Tallahassee—so the nomadic Pellegrino tribe's number decreased from ten to eight again. In 2002, they settled in the Atlanta metro area western suburb of Cobb County, notorious for its racism to the extent that many of Rich's Black friends said they would not visit him because "DWB" ("Driving While Black") was a crime there. In fact, Cobb was known to stand for *"Come on Black boy," "Caught on Bail Bond,"* and *"Count on Being Busted,"* and it had lived up to those labels for people of color for decades.

A year later, when Rich first met with the Cobb Police Chief and asked him about those allegations of and reputation for racism, his department attorney, who was in the meeting, quickly answered stating that the department's philosophy and motto was *"We sweat the small stuff."* He further explained that while other metro area police departments might give warnings or citations for minor violations, Cobb Police Department arrests you. He also implied but didn't say outright that Black folks commit more crimes, so they are more likely to get busted and arrested (which is blatantly false, though a widely held white supremacist lie disproven by independent research. Also, Rich knew from his life experiences, as he was part of criminal syndicates earlier in life, that white people commit more crimes of all types, including selling more drugs, but are less likely to be caught doing so. Now, years later, things have changed for the better in Cobb through two decades of fighting for such change, however Cobb PD still gives the same excuses when asked about the disproportionate number of Black arrests and citations.)

When Rich pressed the Police Chief further and asked about racial profiling, he denied its existence. Rich then asked, *"Ok, so you sweat the small stuff. I am white and I speed like a NY driver and never get stopped. Is it just a coincidence, or does my whiteness have something to do with it?* The chief replied with a hearty laugh and said, *"Ok, give me your tag number and car description and I will tell my traffic enforcement division to look for and stop you."* To them all this was a big joke because that is how they always did things in the South, and here is this northern "Yankee" questioning them. Later, when he got to know them better, Rich suggested, *"OK, if you are going to "sweat the small stuff" with the public, how about if we community activists and citizens start to "sweat the small stuff" with police officers, watching and calling out their every suspicious and sometimes illegal moves.*" They didn't like that or laugh at that but got Rich's message and knew he meant it! ***They were Equalized!***

Rich and family moved into the more diverse and affordable area of South Cobb. It was still majority white, many with confederate flags adorning their homes and vehicles. But that was gradually changing with the slow but steady influxes of West Africans, then Latinos, and then Black Americans, pretty much in that order. (Now, 20 years later, people of color are the majority and whites are the minority.) "White flight" also gradually occurred, with those whites who could afford to move to more affluent and white areas of East Cobb fleeing there, or moving to more western, rural counties, while poorer whites remained and simply dug in, hoisting their confederate flags higher and likely arming themselves in fear of the diversity and "invading hordes." (Rich and other community activists believe that their advocacy work in making Cobb a more welcoming place for minorities helped to fuel and attract this influx of people of color, moving it one step closer to becoming a ***Beloved Community.***) Rich and family had learned, in all of their travels and moves, that the more diverse a community the better, for many reasons, but the chief one being that is the true strength, uniqueness and destiny of America—it's incredible diversity. They were a bit weary from continually moving around the country teaching and seeking their "*Beloved Community*"*,* and now that the family was complete—all ten of them--- they decided to finally put down some roots and build their beloved community right there in South Cobb.

Episode Five: "Babyland" Beloved Community, Austell, GA

Once settled in Cobb County in the small town of Austell, together with some Bahai friends they adopted a nearby neighborhood called "Babyland" for a community development project. Though nestled in the middle of a modern and developing suburb, it was a throwback to earlier days with some older homes not even having basic amenities like functional utilities, next door to more modern homes. The residents were mostly Black and related to each other, with a sprinkling of poor whites and Latinos--- a perfect mix, Rich believed, to start and build a Beloved ***Community*** development initiative. (Legend had it that the neighborhood derived its name, "Babyland," from the fact that during Jim Crow segregation Blacks were not allowed in the white hospitals so the midwife delivering Black babies at her home was in that neighborhood.)

A diverse team comprised of Rich, his family members, and some Bahai and other friends, started the "Babyland" initiative, befriending, listening to, and learning from the residents by walking the streets, in the neighborhood park, and going door to door. The residents were very friendly and welcoming and, once trust was built, very willing to open up and share their hopes and dreams since really no one in government paid attention to their needs and they felt neglected. Based on what the team learned from a lot of listening (which is the basis for any successful community development initiative, otherwise it is just another top-down, "white-savior" mentality, super- imposed "help", which is often not helpful or sustainable at all), they started children's and youth classes and activities based on Bahai oneness and *Beloved Community* principles, and helped find jobs for residents, and transportation to jobs, healthcare and other services (since they were not on the bus-line). Eventually they lobbied the county to get bus service established there, and connected the residents with other social services, including housing rehab to help upgrade and repair their homes. The City of Austell began to take notice and was so impressed with this grassroots development work that it donated a house it owned nearby to serve as a community center. The local church leaders also took notice, joining in to support the efforts, but also were skeptical and cautious since they were not used to working with each other and definitely not the diverse team members, some of whom who were not "Christian" in their view (a prime example of religious bigotry).

Eventually, the pastors wanted to take over control and manage the initiative, and helped form a more formal community organization, "Babyland Improvement Group" (B.I.G). Rich and team then took a more supportive rather than leadership role, since they didn't live in the neighborhood and wanted it to become self-sustaining with the local residents leading. The initiative thrived for a few years, gaining regional and national attention as community organizers came from near and afar to visit and learn. Ultimately, however, it ended due to disunity within the ranks of the formal leadership, who were not used to working with unity in diversity and the cooperative principles of building *"Beloved Community"*. Some good things remained though, as Rich and team made some lifelong friends there, helped some families to become self-sustaining, and a local resident they helped empower were elected to City Council, so the neighborhood's needs were no longer neglected.

Some of the key lessons learned from the "Babyland" development initiative, include:

1) It is difficult to sustain a community or neighborhood development initiative without residing directly in that community or finding grassroots resident-champions who live there. And religious pastors are not necessarily good resident champions. (Though Rich lived only ten minutes away, it might have been hours because it being two different worlds. This is a mistake made too often by "outside" helpers who don't take the time to listen to the people being helped,

and therefore apply remedies that may or may not help or are extremely short term and not self-sustaining.)

2) Never assume that people from diverse backgrounds or even of similar backgrounds but from different families, churches, and organizations know how to work together cooperatively and to resolve their disagreements amicably and fairly. Americans have not been trained to do this, and have actually been conditioned and trained to do the opposite and compete rather than cooperate, to engage in one upmanship, and to use whatever tactics necessary to "win," whether in business, politics, school, sports, religion, etc. So, there is a lot of training, guidance, and structure necessary to unlearn some of these behaviors and replace them with "cooperation" and "unity in diversity" when working together in coalitions and as one community. (Rich had learned such cooperative, consensus building, and conflict resolution methods in Bahai assemblies, from Dr. King's deputies and his organizations, and from leftist organizations.) Americans are so divided by religion, church, politics, race, gender, class, education, etc. that we have to learn, or relearn, our "oneness," the concept we are born with but has been stripped from us gradually by our institutions. "Divide and conquer" the masses has been the elites' motto and successful tactic since America's founding, which is why they invented and promoted the false concept of different races in the first place, and also the false concept of competing religions.

3) Many people who are poor want to work and better themselves. In most cases they are poor due to circumstances beyond their control and should never be blamed for being poor, as is the case in most of America. They are not lazy—in fact, those who accuse them of that would likely not be able to endure the struggles and suffering they experience, especially the working poor. Aid agency workers, whether government or non-profit, often have condescending attitudes toward the poor when they are applying for assistance—another example of when help is not really help.(Many times when Rich had applied for assistance, whether for his own family or for others, he had to *EQualize* the aid workers who, through their own bigotry and class supremacy, thought they could treat those whom they considered to be beneath them rudely. Rich would often tell the rude ones, *"If you don't like working with and for people then get a different non-public facing job, like stocking shoe store shelves."* **They were EQualized!)** Regarding the laziness issue, Rich found jobs for some of the "Babyland" young adults in a chicken processing plant twenty miles away—very difficult and backbreaking work—and, due to lack of public transportation and before he could arrange rides, they rode

their bicycles for hours there and back, in addition to working gru-eling shifts at the plant. Not one of the poor's detractors could or would endure that, so, really, who are the lazy ones? This has never been the land of opportunity for the masses in America, and the sys-tem is and was always rigged that for everyone who "makes it," ten don't, especially BIPOC folks (Blacks, Indigenous, People of Color). Dr. King outlined how white Americans, even many of the lower or middle class, were given every benefit---land grants, affordable hous-ing, free or subsidized higher education—all denied to people of color. He said what America has is *"Socialism for the rich and capitalism for the poor."* And: *"It's all right to tell a man to lift himself by his own boot-straps, but it is a cruel jest to say to a bootless man that he ought to lift himself by his own bootstraps."* **He Equalized them.** And: *"The curse of poverty has no justification in our age. It is socially as cruel and blind as the prac-tice of cannibalism at the dawn of civilization…"* --MLK

Episode Six: "The Secret": Power of Attraction

Rich's marketing consulting business was providing for the family, but just making ends meet, so he decided to explore additional revenue streams. Always creative and entrepreneurial, he sought opportunities that would not detract from the time spent with family and community building. As always, the Universe placed in his path the people and learning resources that would assist him in that quest—which he would soon learn was due to the *"power of attraction and manifestation."* In fact, he had been utilizing those concepts and powers for most of his life without consciously realizing it. He met a Bahai friend and self-made technology millionaire, Raj, from India. Raj wanted to help others of all backgrounds, including Rich, to increase their wealth so they could help others with whatever noble goals and endeavors they had planned, since the ultimate goal and station for Bahais and other spiritually oriented souls is service and servant leadership. Rich offered to help Raj fulfill his mission of teaching others entrepreneurship and economic self-determi-nation, and he recruited friends and colleagues to attend Raj's introductory presentation at his luxurious home in one of Atlanta's most affluent areas. For that presentation, Raj first showed the relatively new movie entitled *"The Secret"* based on the book of the same name by Rhonda Byrne about the *"power of attraction."*[68] Watching that movie, and during the discussion of it afterwards, Rich realized that it was really the story of his life's journey of learning, opportunities, and adventures, and that, in fact, he had been utilizing those concepts and powers for most of his life without knowing it. Now that

---

[68] For more on "The Secret" book and movie go to https://www.thesecret.tv/.

he could put a name to it and learned that the powers outlined were as veri-fiable as gravity, not only with spiritual proofs but scientific ones, he was determined to learn how to consciously use these powers to plan, fulfill and manifest higher goals, and to teach others how to do the same. So, for almost a year, he held regular, well-attended, and diverse gatherings at his home showing the movie and helping participants set goals based on the principles of attraction-- *"The Secret"*. He also decided, at his family's and Raj's urging, to use "the Secret" principles to focus on the goal of substantially increasing his family's economic wealth. Although Raj also offered him the opportunity to partner and manage some of his lucrative businesses, both in the U.S. and India, that would have required excessive time and travel away from his fam-ily and community, which he was not willing to do. However, he agreed to join some colleagues in the world of high-stakes business financing, which involved "shark-tank" like meetings to match investors with start-ups and later stage companies. He learned a lot (but mostly about the cut-throat, com-petitive, greedy, and sometimes fraudulent nature of capitalism and finance) and came close to overnight wealth a few times. His team had some multi-million-dollar deals, which, if closed successfully, would have provided some million-dollar commissions to Rich and team. But they all fell through, caus-ing some potential investors and entrepreneurs to lose significant sums. And Rich realized that there were no ethics in that field, so it was not for him. At the same time, one of his long-term goals was about to be fulfilled, in a pretty big way…stay tuned. But first, some of his key take away learnings from study and practice of the "power of attraction"—the *"Secret"*:

1. Generally speaking, whatever you focus on you get (except there are some safeguards if what you want is not good for you, but that is only if you believe there is a Higher Power, above or greater than the power of attrac-tion). This also means if you focus on and put energy towards what you don't want then you will likely get more of what you don't want because the force doesn't know if you want or don't want something---it just assumes that whatever you are focusing on is what you want. So, if you focus on negativity, you will get more negativity, and if you focus on positivity, then you will get more of that. (This does not mean to deny the negative things which you witness or experience but enables the use of positive energy to help overcome the negatives which must be identified.)

2. There is enough! That is, the Universe made sure that there is enough of everything that we need in the world to go around, so the only reason for some to have and some to have not is greed and hording by those who have. If people just believed and worked with this concept there would be no more basis for economic wars. However, due to the excesses of mainly Euro-American materialism and greed, exported worldwide, this natural abundance

is rapidly becoming depleted, and the natural balance of the world is completely out of sync causing coming calamities as evidenced by climate change and related increasing disturbances. So, it is imperative to get back to a sustainable balance. (Back to one of Rich's favorite mottos to live by, the Ghandi quote: *"Live simply so that others may simply live."*)

3. Life in all its forms is energy, so if you learn how to harness and channel energy in positive ways, you have mastered life. This is taught in all the true religious and spiritual paths that Rich had studied and practiced, in many ways using the tools of prayer, meditation, chanting, yoga and similar practices. Also, all of the arts are another potent tool for channeling energy. And energy healing is real!

Episode Seven: Hurricane Katrina & the Common Ground Collective

In August 2005, the huge and destructive Category 5 Hurricane Katina hit New Orleans, Louisiana, causing at least 1800 deaths (mostly people of color and the poor) and over $125 billion in damage. The poor response to the devastation and lack of water and food showed how unprepared Americans, especially in the cities and all levels of government agencies, were. In its aftermath, the city was lawless and armed militias and gangs ruled the streets. (A must read is the book by scott crow, *"Black Flags and Windmills: Hope, Anarchy, and the Common Ground Collective"*, which depicts true stories of survival in the storm's aftermath, and what we should be building and preparing for now in our communities before the next storm or disaster hits; this dovetails to what Rich had been working on for decades—intentional communities and collectives.) In Atlanta, thousands fleeing New Orleans filled hotels to the brink and Rich and family went to one of these large hotels on regular occasions to make sure the families were taken care of and were matched with longer term residences in people's homes. (The silver lining was that many white families in Cobb County opened their hearts and homes to fleeing New Orleans families, who were mostly Black and many also poor. This was likely their first time having Black folks in their homes and it could only serve to open minds and humanize each other—a good thing because that is how prejudice and personal racism is solved. ***They were EQualized!***)

Episode Eight: Bienvenidos Inmigrantes/Welcome Immigrants/The CIA

Rich and family, together at times with his teaching team "the Eagles," had been traveling and teaching the spiritual principles of oneness, unity, justice, and beloved community for decades in towns around the U.S. and in the Caribbean, mainly in Black and Indigenous communities. Using the "each one, teach one" method, they had positively impacted and transformed many individuals and neighborhoods. Though he loved teaching one on one, or in small groups, especially on the streets of the ghettoes, barrios, and reservations, it had been Rich's goal to also reach and impact larger numbers of people, the masses, to move America closer to its destiny of unity in diversity and servant leadership to the world. He knew that America has a celebrity and media driven culture, so he used the power of attraction methods to focus on and envision how to reach and use prominent people to help spread the message. Sometimes the answers come unexpectedly and in ways one could not predict. (This is where he saw a Higher Power guiding his use of the power of attraction away from focusing on developing material wealth and toward the fulfillment of his goal of reaching prominent people with the message of oneness. He also realized the importance of being in tune with your spirit so that when a door of seeming opportunity opens you can step through it and try it out. If it's not the right door you can always go back, but if it is and you don't try it you will have missed a golden, God, or Universe-given, opportunity. The potential wealth door was not for him, but at least he experienced and learned from it. This next door was what he was *actively* waiting for--- there are two kinds of waiting—active and passive. Active waiting means that you are using the tools available to focus on achieving your goal and acting as if it is already fulfilled.)

Here is how it happened: It was the December 2006 holiday break and Rich and family were relaxing and enjoying the holiday season. The local news was on the TV. They had been seeing many anti-immigrant news stories and political ads for months fueled by fear-mongering, racist, xenophobic politicians and gobbled up by many Americans, mostly white on the right, who were seeking new boogeymen to be afraid of and target since their hate for and fear of Muslims had cooled off a bit.(Close-minded, ignorant, and racist Americans, really "haters", always seem to need such boogeymen to blame their problems on so they don't have to look in the mirror and accept responsibility, and the corrupt politicians eagerly feed them their demons. And of the two major political parties, though it used to be the Democrats centuries ago, it is now the Republicans who have adopted hate of these manufactured demons as their central platform. Sadly, they keep sinking deeper in the depths of that hate and further and further away from their true conservative and libertarian roots.)

Rich was already feeling that this brewing anti-immigrant fever and furor was about to become the new civil rights battles, this time targeting brown-skinned people coming from south of the border (many of whom were also mixed Native American). But, like most Americans, due to language barriers and lack of knowledge about immigrants, Rich was still on the fence about jumping into the fray, as he was still busy defending Muslims and Islam, and his own Black family and friends (who have always been a target, and still are). However, this newscast was about how a neighboring county, Cherokee

County (how ironic a name), had just passed an ordinance stating that anyone trying to rent a home or apartment there had to prove their citizenship. This was the last straw, totally unconstitutional and racist—an example of rampant and arrogant white supremacy. (Rich half-jokingly said they should have passed an ordinance stating that anyone wanting to rent a home there had to prove Cherokee heritage 😊.)

Rich gathered his family in the living room and said, "We have to do something to welcome these embattled immigrants and show them that at least some Americans are not haters and are appreciative of their contributions to our community and country." (They later learned that most of the undocumented immigrants were imported here by government and businesses, who disregarded the complicated immigration laws to get cheaper and more productive labor, just as all immigrant groups were before---the Irish, Germans, Italians, etc. Also, most of those European immigrant groups were considered or were "illegal," so apparently the haters targeting these new immigrants forgot where they came from and how their ancestors got here. Twelve million people didn't sneak into America from Mexico and further south—they were brought and welcomed here by Americans and American businesses, at all levels, and there is extensive proof of that, right here in Atlanta and nationwide. As of the writing of this book, the thousands who are fleeing here now are refugees of our foreign economic policies which have devastated their countries, so it is simply karma and fair for us to accept and welcome them.)

So, Rich and family started, in their own neighborhood first, visiting homes where Hispanic and other immigrants resided and welcoming them to the neighborhood and the country. Then, they made posters stating *"Bienvenidos Inmigrantes/Welcome Immigrants"* and their entire multi-racial family, including some of their children's friends, spent the entire holiday season standing on the corners of busy intersections in Cherokee and Cobb counties waving those signs welcoming immigrants. They were pleasantly surprised by the positive reactions of many of the passersby, including many white and Black residents. The police even assisted rather than obstructed by guiding them to safe places to stand near the traffic. Before long, every major media outlet in the country was on their doorstep, including many big city newspapers like the LA Times and Boston Globe, since the Associated Press had spread the word about this new immigrant welcoming initiative. They told Rich, much to his surprise, the reason they were there was that they had never seen anyone doing this before, especially White and Black folks going out on the streets to welcome immigrants as he and his family were doing. And, after the media reports, representatives of all major civil rights leaders and organizations—Al Sharpton, Jesse Jackson, NAACP, SCLC, the King Center, etc., as well as the already established pro-immigrant and Latino organizations, contacted Rich and wanted to support and be part of this welcoming initiative, which was quickly becoming a movement.

Almost overnight, Rich's goal of getting the message of oneness and unity out to the masses through prominent people and organizations was fulfilled---the power of attraction! Local Atlanta area immigrant organizations, primarily GALEO (Georgia Association of Latino Elected Officials) and GLAHR (Georgia Latino Association for Human Rights), offered to mentor and train Rich in his new role as a spokesperson and advocate for immigrant rights. This assistance he gladly accepted since he knew little, like most Americans, about immigration laws, history, and policies, and why and how large numbers of undocumented immigrants, especially those from south of the border, were living and working in America. (Note that the term "illegal immigrants" is not used for several reasons, the main one being it is a bullying term only used to dehumanize these good people, many of whom are refugees fleeing violence and economic devastation caused by U.S. foreign policies and interventions in their countries. So, since NO ONE knows the accurate status of any immigrant until they have their day in court and the only distinction between any immigrants are those who have their documents to remain in the U.S., and those who don't yet, the proper and less dehumanizing term is "undocumented". AND NO HUMAN BEING IS ILLEGAL OR IS AN ILLEGAL, unless we all are! *We are Equalized!*)

Rich also learned, by studying American immigration history which is central to American history since this is a country composed of and settled by mostly immigrants, that most of our European immigrant ancestors from Italian, Irish, German and other ethnicities, were considered "illegal immigrants" or worse by the dominant WASPS--White, Anglo-Saxon Protestants-- of the time, so it is a case, for many haters, of forgetting or hiding where they came from and how they got here. (And none ever considered themselves "white" but whatever ethnicity they were. "White and Black," and the whole concepts of race and racial superiority, were terms and concepts invented by the elite in Europe to justify the transatlantic slave trade and then were adopted by the American elite for the same purpose.)

As he delved more deeply, Rich was about to learn some startling facts about his own Italian family's immigration story and that of many Italians. When he was contacted by a producer of a national Fox News talk show in New York to possibly be a guest on that show, his mother revealed that her father, Rich's grandfather, like many Italians who were merchant marines, had jumped ship and were trafficked into the U.S. through Canada with forged documents. He also learned it was for that reason that the derogatory nickname Italians were called, and Rich had been called by those of other ethnic groups his whole school life, "*WOP,*" stood for "*Without Papers.*" So, it became hilarious to Rich that many Italian Americans, including those in elected office, all of a sudden were against undocumented immigrants. They either didn't know their own family and cultural history, or conveniently forgot. And the same goes for Irish Americans and many other ethnic groups here. **They are Equalized—big time!**

As he studied and learned more, Rich was shocked but not surprised to find proof that the twelve million undocumented immigrants in the country at the time (which, he also learned, were composed of many ethnic groups from around the world, not just Latinos from south of the border) were invited here either directly or indirectly by both U.S. government, at all levels including state and local, and by many U.S. corporations. They hadn't snuck in over the border as many haters had indicated, and many had expired work visas which the companies and government agencies neglected to renew just due to bureaucratic failures.

One case in point that Rich witnessed personally is when Atlanta hosted the 1996 Summer Olympics. The city was behind deadline in building the necessary Olympics infrastructure. So, city, state and federal officials desperately reached out to the Mexican Consul General at the time, Teodoro Maus (who later would become, as the leader of GLAHR, one of Rich's mentors and close friends), asking if his country could send skilled and unskilled workers to help them meet their deadline in exchange for legal residency for some or all of them. They came and saved the day, but the Georgia and U.S. officials didn't keep their part of the deal (just another example of the American history of broken treaties and promises, using and abusing and then blaming the victims). So, the workers ended up living here undocumented, which happened routinely. Some of those same officials who had begged them to come, later, when immigrant bashing became popular among the white right and they needed a boogeyman to blame for their economic or political woes, were some of the loudest voices calling for immigrants to be rounded up and deported—how corrupt and racist! (But that is the story of America—both home and abroad, to exploit people, especially people of color, and then cast them aside. It is the story of slavery all over again.)

To formalize and channel all of the pro-immigrant support and goodwill pouring in both locally and nationally, Rich formed a coalition (which became one of his trademarks and titles, as a "Coalition Builder"). The Cobb Immigrant Alliance (CIA) was born, comprised of local, regional, and national organizations assisting immigrants to be welcomed into our society in spite of the hateful and violent rhetoric launched against them by haters and bullies at all levels. This support and acclaim came not without some notoriety, since there were (and still are) plenty of anti-immigrant haters stirring up the fears of the ignorant, even to the point of inciting violence. Rich and his family were targets of death threats by white supremacists who feared the "browning of America" by what they called the "Hispanic hordes" invading the country. This was fueled by conspiracy theories, not the least of which is *"The Replacement Theory"*, which the far right, white nationalists claim is a plan by government elites to replace whites with people of color through immigration and other policies and means.[69] (The interesting thing is that this *is* happening, not by anyone's plan, conspiracy, or design, but by that of the Universe or God or Nature—whatever higher power or natural order of things, or purveyor of karma, you believe in. And clinging to and trying to protect their "whiteness" is especially absurd since there really is no such thing as different races or whiteness—that was an invention of Europeans adopted by the American elite--- and the whole world is progressing toward oneness and back to the concept of one human race. *We are all Equalized!* So really, who cares about the diversifying and mixing of the so-called races unless, of course, you are a white supremacist. Sadly, the American conservatives and Republican party in America appear to have adopted these concepts of white supremacy as part of their platform as the only way they think they can win elections is to spread fear and hate of "the other." *They are being Equalized.*)

Some of the highlights of this exciting period of rapid growth in this next stage in Rich's and the country's progress toward the Beloved Community, include:

1. In doing this pro-immigrant work, a labor of love, Rich came to meet and learn from and about people from all cultural backgrounds—the true strength of America—unity in diversity, as there are rather large communities of undocumented immigrants and refugees not only from south of the border but from Eastern European (former Soviet), Asian, Middle Eastern, Pacific Islander, Caribbean Islander, and African nations. Each had their own story of how they got here and their struggles to get papers and legal status. It was clear that this is the next stage in the progress and development of America's destiny as the multicultural "salad bowl" of the world, in which diverse cultures mix but remain distinct in some respects, as opposed to the "melting pot" in which those cultures assimilate and mix to become one new culture. That was the goal of assimilation in the past but in modern, woke viewpoints, it is inherently a white supremacist concept because those espousing it assume that white, Euro-American culture is the standard and model that everyone else should follow, which is far from the truth. *It is EQualized. (*Whenever Rich spoke to groups of immigrants, wherever they were from, he emphasized the fact that though

---

[69] Read about "The Great Replacement" and "The Replacement Theory" at https://en.wikipedia.org/wiki/Great_Replacement

they may have come to America for some of its economic or educational benefits, their other purpose here is to teach Americans about the world and their cultures because Americans are largely ignorant about anything outside of their borders--as well as of many things within. And there is no excuse for this because even if one cannot afford to travel outside of the country there are so many wonderful ethnic communities right here who express their cultures through festivals, foods, and other events accessible to anyone who wants to learn and experience.)

2. Black-American friends of Rich in California applauded the immigrant welcoming work he and his coalition were doing but warned them to develop strong "Black-Brown" relationships ("Brown" representing all other ethnic groups not identified as White/European or Black; another way of saying "people of color") because some, particularly Latinos and Asians in California, when they got their rights and assimilated into white American culture, turned around and joined the racist chorus and discriminatory actions toward American Blacks. Many come to this country already infected with a racist bias against Black Americans due to American media and government propaganda exported around the world depicting Black Americans as inferior, so they will likely have some unlearning to do. And the pressure for them to assimilate into the dominant white culture further aggravates the situation. Rich often says, "Let *me be very clear— while all non-white peoples are discriminated against in America, Black Americans are still the victims of the most racial bias and discrimination, as it is institutionalized in every system and entity here, and has been for centuries*" Therefore immigrants, who have had less indoctrination and conditioning in this regard, have an important anti-racist role in eliminating this structural racism.

So, Rich and his Cobb Immigrant Alliance started a Black-Brown Coalition to bring Black Americans and immigrants of all colors together to begin a conscious antiracist effort to reverse the racist trends outlined above. Their work was studied by universities and think tanks, and won regional acclaim, outlined in a publication titled: *"Building Black-Brown Coalitions in the Southeast".*[70] Under the auspices of their broader "Cobb United for Change Coalition", which Rich co-founded, they hosted town halls to discuss Black-Brown unity, and worked successfully with Cobb Police to eliminate Black- on-Latino crimes of opportunity in most neighborhoods.

---

[70] *"Building Black-Brown Coalitions in the Southeast—Four African American-Latino Collaborations" can be read at* https://www.intergroupresources.com/rc/Alvarado%20and%20Jaret%202009.pdf

3. Haters in the Georgia State Legislature and Governor's office passed a draconian law (patterned after other "red" states' similar laws) stripping undocumented immigrants of driver's licenses (against the wishes of most law enforcement agencies and the common sense of public safety, which proves hate ultimately makes people go against their own self-interests). It also gave those agencies the right to inquire about every Georgia resident's citizenship status---again, a right and practice which most state and local law enforcement agencies did not want because in order to both prevent and solve crimes, they knew they must build trust with the community, especially communities of color and immigrant groups. They knew that enforcing these foolish laws would extremely damage that fragile trust.

So, Rich and his CIA, as well as other coalitions he was involved in, met with local law enforcement agencies, and agreed to help continue building bridges of trust between the immigrant community and police as long as police did not enforce those draconian laws, which they agreed to stop doing. That is, all except the Cobb Sheriff at the time, Neil Warren, a far right, racist, white supremacist and throw back to the days of Bull Conner and other corrupt, racist Southern sheriffs who enforced Jim Crow laws and continued doing so even after their abolishment. His idol was Arizona's infamous Maricopa County Sheriff Joe Arpaio, convicted criminal and racist for his crimes against immigrants and people of color. Like Arpaio and only a handful of other law enforcement agents around the country, Warren contracted with the notorious federal agency, ICE (Immigration and Customs Enforcement), which itself had a history of brutality and abuse, to deputize his deputies as immigration agents who could deport undocumented immigrants who passed through his jail—even for minor crimes of not having a driver's license. So, the Cobb police, in a major victory for Rich's coalitions, agreed not to arrest undocumented immigrants and to instead just give them citations for minor crimes so that the Sheriff and his deputies could not get their hands on them to deport them. (In many American counties there is a police force which enforces the laws and a Sheriff's department which runs the jails and performs other supportive tasks.) Police in other jurisdictions around metro Atlanta and the state followed suit, rendering those hater laws unenforced.

That racist Sheriff was eventually voted out of office, after too many years there, and replaced by a much more progressive one, again, thanks to efforts by Rich, his fellow activists, and their coalitions.

Due to this collaborative work, Cobb County went from being one of the top three worse unwelcoming localities in the country for undocumented immigrants, surpassed in the number of deportations annually by only two other areas nationwide, to one of the most welcoming with one of the fewest number of deportations. (This really upset the haters in Cobb and Georgia as **they were EQualized!** But what their hatred blinded them to is the fact that almost every deportation breaks up a family, as a large percentage of immigrant families are mixed status, some documented and some not, and leaves children without one or more parents, which has a devastating effect not only on them but on the entire community.)

In the Bahai and MLK spirit of always reaching across the political and ideological spectrum to try and achieve oneness and unity, another significant accomplishment that Rich and his coalitions achieved was the support and collaboration of more conservative groups, including but not limited to Libertarians and Chambers of Commerce and other business association (who knew that their businesses could not survive without undocumented immigrants), and even some evangelical Church denominations which knew that the Bible says to welcome all immigrants (since, in fact, Jesus Christ was one).

4. Let's talk about the myths the haters spread about immigrants and immigration in order to hide and disguise their hate and racism as concern about Americans and America. Rich researched the anti-immigrant organizations who helped lawmakers craft the draconian anti-immigrant state laws, and who successfully blocked decades of bi-partisan efforts to craft comprehensive immigration reform laws which would have granted limited amnesty to millions of immigrants living in the shadows but earning their right to stay by working hard to build this country (just as all similar immigrant groups did before). He discovered the shocking but not surprising fact that their leaders unabashedly embraced Eugenics-- a discredited ideology that perverted the methods and legitimacy of science to argue for the superiority of white Europeans and the inferiority of non-white people. This was the basis of Nazism and is the basis of white supremacism in America.[71]

Here are some of the facts about undocumented immigrants Rich also discovered and promoted countering the haters' lies: a) They produce less crime than citizens do and the communities where they reside in largest numbers have the lowest crime rates. (So much for the lying, corrupt, hater, 45th President, who characterized them as criminals.) b) They are an economic boon to every state's economy where they reside, paying more in taxes and

---

[71] Read more about Eugenics at : https://www.genome.gov/about-genomics/fact-sheets/Eugenics-and-Scientific-Racism and https://en.wikipedia.org/wiki/Eugenics .

getting little in return, working for lower wages and producing more, doing jobs that no one else want and not taking jobs away from Americans but actually, through their spending power, creating more jobs for Americans. (All of that has been confirmed, not only by independent national research organizations, both liberal and conservative, but also by state audits, including red states like Texas and Kansas.)[72] It has been proven that they are an asset in every way, and no liability, except, of course, they are contributing to the "browning" of America (which scares the shit out of the white supremacist and white nationalist haters who have infiltrated every level of government and society. It is time for them to come out of their closets, and take off their hoods, which many did after the election of the 44th President, Obama –the first Black one-- with the permission of the 45th President, the king of haters and white nationalist supremacists.)

5. The hateful rhetoric and actions of white supremacist, white nationalist, racist, anti-immigrant haters (who no longer wear white hoods but business suits in the halls of Congress, the White House, and corporate board rooms, and uniforms in law enforcement agencies) incite their followers to violence, not only against immigrants but against those who defend them. So, it is completely disingenuous for them to cite the reason they are against so called "illegal immigration" is because they support "the rule of law." That lie is the furthest from the truth since many of these haters at all levels are the biggest lawbreakers and follow the law only when it suits them and their hateful beliefs. The elitists follow only one law-- *the Golden Rule—he who has the gold makes the rules.*" And they incite their followers to violently break the law, the greatest example of which was the January 6th insurrection after the last Presidential election.

Every time Rich was interviewed by the media defending immigrants and dispelling the myths about them, he received death threats, via phone, email, and in person, with some even attacking his home, children, and pets. One time he went out onto his porch where his two youngest children had been playing a little while earlier, to find an effigy of him hanging attached to a canister with some white powdery substance. Rich and his family had to be evacuated by the police haz-mat team to determine if the powdery substance was dangerous. A crime lab later determined it was not, but definitely the haters' message had been sent—all meant to bully and intimidate them to stop speaking out against hate and for immigrants and other marginalized communities and peoples of color. Another time Rich found his children's

[72] For more myths and facts about immigrants read: https://www.pbs.org/newshour/classroom/app/uploads/2013/11/mythsandfacts.pdf and https://www.carnegie.org/our-work/article/15-myths-about-immigration-debunked/

dog, which had been in the front yard, murdered with a slit throat on his front doorstep. And his car was defaced several times, both when parked at home in the driveway and when parked in public places, with Nazi swastika symbols carved into the paint.

When people called with threats, Rich would try to engage them and turn it into a respectful conversation to find out what motivated their fear and hate. A constant refrain from poor white folks was placing the blame on immigrants for their poverty, loss of a job, or other hard luck (blame incited by corrupt, hater, conspiracy theory politicians and FOX news commentators). Rich would offer to help them through his organizations and coalitions, since they helped all people regardless of color or status, however one condition was that they drop the hateful rhetoric--but few would agree to that condition. He had learned from Dr. King and all the spiritual prophets that the best way to diffuse hate is through love, though difficult to do in the face of threats to your life and your family. That often involved utilizing "tough love" which means not allowing someone to bully you or others while also letting them know that you will be there for them once their bullying behavior ceases. All of this is easier said than done, but Rich's spiritual and martial arts training helped in learning non-violent ways of deescalating violence. Sometimes this "tough love" meant he and his coalition had to physically protect immigrants from those who sought to intimidate and bully them. For example, there were a few spots where "day laborers" would stand every morning waiting for people or companies who needed a laborer for a day to pick them up. Some of the immigrant haters would try to form circles around the laborers while taunting them and trying to scare away would be employers. So, Rich and team gathered in groups and surrounded the haters, providing a human barrier between them and the immigrant laborers. Eventually the police would have to come and disperse all of us, both the haters and protectors, in order to avoid violence, and then they would do their job and protect the day laborers from further harassment—our mission accomplished. ***They were EQualized!***

Violent threats against Rich gradually ceased or greatly diminished due to, he believed, two reasons: A) Threats didn't work to quiet his outspoken and public advocacy work; it only got louder. B) A local conservative newspaper columnist began writing humorous spoofs of Rich and his advocacy, casting him as a harmless buffoon who had lost his way. This likely reduced the haters' fear of him. Eventually Rich wrote to that columnist thanking him for this, though it was not his intention. (One important note: Rich was grateful that he always had the strength of coalition partners behind him as it is much easier to carry on the work of social justice with that kind of support. One such partner, the local Nation of Islam group, upon hearing about the threats on Rich's family, offered to send their security team to surround and defend his home. Another partner, the Cobb Southern Christian Leadership Conference (SCLC), national civil rights organization founded by MLK Jr., provided constant moral support. One of Rich's friends and mentors from SCLC, a former street gang and Black Panther member from Philadelphia, Dr. Ben Williams, always reminded him and other activists of the Rudyard Kipling quote from Jungle Book, that *"the strength of the wolf is in the pack".)*

6. Though engagement in this advocacy work was a labor of love for Rich and family and a crucial step in his journey to knowledge of self and country, he received many awards and accolades from local, regional, and national organizations for it (and still does). One of his proudest was received from Atlanta Latino newspaper and media group who chose him as their first non-Latino, "Latino of the Year" in 2007, and here are excerpts from their article announcing this honor, which is framed and hangs in Rich's home:

He is a white male of European descent, doesn't speak Spanish, isn't married to a Latina, but to an Afro-Caribbean woman. He wasn't born in Latin America, but in the capital of the world, New York City, he is Rich Pellegrino, Atlanta Latino's Person of the Year for 2007. But despite his lack of direct connection with the Latino community, exactly one year ago, Pellegrino, his wife of 25 years and their eight children (ages 24, 22, 21, 19, 17, 15, 9, and 6) began what he calls a "family movement" to help immigrants.

"We are all immigrants," Pellegrino frequently says, despite the fact that his parents were also born in the United States and three of his grandparents were Italian.

Pellegrino's "family movement" started last Christmas when he read the news in local newspapers about the various regulations that Georgia's counties were trying to push through to supposedly counteract the problems being caused by undocumented immigrants. The final straw was the proposal to prohibit the lease of apartments to people who were not legal residents or citizens of Cherokee County.

"That woke me up. They wanted to fight illegal immigration with illegal unconstitutional laws, when hate and fear have to be healed with love and welcome," says Pellegrino, who was out on a street corner in southern Cobb County with his family the very next day, carrying bilingual signs that said, "Welcome immigrants. Bienvenidos inmigrantes."

A few days later, the Pellegrinos did the same in Cherokee County. The response was favorable in both cases. "White and black people honked and waved," says Pellegrino. "We did get a few fingers, but the response was mostly positive." That was only the beginning of what was to be an entire year dedicated to working with people and organizations that defend the interests of immigrants. 2007 was a year of intense work that awakened the interest of media outlets like Fox News, LA Times, the AJC, and more, who found Pellegrino's story to be far from conventional: an American defending the rights of immigrants.

Specifically, Pellegrino provided the spark for the "Labor of Love" campaign, the peaceful event that brought together hundreds of people in Centennial Olympic Park, where community leaders distributed pamphlets on their work and invited participants to place red, white, and blue carnations in a gigantic heart of 7,000 flowers as a show of goodwill and encourage authorities and the local population toward dialogue, integration, and working together. "Rich was the one who pulled the event together," says Teodoro Maus, one of the activists who participated in the event and one of those who nominated Pellegrino for this award. "He started out by convincing skeptics, and later coordinated all of the logistical details such as permits, dates, etc."

A LIFE OF SERVICE

It's no coincidence that Pellegrino has taken such an active role in defending undocumented individuals, given his lengthy and consistent track record in serving others. He has been the founder, director, member, and collaborator of several non-profit humanitarian organizations, including crisis and referral centers, community food pantries, homeless and women's shelters and resource centers, addiction prevention and treatment clinics, faith-based initiatives, United Way committees, and more – and immigrant aid organizations as well, starting this year.

His vast experience in community service and his countless travels, as well as the six years he spent in the Caribbean (his wife is originally from St. Vincent) and a life dedicated to the study of spiritual practices have led him to write and publish professional and faith-based articles, newspaper columns, training materials, courses, and booklets. He has also produced and hosted faith-based self-help radio and television programs and series.

A SPIRITUAL MISSION

Pellegrino emphasizes that his intervention in defense of the immigrant is a spiritual mission. "There are many misconceptions about Latinos and prejudice, but especially all kinds of fears," says Pellegrino. "Information helps, but it doesn't heal the heart." According to Pellegrino, to combat their own pain, people attack those who are different when they are perceived as a threat to their dominant position. The same situation has repeated itself over and over again through history – first with European immigrants, then with blacks, then with Muslims, and now with Latinos. However, Pellegrino has not lost hope that the outcome will be positive, even though the journey is a difficult one. "I believe this will be the quickest time that as a group we hate somebody and then we forget about it," says Pellegrino. "The sad thing is that (in Georgia) it will get worse before it gets better."

WHAT'S NEXT

While the situation is still changing, Pellegrino is preparing to finalize in 2008 two projects he began this past year and is continuing his work as a mediator and coordinator of activities aimed at reducing tensions between Americans and Latinos.

The first project is the establishment of the Atlanta chapter of Healing Our Nation, a nationwide organization dedicated to promoting the resolution of disputes through peaceful dialogue.

The second project is the publication of The Survival Manual for Latino Immigrants (Manual de Supervivencia para Inmigrantes Latinos), a booklet that will include an historical timeline of immigration in the United States and practical information for Hispanic immigrants.

As a man of faith, Pellegrino feels that his work and the work of all those who support the cause of immigrants will help people resolve issues in ways that bring benefits to all. "I believe the arrival of Latinos is part of a greater plan of the Higher Power for this country," says Pellegrino. He also says that he is available to provide an ear or assistance to anyone who needs a hand. "Please include my email, which is pilgrim1@mindspring.com because my last name means 'pilgrim,'" says Pellegrino. "I think it's a cute coincidence.," he concludes.

7. Though he had previously authored many articles, papers, newspaper columns, pamphlets, training materials and courses, this period of Rich's pilgrimage to becoming the "Woke Equalizer" was capped with the publication of his first book, in English & Spanish, Immigrant Survival Manual/MANUAL DE SUPERVIVENCIA PARA INMIGRANTES, in 2007, excerpts of which follow:

Latinos & Immigrants: "Why Are We Being Attacked?"
"How Can We Survive This Period of Anti-Immigrant Senti-
ment?"

A SURVIVAL & ADVANCEMENT MANUAL FOR
IMMIGRANTS TO THE UNITED STATES OF AMERICA

With a Special Section for All Immigrants (Most Americans)
entitled:

"A Reminder & Wake Up Call: How We Can All Survive & Advance Together"

Written & Compiled by Richard A. Pellegrino, Italian American
Chief Translator: America Gruner

INTRODUCTION: *"WELCOME TO THE UNITED STATES*
OF AMERICA!"

"E PLURIBUS UNUM"

We know that many of you have been here for a long time, and some
have just arrived. You may have been initially welcomed in different ways–
by family members, employers, and others–though recently some Americans
may have made you feel unwelcome and under attack. (There are a few who
unfortunately make a lot of hateful noise arising out of their own fear of
change, the unintended consequence of which causes pain and suffering to
others–a situation which every new immigrant group to this country had to
endure.) So, on behalf of most ordinary Americans of all colors and backgrounds, who are all descendants of immigrants, we are happy that you have
come and are grateful for your significant contributions to this great country,
and ***WE WANT TO WELCOME YOU!*** One reason we produced this
booklet is because of our firm belief that your coming is no accident, that
you came here to both benefit yourselves and this country, and that, if you
are not yet a citizen or permanent resident, in the very near future you will
begin the path to becoming a citizen of this ongoing "melting pot experiment" called the U.S.A., still very much a work in progress. In the meantime,
whether you are already a citizen or not, we want to help you survive and
even advance during this period of anti-immigrant sentiment (which, as mentioned above, has nearly always happened to new immigrant groups when
they first came to this country; see Chapters 1 & 2). This is also an expression

of our great appreciation for and admiration of your many contributions to our country, through your hard work & service, family values, intellectual and educational attainments, and vibrant cultures (including tasty foods ☺).

And please, no matter what your temporary status is, do not let anyone label you as "illegal," or "an illegal immigrant," or "illegal alien," for several important reasons:

1) No human being is "illegal." Certain actions and behaviors may be against the law, hence illegal, but a person, even if he is convicted of a crime, is not "illegal."

2) If you have not been charged with or convicted of a crime by any court, in this country and legal system you are innocent until proven guilty in a court of law and only by a competent court of jurisdiction, hence no individual Americans, including individual elected officials, media personalities, local law enforcement personnel or even Immigration agents can claim or decide that you are guilty of any crime. As an individual human being living in the U.S. no one can take away your right to life, liberty, and the pursuit of happiness without due process by a court of law. (See Chapter 7, Legal Survival & Advancement, for more details.)

3) Labeling groups of individuals derogatory names, like "illegal immigrants," is a way of trying to dehumanize them in the eyes of others, enabling the name caller to feel superior and trying to make the targeted individual or group feel or appear inferior. It is really a form of bullying others, and, as I tell my children about bullies: they are not happy with themselves and their lives, so they pick on others to hide that fact. So do not listen to or pay any attention to anti-immigrant bullies, they are a small minority. Most Americans who are worried about "illegal immigration" are being manipulated by these bullies, through fear tactics and misinformation spread largely by talk radio and TV show personalities who make money as professional bullies and haters. When most Americans realize this fact, and the fact that you are human beings just like them who are trying to raise their families and work hard to build this country, they will welcome you and abandon the anti-immigrant rhetoric and those who espouse it. (This has already happened to some extent in the recent Presidential election as the candidates who were most anti-immigrant were cast aside by the voters, leaving only those candidates who promised Comprehensive Immigration Reform which includes a path to citizenship for our current undocumented immigrants.)

4) In fact, as you will see in Chapters 1 & 2, many of the current Americans' ancestors were characterized as "illegal immigrants", or worse, by the dominant groups of the time. How soon we forget! And, according to the Native Americans whose land was stolen from them

by most of our ancestors, we are all "illegal immigrants."
So, do not accept the negative labels and keep your heads high and proud without ever stooping to the level of your detractors!

In Chapters 1 & 2 of this booklet you will find a brief history of immigration to this country and a history of the prejudice and discrimination which every immigrant group had to endure at the hands of the dominant group(s) of the time. It is important to learn about the environment in which you are living and some of its history in order to both survive and advance in it. It is also important to know that you are not the first group to be targeted with prejudice and negative stereotypes. In every country there are some prejudices against one or another group, which have often been institutionalized into systems of racism and discrimination.

In Chapters 3-8 you will find tips for both survival and advancement, some of which are common sense but always bear repeating and reminding, and some of which one only learns after living in this country for a while.

Chapter 9 is a special section dedicated to all immigrants and ancestors of immigrants to this country, meaning all Americans, with tips on how we can all get along and cooperate to continue growing this country to its great moral destiny.

In Chapter 10 we try to provide resources and references which you can contact for further information and assistance, however, since this list and the information in this booklet is not exhaustive, if you cannot get your questions answered or needs met, we will provide a referral number where you can reach us or leave your message with your unresolved questions or needs which we will research and respond to.

Table of Contents

(Note: Rich self-published this book at a cost of $.35 cents each so that he could keep its cost down in order to distribute thousands freely or at $1.00

or less, which was accomplished.)

Episode Nine: Obama/Hope and Hate/ Marietta, GA

This opening and tumultuous decade of the new century and millennium culminated in the historic 2008 election of the first Black President, Barack Hussein Obama. Not only was he Black, but his father was a Black African immigrant and Muslim, and his mother was white, so he had all the diverse, cultural elements that make America great and the hater white supremacists, who tried everything in their power to cast him as un-American, despise. **They were EQualized.**

It was a time of great hope for change for many, which Obama's campaign slogan reflected, *"Sí se puede/Yes We Can"* (borrowed from Cesar Chavez, Delores Huerta, and their United Farm Workers organization of the 70s, who had one of the most successful boycotts in American history). This threat to the concept of white superiority and Black inferiority, which the country had been born and bred on, unleashed a firestorm of hate, which Rich found himself and his family in the crosshairs of again. During the election campaign, Rich sported an Obama bumper sticker on his car (which was always plastered with various social justice bumper stickers and signs), and two white guys in a pick-up truck pulled up next to him at a light, shouting curses at Rich about Obama, and followed and attempted to run him off the road. Rich called 911 and showed the haters he was on the phone and then snapped a picture of them, and they took off before the police got there.

Another more significant incident that was characteristic of the time took place in Marietta, Georgia, the county seat of Cobb, near where Rich and family resided. Marietta had a sordid history in relation to racism as it was the site of a lynching of a Jewish man, Leo Frank[73], and the place where J.B. Stoner and accomplices met and planned the 1963 bombing of the Birmingham church that killed four young Black girls.[74] On one of Marietta's central, busy streets there was a biker bar and grill, Mulligans, which routinely put anti-immigrant and other racist slogans on its prominent display sign, such as *"Wetbacks go home"* or *"Border Patrol Eats Free"*. One day, Rich and family were on a family outing in Marietta and when driving past Mulligans, they slowed to read their sign's latest racist slogans. On one side it read *"Democratic Dilemma: A boob with nuts or a nut with boobs"* (referring to Obama and Hillary Clinton, who were running against each other in the Democratic presidential primary).

The other side of the sign read, *"Obama T-Shirts for Sale---Really."* Rich had

---

[73] Read the story of Leo Frank at https://en.wikipedia.org/wiki/Leo_Frank

[74] Read about J.B. Stoner and the bombing of the Birmingham church: https://en.wikipedia.org/wiki/J._B._Stoner

always wanted an excuse to go into the bar to see what it was like on the inside (which he had heard housed racist KKK and other memorabilia) and to see if he could strike up a conversation with the owners to determine if they were intentionally racist or just thought it was all a good joke (which is still racist anyway). So, he stopped in the parking lot and he and his oldest daughter went into the bar. Upon entering they were taken aback to find KKK memorabilia on the walls, and, walking over to the bar, they saw the "Obama" t-shirt hanging there for sale---much to their surprise it was Obama depicted as Curious George, the cartoon monkey!

Completely shocked, they asked the white, female bartender for the owner. She said that he wasn't there, and she was the manager and asked how she could help. Rich asked her if she knew how racist that t-shirt image was, and she laughed and said it was simply playful fun. Rich told his daughter *"Let's get out of here"*, but, before leaving, they bought one of the t-shirts so they could show it to others and the media. As soon as they exited that building, they went straight to a nearby Black church where Rev. Dwight Graves, pastor and SCLC president, presided, and told him the story, showing him the shirt. He was shocked that this could be happening in 2008 and only a few blocks from his church in a mixed-race neighborhood. He asked Rich to immediately accompany him for a visit to the bar, which he did. (Dwight was a large, dark-skinned Black man, and a military veteran.) They went in and tried to engage the bartender/ manager and some other white patrons in a dialogue regarding why that shirt is offensive and should be removed, to no avail. Trying to be friendly and change the subject, and apparently not knowing how to converse with a Black man, the patrons started asking Dwight the typical stereotypical questions---do you play basketball or football (as if that was the only profession a large Black man could hold). Dwight was getting more agitated by the minute by their racist ignorance so Rich ushered him out and home before there could be any confrontation.

Rich and Dwight called an emergency meeting of their coalition which, due to the gravity of the situation, was a full house, and they planned a protest at Mulligans to demand that they stop selling that racist T-shirt. When other like-minded organizations around Atlanta heard the story, they joined the effort. The protest, on very short notice, was well attended by a diverse crowd and all of the Atlanta metro media, plus some national media. This upset the bar owner and he tried to hide, refusing to agree to their demands. The story went viral nationally and globally, and Rich and his coalition partners were interviewed by every major national and international news media, causing Mulligans to get bombarded with calls asking them to cease and desist. (It was a case of *"no justice, no peace"* for the bar owner and his family. **They were EQualized.** Rich had been involved in many media events and interviews over the years, but that was the largest one ever, as the news went viral— before that was even a thing-- and he got interview requests from all over the world.)

Before this incident some of the civil rights and advocacy organizations in Cobb and metro Atlanta did not work well together cooperatively, and some competed. However, they all came together in unity for this, so Rich, Dwight and others helped form a new, more inclusive, and unified coalition, which they all joined, called Cobb United for Change (CUCC).

Rich, besides helping to organize and lead the new and expanded coalition, also became an active SCLC member, serving with and under his friend and mentor, Rev. Dwight Graves and continuing to learn, in more depth, about the real MLK and Kingian non-violence and beloved community principles and strategies. Over the next few years, the CUCC would become a model for other county coalitions addressing many issues and hosting related events, including but not limited to police racial profiling and brutality; gun violence and buy-backs; immigrant bullying; healing racism workshops; candidate forums; town hall meetings; Black-Brown dialogues; GOTV(Get Out the Vote); legislative advocacy; cop and court watch; youth workshops; eviction and foreclosure prevention; criminal justice and prison reform. (Back at Mulligans, after the racist t-shirt protest and the widespread outcry against the racist statements on their signs, they finally ceased displaying them after years of residents' complaints to the City of Marietta, which did nothing. So, once again, the people took power into their own hands and did the work the weak politicians refused to do. *They were EQualized!)*

To close out this decade, Rich's family entered a new stage with the birth of their first two grandchildren, both girls. That continued the trend of his female-dominated family, with spouse V, six daughters, and now two granddaughters (so Rich has had a lot of training at home in how to abandon one of the other scourges of our society—patriarchy! *He is EQualized!)* And they are strong women! (In the old days the Italian father had to protect his daughters from the guys who wanted to court them, however, in this new age, Rich often said, only half-jokingly, he had to protect the guys from his Amazonian daughters who might intimidate and scare them away, and then they would never get married 😊.) But as the Bahai and all progressive writings state, until women get equal rights and are in every position of leadership in our society, humanity will be like a broken-winged bird that cannot fly adequately. Therefore, "women's liberation" is really men's and society's liberation, just as freedom from racism and all the other isms frees us all. To begin this tradition of women's leadership in Rich's family, their eldest daughter was the first ever person in his immediate family to graduate college with a bachelor's degree (in International Affairs, from Florida State University, 2007.)

The woke musical soundtrack of this decade was provided by artists such as Eminem; Drake; Taylor Swift; Alicia Keys; Cold Play; Michael Jackson; Jennifer Lopez; Lady Gaga; Black Eyed Peas; Mariah Carey; 50 Cent; Maroon

5; Ne-Yo; Katy Perry; Usher. The decade ended with the premature death of superstar Michael Jackson in 2009. *"Michael Joseph Jackson (August 29, 1958 – June 25, 2009) was an American singer, songwriter, dancer, and philanthropist. Dubbed the "King of Pop", he is regarded as one of the most significant cultural figures of the 20th century. Over a four-decade career, his contributions to music, dance, and fashion, …made him a global figure in popular culture. Jackson influenced artists across many music genres; through stage and video performances, he popularized complicated dance moves such as the moonwalk, to which he gave the name, as well as the robot. He is the most awarded individual music artist in history."*[75] Rich and family didn't realize what a profound effect his music and artistry had on them, and on the whole world, until his passing, so to both mourn his loss and celebrate his life they joined forces with a youth group at the local County recreation center and put together a show featuring the youth performing Jackson's songs and dances. It was a tremendous success and inspiration for all who participated, and their audiences. (This is another example, and a very profound one, of how music and the arts unite the hearts of all peoples, and the world, as evidenced by the extent of MJ's fanbase worldwide.)

---

[75] Read about the life of Michael Jackson at: https://en.wikipedia.org/wiki/Michael_Jackson

I AM NOT WHITE

7 SECOND DECADE OF THE NEW MILLENIUM (2010-2020)

"The 2010s (pronounced "twenty-tens" also known as "The Tens" or more rarely "The Teens") was a decade that began on January 1, 2010 and ended on December 31, 2019. (And for the purpose of this book, we are adding the first two years of the next decade, to bring it up to date to 2022.)

The decade began amid a global financial crisis and subsequent international recession dating from the late 2000s. Economic issues, such as austerity, inflation, and an increase in commodity prices, led to unrest in many countries, including the Occupy movements. Unrest in some countries—particularly in the Arab world—evolved into socioeconomic crises triggering revolutions in Tunisia, Egypt, and Bahrain as well as civil wars in Libya, Syria, and Yemen in a regional phenomenon commonly referred to as the Arab Spring. Shifting social attitudes saw LGBT rights and female representation make substantial progress during the decade, particularly in the West."

"China, along with launching vast economic initiatives and military reforms, sought to expand its influence in the South China Sea and in Africa, solidifying its position as an emerging superpower...global competition between China and the U.S. coalesced into a "containment" effort and a trade war. The War on Terror continued as Osama bin Laden was assassinated by U.S. forces in a raid on his compound in Pakistan as a part of the U.S.'s continued military involvement in many parts of the world, causing the rise of the extremist Islamic State *(ISIS)* organization... In the U.S., celebrity businessman Donald Trump was elected president amid an international wave of populism and neo-nationalism."

"Information technology progressed, with smartphones becoming widespread. Advancements in data processing and the rollout of 4G broadband allowed data, metadata, and information to be collected and dispersed among domains at paces never before seen while online resources such as social media facilitated phenomena such as the Me Too (and Black Lives Matter) movements (as well as White Supremacist organizations). Online nonprofit organization WikiLeaks (led by Julian Assange) gained international attention for publishing classified information on topics including Guantánamo Bay, Syria, the Afghan and Iraq wars, and United States diplomacy. Edward Snowden blew the whistle on global surveillance, raising awareness on the role governments and private entities have in global surveillance and information privacy. Global warming became increasingly noticeable through new record temperatures in different years and extreme weather events on all continents. At the same time, combating pollution and climate change continued to be major concerns, as protests, initiatives, and legislation garnered substantial media attention and momentum."[76]

Meanwhile, back in America, President Obama, who inherited an economy in recession teetering on the brink of depression, bailed out banks and corporations with massive infusions of cash—the largest corporate welfare in history—because they were *"too big to fail"*, while average Americans received small amounts of stimulus funds. In doing so he saved the country from depression but increased the inequity and disparity between the rich and poor. This sparked the "Occupy Wall Street Movement" which occupied public spaces nationwide to bring light to and protest that ever-widening gap between the rich and poor-- the 1%, who have over 30% of the nation's wealth, while the top 10% have over 70%, vs. the 99%. (From his studies of history, economics and religion, Rich felt that this gap completely unjust and unsustainable, and is the cause of most social ills, so he gladly joined and supported the Atlanta-based Occupy protestors, who occupied Woodruff Park there.) Also, with the increased speed and bandwidth of the internet, the cloud, smart-phones, and social media platforms, information (and misinformation) spread like lightening and what was going on in society could no longer be hidden, especially from the younger generation. With their smart-phone cameras, they were able to record in real time such things as police brutality, racial profiling by law enforcement, and all forms of discrimination which many knew existed before but there was little concrete proof of. This information and these realities were not new but now they were "news," and the traditional media, in order to compete with the new social media and smart-phone cameras, had to begin revealing these same previously hidden unjust truths and realities. ***They were EQualized!***

Everyone became a photo/video journalist of sorts overnight, and we were bombarded with pictures of police and vigilante murders of unarmed Black men and women such as Trayvon Martin, Michael Brown, Eric Garner, Sandra Bland, Amadou Diallo, Tamir Rice, Freddie Gray, Philando Castile, Breonna Taylor, George Floyd, and hundreds more---*"Say Their Names."* This

---

[76] https://en.wikipedia.org/wiki/2010s

forced some police and other agencies to examine their own implicit biases, however most hunkered down, and continue to do so now, in denial and more of the same.

In Cobb County, Rich and his coalitions made some gains but are still fighting the prevailing "bad apples" notion and myth---that there are only a few bad apples and implicit bias, and racism are not systemic. That denial is so ingrained in law enforcement that it may take a generation and new, young, and educated recruits to overcome.

Episode One: DACA and the Dream Act

Rich and his CIA (Cobb Immigrant Alliance) coalition continued to fight for immigrants to stay and work in Cobb County. As part of that battle they fought for Jessica Colotl, an undocumented student at Kennesaw State University who was brought to America when she was ten like nearly a million other children. The racist/hater Cobb Sheriff Warren, together with the ICE gestapo (federal Immigration & Customs Enforcement), tried to have her deported when she was caught by campus police driving without a license (because the Georgia hater legislators had blocked licenses for undocumented immigrants). However, she became a national poster child for these children who never knew their homelands and their only home had been America. Local and national coalitions staged protests demanding that her arrest and impending deportation be cancelled, and she was finally released and allowed to stay, at least until she finished college. Then the same pro-immigrant coalitions, including the Cobb Immigrant Alliance, held demonstrations at President Obama's campaign headquarters in every city demanding that a new policy known as DACA (Deferred Action for Childhood Arrivals), and a new law, the Dream Act, be instituted to protect these children and youth from deportation. DACA was enacted, which provided temporary protections, however Congress could not agree on authorizing the Dream Act due to hater, white nationalist legislators there. That has not changed to this day, so "the Dreamers", as they became called, still have only temporary legal status. Then, the haters at the Georgia State Legislature tried to ban these undocumented students, who consider themselves Americans, from attending Georgia Universities. That measure failed, so the haters at the Georgia Board of Regents passed a policy that they could attend but not receive in-state tuition even though they had always resided in Georgia and graduated from Georgia high schools.

Rich and others were arrested protesting the Regents' bullying actions by laying down in the busy intersections and blocking traffic in front of their downtown Atlanta offices. Other activists and educators helped form a new and accredited private university, not subject to the Regents' racist policies, for undocumented immigrants to attend. (Rich would often call out, in the media and public spaces, the cowardly haters referenced above, at all levels, and their supporters, as barbarians and the worst form of lowlife who bully children and youth who did no wrong, and, in fact, did everything right, including excelling in school while being law-abiding and contributing community members. Those haters are the epitome of bullies and bullying. ***They are EQualized!)***

Episode Two: Black Lives Matter & the Movement for Black Lives

Rich knew, along with every other woke American (and many woke folks worldwide), that Black people in America had been brutalized for centuries by government, law enforcement, mobs, and every other institution, including in both the 20th and early 21st centuries. He was also aware there were certain past "tipping points"[77] in the Civil Rights struggles to end Jim Crow in the 60s and 70s. However, he saw a new potential tipping point in the struggle for equitable and equal treatment, this time for the millennial generation of BIPOC (Black, Indigenous, People of Color) youth and their older supporters, which occurred on February 26, 2012, with the murder of 17-year-old Black youth Trayvon Martin. While walking home from a convenience store in Sanford, Florida, he was shot and killed by a twenty-eight-year-old neighborhood-watch vigilante, George Zimmerman. Zimmerman was acquitted by using Florida's racist "Stand Your Ground" law, which immediately threw that law in Florida and in other states into question and eventual removal. The nation and especially communities of color had had enough, and that shocking acquit along with the realization that any Black person could be murdered without recrimination just for "walking or driving while Black," launched what became known as the *Black Lives Matter* movement and the *Movement for Black Lives*, with young "millennials" leading massive protests nationwide. Almost immediately after that shockingly unjust verdict, the murders by police of Mike Brown, Eric Garner, Tamir Rice, and Sandra Bland, among others—all unarmed Black men and women-- were broadcast virally through social media and the news. (Since 9/11 the government had suspended many privacy protections, under The Patriot Act and similar draconian new laws, and was watching and tracking Americans like never before. However this period witnessed the beginning of what Rich and others called the "peoples' surveillance revolution", as now the people, and especially the youth, turned the powerful tool of video cameras in their hands and pockets, ready to deploy at a moment's notice and in any and every interaction with police, into a massive "cop watch revolution" and surveillance movement,

---

[77] Use of the term "tipping point" here comes from the book by Malcolm Gladwell " ***The Tipping Point: How Little Things Can Make a Big Difference*** " Gladwell defines a tipping point as "the moment of critical mass, the threshold, the boiling point.": https://en.wikipedia.org/wiki/The_Tipping_Point

depicting police racist and brutality interactions with people of color on a daily basis, and then spreading them like wildfire through social media platforms. Again, this was not "new," but now became "news" through technology in the peoples' hands. This caused the police to get dash and body cameras so they could present their side of the story, which often incriminated them—that is, when they didn't doctor or mysteriously lose their videos or turn off their cameras. And this caused the mainstream media to cover and broadcast these racist and brutal incidents to a greater extent than ever before, in order to compete with the social media platforms.) Rich, like countless millions of others, had had enough and helped organize and participated in these protests held in the Atlanta metro and Cobb areas. Together with some of his family members and many fellow citizens, they took over the streets, chanting slogans *"Say their names," "Hands Up—Don't Shoot;" No Justice-No Peace--No Racist Police", "Black Lives Matter",* among other chants of the time.

Rich met and worked with many of the young millennial activists, who naturally distrusted him as he was an old, white, straight male, so he had to work hard to gain their trust. (This was not surprising to him because when he was a young activist in the seventies there was a rule not to trust anyone over thirty. Also, some liberal white activists had a "white savior mentality" and wanted to tell the millennials what to do and not do, injecting white supremacy and arrogance into the equation. Even some of the older guard, Black activists, who were also mistrusted due to their age, fell into the same trap of trying to direct and lead the youth rather than supporting them.) Although there were a lot of challenges and necessary learning taking place on how to work together both interculturally and inter-generationally, sometimes through conflict and then resolution, it was an exciting time and one Rich had been actively waiting for since the seventies and the last youth-led revolution. He knew that without the energy and audacity of youth there would be no revolutionary transformation. The country had not experienced that since his generation of youth, as subsequent ones had been co-opted, along with their parents, by money and materialism.

Rich had worked hard in Cobb County to build bridges between the police and the immigrant community and other people of color. Great progress had been made, mainly for the immigrants who were not profiled and targeted as before, but not as much for the Black residents, though it was better than when he had moved the years earlier. It was decision time, though, as he became more directly involved in defending Black victims of profiling and police brutality, both locally and nationwide, and that often put him in direct confrontation with the police. To avoid disturbing the alliances and good relations between the immigrant community and the police, Rich decided to hand over the reins of the Cobb Immigrant Alliance and other pro-immigrant organizations to trusted others, so that he could focus on building bridges between the Black community and the police. (Rich also realized that his own children and grandchildren, though mixed, are considered Black and could be victims of the profiling and brutality, so it was close to home and personal. His white privilege did not necessarily shield them—a fact that was borne out by incidents to come.)

Then Rich's world changed again, opening his eyes wider and bursting his bubble of white insulation through a string of incidents, two of which would completely change his perspective on law enforcement. While videos showed unarmed Blacks being routinely murdered by police around the country, police in nearby Atlanta and metro area counties were routinely gunning down unarmed Black men and women there too--Anthony Hill, Kathryn Johnston, Oscar Cain, Jamarion Robinson (executed, shot 76 times, by a combined task force of federal marshals and local police), Gregory Towns, Deaundre Phillips—to name a few. (*"Say their names".*) One example of the disparate treatment of Blacks and whites by Cobb Police was a young unarmed Black robbery suspect who was shot when he ran away from police and hid in his apartment's bedroom closet. The police fired into the closet killing him though he was no threat. The same month several white teens were out drinking and joy riding, driving erratically, when a Cobb police officer on a motorcycle attempted to pull them over. They refused to stop and fired gunshots at the cop but were eventually surrounded and stopped by other patrol cars. They were unharmed and seen laughing as they were arrested.

Fast forward a few years and the same disparate treatment again—a young Black man running away from police was shot in the back and killed, and another one shot and killed in his car after a chase by police. A month earlier, a white man who barricaded himself in his house and was shooting at police and neighbors was arrested hours later unharmed. (When it comes to American law enforcement, and all-American institutions, ***"Black Lives Don't Matter,"*** and never did, hence the need for a whole movement stating emphatically and without equivocation, ***"Black Lives*** (do) ***Matter." They are EQualized.*** And for the haters, or well-meaning non-haters, who try to counter with *"All Lives Matter"* -- which is hilarious since most using that phrase don't think the lives of immigrants, Muslims, LGBTQ, etc. matter— the answer is, ***"All lives will not matter until Black Lives Matter."***

Anyone who has a problem saying the phrase *"Black Lives Matter,"* has a much larger problem, just as anyone who cannot say *"I am antiracist"* has a problem, is inflicted with that insidious disease, and is in denial. Fact is, all Americans are infected with it, including this writer, the only difference being those who acknowledge that fact and are working to dismantle it within their own selves and in our institutions, and those who deny it. ***They are EQualized!)*** Back on the "Cobb plantation" (as Rich's mentor and friend, Dr. Ben Williams, Cobb SCLC President, always half-jokingly calls it, since Cobb and most of America is still organized with a plantation mentality and structure), though things were getting better for all people of color, thanks to the hard and sacrificial work of Rich's and friends' coalitions, two incidents, both in 2015, would serve to erase some or much of that progress, one in Rich's mind and attitude and the other in the community.

Episode Three: The Pellegrino Homestead—Under Attack by the Police

After collaborating closely with the Cobb Police for nearly a decade, building bridges between them and the community, especially communities of color, Rich knew a lot of officers and most of the command staff by first name and had even been to some of their weddings and other celebrations, as well as their lunch and dinner tables. This served to re-humanize them in Rich's mind, as he rediscovered the people behind the badges and uniforms. He had grown up to respect and revere them to a significant degree, with his police officer father and father's police friends and families as his extended family, spending most holidays and summers as a child with them. Then the seventies happened, with rampant police brutality and injustice against anti-war and antiracism protestors, which Rich not only witnessed but was on the receiving end of. So, the police became, in his eyes and eyes of millions, "*the pigs.*" (In response, his father and his entire precinct had t-shirts printed with a picture of a pig and the caption: "*P.I.G.s: Pretty Intelligent Guys*" which they proudly wore at both off and on duty events. While that may have been a clever way to diffuse the tension, at least for them, it was also a bold indication of their complete denial of the extent of their dysfunction.) That negative perception of police had cooled off a bit for many until the advent of the cell-phone camera in the new millennium and the constant stream of videos depicting police brutality again, mainly against people of color (which had never stopped but was not as exposed). Though these perpetrators in uniform became "*pigs*" again, in Rich's eyes, he, like most of the nation, subscribed to "*the bad apple*" theory--- that those officers who carried on racial profiling and disproportionately stopped, harassed, cited, arrested, beat, and murdered people of color, many whom were innocent, were just "bad apples" and the rest of the tens of thousands of police were good men and women, protecting and serving without bias.

That perception and belief was severely rattled and changed in early 2015. Rich was up one night after midnight writing articles and correspondence when one of his grown kids ran into his room and said that there is a police cruiser in their driveway with its flashing blue lights on. It was behind his daughter's car, which had just pulled in returning home from a full day and night's work. (She was just in the process of changing residences and was staying with her parents for a few nights until moving into her new apartment, so her car was packed tight to the hilt with all her belongings.) Rich went outside and as he was walking toward her car, the officer, a young Black male who Rich did not recognize, yelled at him a command to stay back, stating that he has it under control and it's just a broken taillight. (He shouted at Rich so rudely, in his own driveway, that Rich was shocked and felt it was out of character based on other police interactions for minor traffic issues, and the fact that most Cobb police knew where he lived, so he thought that something else was at play, but still complied.) So, Rich stood back expecting the officer to wrap it up quickly so they could all go about their business, at nearly 2:00 am, on this cold, below freezing, morning. However, Rich noticed the officer conversing with his daughter, seemingly heated or animated at times, and it was dragging on. Then, he saw another police cruiser pull up with flashing lights, and then a third, and he knew something was up if they had called for back-up. By then his two grown sons and wife had joined Rich on the front lawn, along with some daughters, all wondering what was going on. The other officers who arrived on the scene knew and were known to Rich. They first huddled with the original officer, then walked up to Rich and family asking them to continue to stand back and down and let the original officer do his job without interference. They said he now suspected drugs and Rich's daughter was not cooperating by refusing to open and allow a search of the vehicle (which would have been impossible without unpacking and placing on the wet ground all her personal belongings). At this point of absurdity, Rich told them "Hell no," not in his driveway, at 2:00 am, in the freezing cold. Rich assured them there were no drugs and said to halt this whole event and call a supervisor immediately. (Meanwhile, he called their commanders whose personal numbers he had on speed dial, all the way up the chain to the Chief—leaving frantic voice messages because no one answered due to the lateness of the hour.) By this time there were eight police cruisers there and a crowd of police restraining an agitated crowd of Pellegrino family members. They were all arguing, and Rich was telling the police in no uncertain terms that this was a fiasco and ordering them off his property until a supervisor arrived. Then, the daughter, who the initial officer had told to stay put in the car with it turned off, was super tired and now freezing cold after working a whole shift and sitting in the below freezing weather, grew weary of all the wrangling outside with no resolution and opened her car door and attempted to step out. Then, all hell broke loose as several officers jumped on her attempting to handcuff her, telling her she was under arrest. She fought them until they got on top of her in the mud while we were also trying to pry the officers off her. Others were attempting to restrain us, all while a couple of family members were filming this fiasco. It was a mini riot, all over an alleged broken taillight and an overzealous "war on drugs" officer. Eventually they threw Rich's handcuffed daughter in the back of a patrol car, and, instead of searching the car there, a tow truck pulled up and tried to back into the driveway. Rich blocked its entrance and told the driver and officers to get lost, and that he will see them in both the judicial courts and in the court of public opinion through protest and the media. Then, finally, the supervisor arrived and explained that the car and its contents were now considered evidence so they would have to tow it to the precinct to search it. Rich's response was *"Go to hell, where were you an hour ago when this whole fiasco started and could have been avoided!"* He eventually let them take the car as he had to focus on calming his family members, some of whom were reacting violently against the bullies with badges who had brutally harassed and harmed their sister (whom they transported to the county jail, and Rich's focus shifted to getting her released.)

Later, Rich realized that he had to have this traumatic experience to finally finish bursting his white and blue insulated bubble and to know first-hand how innocent people, especially people of color, are treated and criminalized every day in this country, not by a few bad apples but by a rotten law enforcement system and mindset which infects almost everyone in uniform, enabling and rewarding them to criminalize innocent people. And the color of the officers' skin doesn't matter because while in uniform it is not white or Black--it is blue. In the ensuing days when Rich met with every level of command in the Cobb Police Department, and they all defended the actions of their officers in this encounter with his daughter and family, he realized how far gone the system was and how it was the cause of crime rather than the solution to it.

Here are the key learnings Rich took away from this unfortunate but necessary encounter:

1) Rich's initial reaction was *"If this is how they treat friends, how do they treat strangers."* He had spent nearly ten years helping to build bridges of trust between the police and communities of color there, and that trust was shattered in a one-hour encounter, never to be regained again. Now, he doesn't trust any law enforcement officer or agency until they are thoroughly vetted against the standards shared below. But he felt it was good that the initial officer did not know him and that the others didn't show him special treatment because he needed to know how they treat others, especially people of color. Though he abhors both violence and guns, his initial visceral reaction was one of feeling helpless to defend his own family against such terrorism and the need to arm himself and his family, not against criminals but against the police, a reaction shared by several family members and many community members who have suffered similar or worse trauma at the hands of the police. He and his family no longer felt safe in that community and with those police. They understood others' visceral reactions to being bullied and brutalized by those who are supposed to protect and defend them--- the reaction is fight or flight. Rich initially chose flight and decided to explore opportunities to move to other places, in and out of the country, where law enforcement was less belligerent and racist, to protect his family of color. After a

good deal of research, however, he found that this corrupt system of racial profiling and aggressive police strategies, such as pretextual stops, "broken window," "stop and frisk," etc., had infected nearly every community and law enforcement agency. And it was not practical to uproot his large family to move overseas. So, they decided to stay put and protect themselves while continuing to fight for changes. They felt then, and still feel now, to be under a state of attack by law enforcement due to their tactics and attitudes, and until the police consent to mutually agreed upon conditions of a cease-fire, then they are at war. (The war on drugs and the war on terrorism have always been wars on people of color and the poor, and that has not changed significantly for decades.)

When you are at war and under attack, the only way there can be peace is if there is a cease fire, so Rich drew u conditions for such a cease fire, in the flier included below, entitled "**THE MAGIC PILL THAT WILL IMMEDIATELY BEGIN BRIDGING THE GAP BETWEEN COMMUNITY AND POLICE**" which he began circulating, and still does, in the community. To this date, these reforms are still not implemented, so they are still in a state of war.

THE MAGIC PILL THAT WILL IMMEDIATELY BEGIN BRIDGING THE GAP BETWEEN COMMUNITY AND POLICE

IN ORDER TO REPURPOSE OUR POLICE DEPARTMENTS INTO PEACE DEPARTMENTS, AND INITIATE AN IMMEDIATE CEASEFIRE IN THE WAR ON OUR COMMUNITIES & RESULTING RETALIATION AGAINST POLICE, THE POLICE MUST IMMEDIATELY:

STOP all "pretextual" **STOPS** for minor traffic and pedestrian violations, including but not limited to loitering, license plate light, brake light, turn signal, lane change, seatbelt, etc.—and most importantly---DWB (driving while Black or Brown).

STOP all **ARRESTS** for minor traffic and pedestrian violations, including but not limited to loitering, driver's license expiration or suspension, insurance lapse, and possession of marijuana and other controlled substances in small amounts, obstruction, and all other offenses that can be treated with "non-custodial arrest", meaning issuance of a citation. And **STOP shooting unless shot at--**or defending someone shot at--**period!!!**

STOP all *CRIMINAL PROFILING* and street-level crime detection tactics---those are not *"protecting and serving"* but *are* harassment and privacy invasion. Leave the crime solving to the Detectives---and **STOP** saying, "I stopped you because *you fit the description"* or *"look suspicious"*, ESPECIALLY if you are a white officer saying that to a Black person. (This all adds up to *"implicit bias" and "racial profiling"* however you dress it up.)

NOTE: **ALL OF THE ABOVE CAN BE INITIATED *RIGHT NOW* UNDER EXISTING LAW!!!** *And though it may be a difficult pill to swallow for some, everything listed has already been tried with success in other cities!!!*

- Additionally, since WE KNOW that EVERY police department has been infiltrated with KKK members/sympathizers and similar domestic terrorists, so every existing and new officer must pass polygraph tests regarding their beliefs about racism and people of color.
- It is time to stop calling resisting arrest and "obstruction" a crime. OUR COUNTRY WAS FOUNDED ON THE PRINCIPLE OF RESISTING. If the police are willing to take away someone's freedom, there must be cause. It is no longer enough to say "...impeded my investigation" or "...he pulled away from me."
- In summary, the street level *"war on drugs"* ends now (as we know, in practice, it has been the war on people of color and the poor).

IF YOU ARE A CITIZEN OR A POLICE OFFICER AND WANT TO TAKE PART IN IMPLEMENTING THIS SOLUTION IN YOUR COMMUNITY, CONTACT US AT: LABOROFLOVECAMPAIGN@GMAIL.COM or 404-573-1199

2) After that traumatic incident with the police, once the dust and anxiety settled a bit, Rich began analyzing what had happened and why. He knew that his daughter would be okay because she had him and their family to bail her out, help her deal with the trauma, and eventually get her charges dropped or ameliorated so that she could go on with her life—likely with zero trust in police ever again but not much other baggage. However, he asked himself, " What about my neighbor's kid—Black, the same age or younger—from a struggling single parent, one income family, who finally gets his first job and car and then the police randomly harass and arrest him, like they did my daughter, for an alleged broken taillight or small amount of pot"(which he later learned is often a bogus pretext used in "pretext policing" in order to stop someone for

a drug search or other suspected criminal activity.)[78] If that kid is arrested and the family cannot afford bail quickly, he is thrust into the system with grossly disparate and harsher treatment of minorities, and which produces hardened criminals. He loses his job and car, and then is recruited by the gangs and drug dealers to provide for himself and help his family. In fact, he was criminalized by the police, who are the initial gatekeepers into the racist and corrupt criminal justice system, and THEY recruited him for the gangs and drug dealers.

Finally, after five decades of living and learning on the front lines of social justice, the light dawned, and Rich understood. In all his dealings with the police as a community activist, they had always told him that the burden was on us, the community--its parents, spokespeople, and advocates. They said we had to work to prevent criminal activity by providing better parenting skills training, youth activities and alternatives, and other social and economic reforms which are known to prevent crime. This is all still true but is only one part of the story. The police always put the burden on us, taking little responsibility for how their approaches and actions might contribute to criminality. But now Rich knew for sure that they and their policies, training, and attitudes are among the major causes of crime and criminality. When he tried to explain any of this to the Cobb Police command staff, they all, Black and white, defended their officers' actions regarding both his daughter's case and their method of policing. They admitted that that is their most effective method of catching real, big-time criminals—to stop and harass 10 or 20 low-level alleged violators like Rich's daughter to catch the one big fish—the big drug dealer or serial killer. He then asked them this question, which they had no answer for: *"So your method is to profile, harass, brutalize, and criminalize ten or twenty innocent people in order to catch the real criminals?"* This is what they admitted to, and they were either willfully or just plain ignorant about how that could be wrong and even crazy.

When Rich met with the Police Chief at the time, the Chief apologized for his daughter's treatment but confirmed that that is the method of policing they employ, casting a wide net and seeing what they catch in it—never mind that a lot of innocent people and small-time "fish" might be hurt in that process. He used the excuse that they don't have the resources to use more advanced methods of serious criminal activity detection. Rich told him that if they would change their method from casting a wide net, which disproportionately targets people of color, to more precise methods of crime detection,

---

[78] "One of the longstanding problems in policing has been the pretextual use of low-level traffic and pedestrian stops as a strategy to address more serious crime. While there may be some limited role for pretextual enforcement to investigate specific serious crimes, its over-use has exacerbated racial disparities in policing; unnecessarily pulled individuals into the criminal justice system for very minor misconduct; generated a great deal of distrust between police and communities; and done very little to address serious violent crime." https://www.policingproject.org/pretext-legislation

he would lobby the county and state for the resources needed to make those changes. But Rich received no commitment from him—it was only lip service. The Chief did set up a meeting for Rich with his command staff to discuss those options (as he was about to retire anyway and had little skin left in the game).

That meeting with the command staff, to which Rich brought several other community advocates, was a fiasco. It erupted into a shouting match because the command staff were insulted by even the hint that they do anything wrong and should change any tactics or attitudes (which are so entrenched and ingrained in policing, along with implicit biases, for decades). Rich knew than that the only way to get real change was to clean house and start over, which was not likely in the short term.

So, regardless of the existing law enforcement establishment's resistance to progress and change, Rich and other advocates insist there must be major three-part reforms in order to experience any positive change: A) Family and community training B) Law Enforcement policy, training, and practice reform C) Legislative policy change aimed at reducing poverty and mass incarceration.! **They are EQualized!**

3) Rich had always worked to diversify the police force and had felt that a more diverse force of women and officers of color would make a big difference. However, now he knew that if you put good people into a corrupt system, led mostly by those who have been corrupted by that system, you will corrupt the good people no matter their color or gender, and they will be "blue." As the Bible states, only a fool pours new wine into old wineskins expecting the new wine to remain unspoiled. (Read the book by James Forman, *"Locking Up Our Own"* for ample proof of this.[79])

4) Rich remembered that the Cobb police command, most of whom were there for decades, had bragged to him about their law enforcement training from ex-military trainers. One such trainer was very popular around the country and promoted a warrior mentality versus a guardian mentality, an attitude which has now been found to be toxic and violent. The warrior mentality puts emphasis on fighting crime and officer safety, viewing alleged lawbreakers as the enemy with the assumption that they are already guilty. Law enforcement officers with this mentality often see police forces in military terms: they are soldiers fighting an enemy force, namely crime, and view the public, especially people of color in this racist country, as enemy combatants... On the other hand, a guardian mentality puts emphasis on protecting and serving all com-

---

[79] Forman, J., & Jr. (2018). *Locking up our own.* Abacus.

munity members. For any meaningful reform to take place the command staff leadership must be well grounded in the guardian mentality, otherwise the brutality continues. Also, due to the above, drawing officers from the military, especially those who have seen combat duty, is the worst practice as many suffer from PTSD and related disorders and it will be especially difficult for them to convert from a warrior to a guardian mentality.

5) Rich researched and studied other reforms which have proven to work. One is pre-arrest diversion (P.A.D.), meaning that for certain low-level crimes the suspect is not arrested but transported to a substance abuse or mental health facility, or similar provider. This is restorative justice versus punitive justice. Here is the description from the Atlanta P.A.D. site*:" **The Policing Alternatives & Diversion Initiative** *works to reduce arrest and incarceration of people experiencing extreme poverty, problematic substance use, or mental health concerns, and increase the accessibility of supportive services in Atlanta and Fulton County. PAD fosters a new approach to community safety and wellness by providing an alternative to punishing people for what they do to survive. Instead, we connect with people as people, address their basic needs, and work with them to reduce harm to themselves and their neighbors. We believe communities are safer and healthier when people have what they need to not only survive, but to thrive."* [80]

6) Since Rich knew that the real culprit driving much of the police militarism and brutality was the war on drugs, he researched alternatives and found a decade long experiment that worked. A decade ago, the country of Portugal had the worst European crime rate related to drug abuse and trafficking and one of the world's highest drug addiction rates. To combat that, they employed the usual aggressive tactics of the war on drugs, which hardly put a dent in the problem-just as it has failed here. They then legalized not only marijuana but all drugs and put the resources previously spent on the war on drugs into treatment and prevention programs. They now have one of the lowest crime and drug addiction rates in the world. It is time we admit we don't have all the answers in this country and learn from others. *"Get tough on crime"* and the *"war on drugs"* don't work and increase crime and drug addiction.

7) Finally, Rich came to the realization that the current law enforcement system is a set-up for failure for many reasons including its history and founding purpose--which, initially, was to apprehend runaway slaves, and then, to defend companies from union strikes and protests over their slave labor practices. Beyond history, the two other failure factors are its current outdated leadership and our unrealistic expectations as citizens. We expect the police to solve every problem and call 911 for

---

[80] Read more about "pre-arrest diversion" programs at https://www.atlantapad.org/ .

many we can solve as neighbors, families, and communities ourselves. We complain about them profiling the Black community when local Cobb statistics, especially in diverse South Cobb, show that 90% of the 911 calls are Black people complaining about other Black people and then they expect mostly white officers to go into Black neighborhoods and know how to deescalate situations which could have been handled by neighbors and families in the first place. We want the police to be tough on crime but not tough on us or our children. We have created a perfect storm of contradictions, which they are caught in the middle of. There are plenty of steps we can take to reduce and address crime in our neighborhoods without involving police. (In fact, after Rich's negative encounter with police he and his family resolved not to call 911 unless it was a life-or-death situation, or an accident which required an accident report, but not for suspicions or minor property crimes. Together with their neighbors, they have been able to handle those.)

Rich believes most officers go into the profession with good intentions to help people, but they are not provided with the training, guidance, and resources to do so. They are also underpaid and should receive a free university degree in criminal justice so they can learn modern and progressive strategies rather than relying on the old guard's outdated methods, which never worked and only made things worse.

That is why, and he may differ with fellow social justice advocate colleagues on this, Rich doesn't think officers who make a mistake in the line of duty, even some fatal mistakes, should be charged with and convicted of a crime that involves jail time unless they deliberately violated someone's rights due to race, class, or other bias, and it is proven beyond a reasonable doubt. Otherwise, they should be suspended and retrained for minor mistakes or fired and lose their post certification for major ones, as they are not fit for the job and should not be able to simply transfer to another agency. Victims of these mistakes should be able to pursue civil lawsuits to get justice and municipalities should properly compensate them without drawn-out trials. (Until the conditions and reforms, he has proposed are instituted, Rich discourages anyone, especially people of color, from joining the law enforcement profession, just as he discourages them from joining the military,

as both are corrupted and set-ups for failure and abuse.) Also, ex-combat veterans should not be employed as police officers unless they go through extra screenings, as many suffer from PTSD from the traumas of war and come into policing with a destructive warrior mentality.

8) Regarding Rich's daughter's case, her taillight was not broken or dysfunctional, so the pretext for stopping her was a lie and allegedly they found a small quantity of marijuana and a couple of prescription pills not in their container. All of that fiasco for nothing, and if it had been

another victim and family, it could have ended in violence and even fatalities. Rich was going to sue them, to try and shock them to their senses, since the only way they are forced to change policies is when they must dole out sums of taxpayer money, but then a new tragedy and travesty happened, much worse than my daughter's.

Episode Four: Nick Thomas Murder—Say His Name

In 2015, Smyrna, Georgia, a small but growing Cobb city, was becoming increasingly diversified as immigrants and people of color were moving there in significant numbers, like other parts of South Cobb. From 2000 to 2012, Smyrna grew by 28%; historically, it was one of the fastest-growing cities in the state and one of the most densely populated cities in the Atlanta metro area. However, its leadership had not (and still has not) reflected that growing diversity, and neither did its police department which was notorious for its speed traps. (Rich and his coalition later discovered that there was no police department budget allocated by the city, so it was funded solely by fines and seizures, a throwback to Jim Crow days.)

On March 24th, 2015, Smyrna officers, under the command of Sergeant Kenneth Owens, had planned to serve a six-month old warrant for $175.00 in probation fines owed by 23- year-old Nicholas Thomas at his place of work in a local Goodyear Tire Auto Repair Shop. But there was one problem. They didn't realize the workplace was not in the city limits of Smyrna but right outside its border, and they didn't have jurisdiction. So, when they arrived there, they called Cobb County police. Together, a combined force of Smyrna and Cobb police raided the repair shop, letting loose dogs, oblivious to the safety of customers and employees, all for a $175.00 fine, while Thomas was in a customer's vehicle moving it in the parking lot. In all this confusion, and again, oblivious of everyone's safety, when Thomas refused to exit the vehicle and drove it in the parking lot to avoid the dogs, Sergeant Owens shot into the car from behind and right into Thomas' head, killing him instantly--an unarmed, hard-working, young Black father of an infant daughter. (Owens later claimed that it was in self-defense and in defense of the other officers. Thomas was unarmed, and the other officers, when interviewed by investigators, stated that they were not in any danger, refuting Owens' story. Witnesses attested to the same fact.)

Upon further investigation into his background, Owens had been a sniper in the military, and he had been convicted of domestic abuse years earlier when he was a Cobb Police officer. Forced to resign from Cobb Police Department, he was nevertheless hired by Smyrna police even though they were fully aware of his record and aware that Federal law states that a convicted domestic abuser was not legally allowed to possess a firearm (another dangerous, and, in this case, deadly, mistake and example of law enforcement agencies and officers not respecting the rule of law and thinking they are above it.) When the Smyrna Police Chief was asked why they hired Owens he said they believe in second chances (but apparently not in second chances or the chance to live for unarmed Black men. That is the whole story of America in a nutshell—second and third and fourth chances for white citizens and "blue" police folks, especially if they are both white and blue-- but no chances for Black folks.)

Much of the entire metro Atlanta community was horrified at this police execution of another unarmed Black man, as witnesses testified that Thomas was never a threat to the officers or the customers. However, the police chief, mayor, city council, and police union all defended and justified Sergeant Owens' actions, attempting to further murder Nick Thomas' character in the process. Rich and others, including Nick's family and attorneys, quickly formed a coalition—the Nick Thomas Justice Coalition, composed of many organizations, including, SCLC--Cobb Chapter; #ItsBiggerThanYou; Moral Monday; Sankofa United Church of Christ; Active Voices; National Action Network; Solutions Not Punishment ;Stop Mass Incarceration; Cobb Peoples Agenda; Greater Works Ministries; United Church of Christ; Georgia Community Coalition; New Order National Human Rights Organization; Occupy Homes Atlanta; Giving a Hand; Southern Anti-Racism Network; Lakeside Family Life Church; Rise Up Georgia; Hello Racism; Powder Springs Task Force; Parental Empowerment Institute; National Coalition to Combat Police Terrorism; Cobb Immigrant Alliance; Saving OurSelves (SOS); Black Lives Matter Atlanta.

They staged street protests and protests at the City Council meetings, demanding justice for Nick Thomas. They shut down the streets of Smyrna and Cobb, all the way to the local Cumberland Mall, and then they took over the entire mall. They attended the City Council meetings in large numbers, at times taking over the meetings so that the Mayor and City Council had to be rushed out and the police and SWAT team pushed the protesters outside of city hall. The Coalition fulfilled its promise of "*no justice, no peace*," disrupting Smyrna streets, businesses, festivals, and government meetings.

However, like most other officers who murder unarmed Black men in this country, Owens was eventually cleared of any wrongdoing by a grand jury manipulated by the District Attorney, who had higher aspirations and could not be trusted to present a neutral and unbiased case. (They later learned from researchers on both the left and right that the whole system of grand juries as independent peer arbiters of justice in this country had been corrupted by the manipulation of District Attorneys who abuse the system. *They are EQualized.*) Then the Smyrna police chief, adding insult to injury, had the audacity to reward and promote Owens to Lieutenant--murder an unarmed Black man and get promoted! (It seemed that nothing has changed since the police were the slave patrols. *They are EQualized!*)

Rich continued to work with Nick's family and attorneys to try and seek justice in the Federal courts, to no avail as a Trump-appointed federal judge dismissed the case, again taking the side of the police. However, Rich vowed never to let Smyrna city and police leadership, and the community forget that they had the blood of an innocent Black man on their hands. So, at every Smyrna city festival and other events, Rich, sometimes alone and sometimes accompanied by others from the coalition, would hand out fliers detailing the Nick Thomas tragedy and travesty. ***Smyrna was EQualized!***

Episode Five: Street Groomers/Brother Haroun Shahid Wakil

At one of the Smyrna City Council protests, the council meeting chambers was packed with Black Lives Matter Atlanta and other Nick Thomas Justice Coalition members, so Rich stood in the lobby helping to provide security for the protestors since there was a heavy police presence (and they later learned SWAT teams were standing ready behind City Hall). Also standing in the lobby and providing security for the protesters was a towering figure of a man (who Rich later learned was Haroun Shahid Wakil, at nearly 7 feet tall and over 400 pounds), Black and dressed in Muslim garb. When arguments broke out at the city council meeting between Nick Thomas' family and the Mayor and City Council, and the police rushed in to evacuate the elected officials and then harass the protestors, Haroun bellowed out loud, nearly shaking the room, telling the police to stand down and making sure they did not abuse the protesters as they were escorted out of the room when the police declared it an unlawful assembly (which it was not, as it was a public city council meeting). Haroun and Rich tried to calm and exit the protesters as they didn't want anyone to get arrested or hurt. When everyone was safe and accounted for, they continued the protest outside on the city hall steps, as the police had barricaded the doors to prevent anyone from reentering, which the crowd vowed to do if the City Council returned and resumed their meeting.

Outside, Haroun and Rich got to talk and learn more about each other, which was the beginning of a long intimate friendship and extended family relationship. (Rich and his entire family adopted Haroun as a family member, who was in his thirties and didn't have any family in Georgia--until his untimely and premature death five years later.) Aaron Bridges, aka Brother Haroun, told Rich the story of how he got to Cobb County from Chicago, and what happened then. He had grown up on the south side of Chicago and was a prominent member of the black street tribe there, the Gangster Disciples—GD's. (Haroun said that "street tribes" and not "gangs" is what they called themselves, to distinguish themselves from the criminal gangs of racketeers in business suits and uniforms, at all levels of society. To this day, whenever anyone complains about the street gang problem or talks about getting tough on them and how they are taking over, Rich asks them what about the gangs in gated communities and business suits and uniforms at all levels of government and society who supply the street tribes with drugs and guns and commit white collar crimes robbing the society of its resources. Of course, the police don't go after them because that is who pays and controls them, whether directly or indirectly. ***They are EQualized!*** Rich used to be a drug dealer and witnessed this first-hand. And later, when he became a consultant for the DEA to help stop the trafficking of narcotics in the Caribbean and beyond—before he wised up to their corruption and the complete corruption and futility of the "war on drugs" ---he witnessed it further. The street-level drug dealers are minor compared to the high-level dealers, mostly white and professionals from all walks of life and levels of government, who make their millions on the illegal drug black market and through the Black and Brown, street level dealers. So, when Rich hears these hypocrites in public office promote "the rule of law" and "get tough on crime," he knows they are just distracting attention away from themselves and their high crimes. ***They are EQualized!)***

Several years earlier, Haroun's mom and aunt decided to move away from the Chicago south side "hood" and start a new life in Cobb County, Georgia. Haroun came with them to leave the violence of the street tribe life, where he was known as "Big A." Soon after arriving in Cobb (where the racist police "sweated the small stuff"), Haroun was arrested for marijuana possession and was sentenced to a year in the Cobb County jail, during which time he studied Islam and became a Muslim. He also joined the new iteration of the GD's--- Growth & Development. To put his newfound Muslim and GD beliefs into action, he formed, under the guidance and with the assistance of renowned, incarcerated civil rights activist and Black separatist Jamil Al-Amin (formerly H. Rap Brown)[81], his own social justice and street tribe alternative organization called Street Groomers.[82]

Through his Street Groomers organization, Brother Haroun organized several Atlanta area young Black men and former "street tribe" members who had grown tired of life on the streets and in the jails and decided to transform their lives and reach out to others in similar situations to help them do the same. They were also tired of seeing young Black men killing each other and racist police harassing, arresting, and killing their brothers and sisters. So, they decided to organize themselves into street patrol units, to unite the "street tribes" and begin taking back the streets from thugs of all types (including those in Blue) and cleaning up their communities. And the Street Groomers was born!

Rich pledged his support of this noble initiative and discovered that

---

[81] https://en.wikipedia.org/wiki/H._Rap_Brown
[82] https://streetgroomers.org/

Brother Haroun and the Street Groomers were in demand in many Atlanta area neighborhoods, and in communities in other cities and states, as positive results were immediately noticed in communities where they patrolled. In addition to expanding the number of communities they patrolled, their next step was to launch enterprises, programs, and projects that benefit and positively transform the youth and communities they served.

Rich had been familiar with the similarly great work of the Guardian Angels[83] street patrols back in New York in the 70s and thought that Haroun and the Street Groomers were on to something timely and needed. He vowed to assist them to fulfill their noble goals by helping to get their work funded so that Haroun could devote himself full time to his mission. Working together, they decided to crowd fund that mission so that the people and neighborhoods they served could contribute, and to start legitimate street businesses selling oils and related products. Rich and family also adopted Haroun as a member of their family since, while in jail, he had lost his mother and aunt, and his fiancée had skipped town with his infant son, so he had no local family. Also, the jail had lost all his identification, so he had nothing to prove his identity. The Muslim Masjid in West Atlanta had purchased a house to utilize as a halfway home for Muslims coming out of jail or in recovery, and they invited Haroun to live in and manage that home. It was in the Bankhead section of Atlanta on the West Side, which was a perfect base, at least initially, for Haroun and the Street Groomers' work.

Rich started a Cobb Street Groomers chapter with Haroun's help, and they worked in some of the high crime areas of Cobb. He also joined Haroun and the other Street Groomers on their street patrols in Atlanta, enjoying some great successes and challenges together. Some highlights of Rich's and Haroun's work and learning together, included:

- One thing Rich had learned early in life as a street drug dealer in New York, but had somehow forgotten or tucked away as he left the street life, is that those on or close to the "streets" have a common, "street sense" and knowledge which is full of practical wisdom about social and political realities that those of us in the relative comfort of our middle-class trappings, whether in the city or suburbs, don't get. The more he hung with Haroun, who was not uneducated at all and was an avid reader of everything and anything related to his mission, the more he learned from Haroun's street-derived intelligence which armed him with uncanny insights on whom and what to trust, and distrust—an imperative skill needed for street survival. One of Haroun's favorite sayings and warnings was, *"Just because you're white doesn't mean you're right, and just because you're Black doesn't mean you got my*

---

[83] https://en.wikipedia.org/wiki/Guardian_Angels

back." **They were EQualized!** People of all stripes had to prove themselves worthy of his trust, as Haroun did not discriminate, and when they did earn his trust, he developed close White and Black, Asian and Latino, gay and straight, Republican and Democrat friends and allies, much like Malcolm X did near the end of his life.

Haroun and the Street Groomers were a prime example of "the Beloved Community" in action in one of the most difficult urban environments. Rich learned or relearned from them how the people can take responsibility and care for their own communities and neighborhoods, and then only need to call the police for major issues. But Americans of all stripes are lazy and want someone else to do the work of building community, which is why policing is a set-up for failure, as are cities, where poor people are stacked up on top of each other and squeezed together in small spaces surrounded by relative affluence, all controlled by "white money" even if the leadership, as in Atlanta, is mostly Black. Who knows the community and neighborhoods better, it's needs and wants, than those who are on the streets? So, any wise public officials, including police, know and respect that and would harness and channel that collective power and wisdom. For that purpose, Rich set up meetings for Haroun and the Street Groomers with the Atlanta police and elected officials to let them know that Street Groomers could collaborate with them, not work against them, and be their "eyes on the streets" to help reduce and prevent crime and homelessness. Those meetings were successful, and the police and public officials began calling the Street Groomers to solve or mediate minor crimes like thefts and drug dealing out in the open which exposed children and seniors to potential violence. The Street Groomers knew that they couldn't tell people not to sell drugs, especially the poor, until they could provide jobs and alternative sources of income for them. However, they could and did tell them to do it more discreetly like dealers do in the more affluent neighborhoods, out of the sight of children, seniors, and the police. That was part of cleaning up or grooming the streets. (And more than once, the Street Groomers witnessed rogue police officers involved in drug deals.)

One time a City Council member's car was stolen, and he called Haroun who had it found and returned to him within days. Haroun also reached out to the affluent white Atlanta community of Buckhead and became close friends with one of its prominent City Council members who had unsuccessfully run for mayor. They worked together on crime prevention by focusing on the youth in the poor neighborhoods, because they both knew that if those youth's needs were not met crime would begin spilling over into the affluent neighborhoods—a phenomena Rich and the Street Groomers called "Bankhead to Buckhead." (That is a prediction which was sadly fulfilled after Haroun's untimely passing, as crime skyrocketed, not only in the high crime areas but in affluent Buckhead as well. Secretly, Rich was happy when this occurred because he knew that positive change would only occur when the white, affluent people are directly affected. 'Just as in the opioid crisis, since white youth are dying in record numbers suddenly it is a priority. That is why we constantly must repeat "Black Lives Matter—too!" *They are EQualized!)*

- One of Haroun's goals for the Street Groomers was to have proactive street patrols in the neighborhoods *before* there was violence. However, due to the sheer numbers of violent incidents, they had to settle for being reactive. So, when there was a shooting in an area they gathered together all of the groups who were active in or near there, including but not limited to the Nation of Islam(NOI), the new Black Panthers, the NAACP, BLM, etc., and together held a unity march through the neighborhood, adding neighborhood members to the march as they walked throughout, especially youth, not in a threatening manner but a conciliatory and peaceful one. Then they met with existing or prospective neighborhood leaders to form a cell of Street Groomers working to organize ongoing street patrols and prevent future violence there. (Rich participated in many of these marches and street patrols, and, when they were occurring, violence and crime decreased in Atlanta but when they paused or ceased, it skyrocketed. One area where there was a constant Street Groomers and NOI presence and positive effect was "the Bluffs" neighborhood, infamous as part of the Southeast's "Heroin Triangle" highlighted in the "Intervention" TV series.)

- Brother Haroun's mission was not only to help prevent violence and injustices against individuals and neighborhoods, but also to call out systemic racism, poverty and injustices perpetrated by public officials in high places (and sometimes loudly and in their faces). He would speak out about this not only in organized street protests but in the City Hall chambers and meetings and at press conferences. And Atlanta had its fair share of corrupt officials who would try to avoid Haroun's spoken wrath by any means. (Dr. Ben Williams, Cobb SCLC President, and Dr. Rashad Richey, popular Atlanta radio and tv host and commentator, and Rich, all three of whom were like brothers to Haroun, can take both credit and blame for his outspokenness and advocacy as they guided him on how to use his growing public advocacy pulpit.) This made Haroun a target of the corrupt politicians, including the Atlanta mayor at the time, who employed their henchmen, including law enforcement, to harass and even imprison him on bogus charges more than once. When they dared do this, Rich and the Street Groomers had a small army of attorneys ready to defend him, supported by troops of supporters who would show up in the courtrooms and outside the jail to protest this mistreatment. However, the stress of these attacks, though Haroun would not admit it, contributed to the deterioration of his health, which was already compromised by both his size and his life-long epilepsy resulting in ongoing seizures. (Alternating between the roles of big brother, fellow activist, and parent, Rich attempted to monitor Haroun's health and get him to specialists to address his seizures, as well as holistic health providers and practices, with only limited success due to his size and the fact that Haroun would not slow down.)

- One uncomfortable truth is that some of the cities with Black leadership were among the harshest on poor Blacks with "tough on crime" policies (often dictated by the white money power brokers), producing the highest levels of mass incarceration and police brutality of Blacks. Atlanta was one of the worst since the time of its first Black mayor, Maynard Jackson, as documented in the book by Black activist and legal scholar James Forman, Jr., called *"Locking Up Our Own: Crime and Punishment in Black America"*.[84] The Atlanta mayor at the time (from 2010 to 2018) was no exception, and, while his administration was rife with corruption, he was not responsive to the advocacy community especially regarding the issues of homelessness and police brutality, including the police murder of unarmed Blacks.

So, Haroun and Rich, together with some other community leaders and advocates, decided to bring the issues right to the mayor's doorstep, literally, in the affluent gated community where he resided. (As one of Haroun's trusted field marshals and advisors, Rich was asked to help organize this. Plus, as his brother and guardian, Rich was always either on his speed dial or present to make sure Haroun was not brutalized or arrested, or to bail him out if necessary.) Word got out about what they were planning so when the Street Groomers and allies arrived at the shopping center staging area near the mayor's neighborhood, not only were there many protestors present on foot and in vehicles, including family members of victims of police violence, but there was an equally heavy police presence of not only Atlanta police, but other metro area police departments which they had called for support. They were determined not to let the protest get into or even near the mayor's neighborhood. Rather than get into a clash with the police, Haroun and Rich decided to hold the protest in and near the shopping center, with full media coverage to get their message across to the mayor and his allies, rather than trying to breach his neighborhood. (They learned other prominent officials

---

[84] https://en.wikipedia.org/wiki/Locking_Up_Our_Own

lived there too, including the corrupt District Attorney who would not prosecute police who murdered innocent civilians, but instead cowardly went after innocent schoolteachers for alleged cheating.) That protest sent the message that they were not going away or backing down and there would no peace if there was no justice in Atlanta.

Then, a couple of weeks later, they were holding a Street Groomers community unity march in a nearby neighborhood that had experienced gun violence. This was on the same night in which there was a huge celebration for a victorious Atlanta sports team taking place far on the other side of the city and attended by the mayor and many public officials, requiring a huge police presence there. After completing their unity march, Haroun, Rich, and the Street Groomers huddled and decided, since they were in the vicinity, to try once again to breach the mayor's neighborhood to bring a protest to his doorstep, since they knew the city and its resources were distracted by the celebration event. So, they assembled a small strike force of about thirty and parked at a church near the mayor's neighborhood. Then they quietly walked a quarter mile to the neighborhood's gated entrance, sending a couple of scouts ahead to see if there was any way to walk into the neighborhood without being stopped or detected by its private security. The scouts reported there was no security present, and a walk-through entrance gate was wide open. So, they quietly slipped into the neighborhood, in staggered small groups of two or three, trying not to draw attention or appear to be a larger group. It was a large neighborhood, with rolling hills and spaced-out affluent homes, and they didn't know exactly where the mayor resided. Some neighborhood residents noticed them though and, realizing that they didn't reside there as they were a mixed group, and it was a predominantly Black area, inquired what their mission was. When Haroun and Rich explained, they were going to protest police brutality and murders, right on the mayor's doorstep, literally, they loved it and said they would guide the group. The neighbors drove their car slowly for the group to follow and took them to the mayor's street pointing out his house from a distance. Haroun and Rich thanked them and saw from that vantage point that the mayor's security detail was parked in a black limo in front of his home. They knew that once they were spotted, the security and the police would arrive on the scene and force them to leave. So, they called the media to let them know where they were and what they were about to do and, at the media's request, they filmed themselves beginning the protest, chanting, and pulling out their signs as they approached the mayor's home. Once they were spotted by the mayor's security, one member of that detail ran into the home and came out with who they later learned was the mayor, who had apparently returned home briefly from the celebration. The security whisked him away in the limo right past the protestors as they chanted and waved their signs at him—what lucky and perfect timing! Rich and Haroun knew their presence there was now exposed, and, with their mission accomplished, they joyfully headed for the community entrance to exit before the police arrived. 'Just as they exited, dozens of police cars with lights flashing and sirens blasting descended upon them, along with media reporters, and they simply resumed walking on the public sidewalks outside of the neighborhood and back toward the church where their vehicles were parked, ignoring the police like nothing out of the ordinary had happened, while granting interviews to reporters now walking with them. Two police commanders got out of their cars and walked with them attempting to also interview them, and Rich, acting as the group spokesperson, told the commanders that they had broken no laws and were simply and peacefully walking to their cars to leave the area. The officers tried to cite laws that had allegedly been violated, apparently trying to intimidate the group, but they firmly but politely told them they were wrong and to leave them alone unless they wanted lawsuits for violation of their rights, and they would make no further comments. So, the police escorted them back to their cars, the group thanked them, and left—laughing all the way, with their mission accomplished. *NO JUSTICE, NO PEACE*, taken to a new level! ***They were EQualized!*** This became the big news of the next day, all across Atlanta—how the Street Groomers and their allies had brought their demands right to the mayor's personal doorstep since he hadn't paid attention when they protested at City Hall! They learned that this was the first time in Atlanta history that this had happened. Both the state and city tried to pass legislation prohibiting similar protests at public officials' homes, but they failed. *No Justice, No Peace!*

- Besides dealing with thugs on the streets (including those in uniforms and business suits), the main other people Haroun and the Street Groomers encountered were the homeless, a constantly growing and diverse population of people living on the streets. This was (and still is) an issue not adequately addressed by city officials and made worse by their apathy and corruption. The Mayor and City Council had recently closed the main homeless shelter, promising to set aside millions of dollars to build a new one. However, they lied and never did, and likely some of that money went into other pet projects and the pockets of their corrupt friends and associates, some of whom were later indicted. Haroun and the Street Groomers partnered with other organizations and became a main distributor of food, blankets, and other necessities directly to the homeless men, women, and children across the city. (Rich views homelessness, and the poverty and lack of mental health care that causes it, as an American tragedy and travesty, and one of the triple evils Dr. King addressed. It is an evil which can be solved, as other countries have done, by taking care of the least among us. It is a symptom of the

148

greed and corruption of the American economic and political system, and the cancerous materialism most Americans are infected with. It is also an affliction of the minds and hearts of those who judge and blame the poor for their circumstances. NO ONE CAN JUDGE another person's situation, mind, heart, motive--as it is hard enough to judge one's own. It is hard to understand how anyone can live and feel comfortable in their own home while there are human beings, people just like us, suffering in the cold or heat, rain, and storms, on the streets around us. To accept that as normal is sick. It is among the cruelest scenarios one can imagine, and any person or elected official who does not cry out and demand change in this regard is heartless. It is not rocket science to fix, as European and other countries have done so. It is just a matter of the will to shift some priorities, just a little. To not do so renders us barbarians, and we have no right to count ourselves and our country as civilized. *We are EQualized!*)

- When Rich and his coalitions needed Haroun and the Street Groomers in the Cobb County suburbs, they were always ready. On one occasion, they decided to hold a protest march and rally regarding the police murder of Nick Thomas and other Cobb police and elected official injustices in affluent East Cobb where many prominent politicians, business owners and corporate CEOs reside in gated communities, and which had never experienced such an event. One of the major alliances Haroun and Street Groomers had made in Atlanta was with the mainly white anarchists and antifa revolutionaries--a throwback to the hippies and revolutionaries of Rich's early days. They would support Street Groomers, Black Lives Matter, and other Black and Brown led protests, bringing their drums and other musical instruments, which amplified and punctuated the "No Justice, No Peace" and other chants, disrupting business as usual. They all came to East Cobb for the march and spontaneously left the streets and went into the strip malls, even marching inside the chain stores, making quite a ruckus until the police arrived and they resumed on the sidewalks. Everywhere people came out to see what the commotion was, and many thanked the protesters for braving that largely conservative area, as no one had done so before.

On another occasion, the town of Smyrna was having its annual Fall festival with booths, vendors and kids' attractions lining the downtown streets and square, which were barricaded to traffic. On the Saturday of the weekend event, Rich went alone to distribute fliers demanding justice for Nick Thomas, murdered by the Smyrna police. While he got some dirty looks from the event organizers and the police providing security, he was not prevented from walking and handing out fliers. The next day, Haroun joined Rich, while some Street Groomers dispersed into the crowd to watch and provide security for them from a distance, as they were accustomed to doing discreetly. Rich and Haroun had barely removed the fliers from their backpacks when the police and event management company personnel surrounded and forbade them from distributing the fliers. They said that it was a private event, and they could therefore place restrictions on what anyone could do there. Rich strongly suggested to them that it was a public event, free to the public, sponsored by the city, on city roads, sidewalks, and parks, and he and Haroun had a free speech right to offer their fliers to those attending in that public space. The police insisted that it was a private event and told them to cease and desist and threatened them with arrest for violating a city ordinance. (Rich knew that this was not only arbitrary, as they would not cite or explain the ordinance, but also racist, targeting Haroun since no one had harassed him, a white man, the day before. Haroun was getting upset, so they agreed to put the fliers away and just walk around and enjoy the festival... To that the police said no, they were not welcome there, and escorted them out of the downtown area.

After they left, Rich called the SCLC civil rights attorney Gary to explain what had happened, and he was livid and said to meet him back there in a couple of hours, and to bring the fliers. When we returned, we met Gary and his wife, also an attorney, both white seniors. He told Haroun and Rich to resume giving out the fliers and to also give him and his wife some fliers for them to distribute. Quickly, the same police and event manager accosted Haroun and Rich and repeated that they were in violation of their orders and were to leave immediately. Rich laughed in their faces and directed them to speak to his attorneys who were standing nearby also giving out the fliers. The police were visibly shocked, their faces turning red in anger, as they realized that they were now "caught with their racist pants down." Attorney Gary told them in no uncertain terms that they were all legally entitled to be there and distribute their fliers in a public space and demanded that they immediately get a police supervisor there to avoid a lawsuit. When the police supervisor came, he apologized profusely and explained that it was just a big misunderstanding and that they were free to be there and distribute their fliers. Rich thanked the supervisor but explained that due to his officers' illegal and racist actions they had been deprived of their constitutional rights for several hours, and the event was about to close, so he asked how they were going to right this wrong. He just apologized again, sheepishly, and they all left.

Afterwards, in discussion with attorney Gary and the SCLC chapter leadership, they decided that Smyrna police and city leadership had to learn how to respect First Amendment free speech and protest rights since this was not the first incident with them, they had encountered. (Days earlier, Rich and his family were distributing the same fliers near the Smyrna police station and an officer attempted to stop them and confiscate and trash the fliers.) So, they contacted a prominent constitutional civil rights attorney in Atlanta to represent them. He was too busy with more important cases involving police and municipal misconduct in other cities but agreed to write a letter to Smyrna police and government officials requesting that a local ordinance be enacted or amended to protect free speech rights, based on the incidents reported. Smyrna ignored his letter, not even offering the courtesy of a reply—the first time in decades of dealing with municipalities that his outreach was completely ignored, which just underscored Smyrna's lack of accountability and transparency, and willful arrogance and disregard for the law. So, he decided to assist one of his younger associate counsels to file a federal lawsuit against Smyrna with Haroun, Rich, and the SCLC as plaintiffs. They were victorious and per the federal court order Smyrna agreed to amend the challenged provisions of their ordinances and will not be able to exclude private citizens from public areas where citizens are engaging in lawful speech under the First Amendment. The court also awarded the plaintiffs damages and legal fees.[85] (Since then, Rich and his fellow activists have been to almost every Smyrna event distributing fliers regarding various issues freely and without harassment, and all people are enabled to do so as well.)

- Haroun and Rich spoke at least once daily, and on February 24th, 2021, a couple of the Street Groomers called and asked if he had heard from Haroun that day. Rich told them he hadn't since the day before, and they said neither had they, which seemed unusual. Knowing that Haroun was often a victim of seizures, they grew worried and one volunteered to go by his house and see if he was there or if anyone had seen him. Upon arrival he called Rich and said the house was locked and no one answered the door but peering through the windows he saw Brother Haroun laying on the floor. He immediately broke in and found him unconscious. He called 911 and the police arrived first but could not conclusively determine if Haroun was breathing or revive him. When the medics arrived, they confirmed that he was not breathing and was already deceased.

A shock of disbelief went through Rich and his fellow Street Groomers, and soon spread throughout Atlanta and beyond. The next hours and days were a whirlwind and blur for Rich as he was consumed with the preparations for a speedy funeral the following weekend since Haroun was a Muslim and

---

[85] Read more about our lawsuit against the City of Smyrna at
https://cobbcountycourier.com/2017/02/smyrna-changes-ordinance-in-response-to-lawsuit-stemming-from-death-of-nicholas-thomas/

that is their tradition. He also began handling the thousands of tributes, condolences, and expressions of loss pouring in, since everyone felt Haroun belonged to them and all felt a personal loss, including public figures, celebrities, activists and community members around Atlanta and the country. Thankfully, Rich was absorbed in helping to field and organize all that, with the assistance of the Masjid and Street Groomers, and his wife and family (who also felt they lost a family member), so he didn't have time to grieve right away. Tributes and proclamations poured in from every level of government. The funeral was held in the Atlanta West End Park near the Masjid, and was packed, including dignitaries presenting the many government proclamations honoring Haroun and his work. Then the crowd of hundreds marched from the West End to the Bankhead area house of Haroun. There a memorial celebration of his life of service was held for hours, with music and speakers offering their remembrances of and praise for the brother they lost, way too soon.[86] The coroner had said his death was from heart failure however, as Rich said in his remarks at the funeral, *"the coroner was wrong as Brother Haroun's heart never failed all the people he loved and served."* And one speaker at the memorial said that he had thought he was Haroun's best friend but now he sees that Haroun had hundreds of best friends!

To this day, Rich and many of his fellow activists still miss Haroun almost daily. When they see any Atlanta area or Georgia injustice or violence on the news their constant refrain is *"if Haroun was here, they would not get away with that"*! (Also, the crime waves are sweeping Atlanta which Haroun had predicted would happen if they didn't work quickly to address the inequities there.)

Episode Six: Atlanta Braves Boondoggle/Crony Capitalism

In his quest for oneness and reconciliation, Rich had always wanted to find a way to work across the aisles and reach out especially to poor white folks who seemed to be among the most abused populations in America, as no one paid attention to their needs and issues except Republican politicians manipulating them through racism and fear to vote on their side. Rich, who is politically unaligned and independent (though he votes most often with Democrats since they appear to have a heart and do not run fear and bullying based, racist campaigns), wanted to find common ground issues and a way to work with both conservative Republicans and Libertarians. He had gained support from Libertarians for his pro-immigrant advocacy since they rejected big government interference in peoples' lives, no matter what their status,

[86] https://www.fox5atlanta.com/news/founder-of-atlantas-street-groomers-remembered-as-a-giant-among-men-with-a-gentle-heart https://www.11alive.com/article/news/local/atlanta-mourns-death-of-community-pillar-haroun-wakil/85-53f70c0a-a6bb-4cdb-a7ac-2a06b9cd4658

however he learned that so-called *"Conservative Republicans"* didn't really appear to be *Conservative* in that regard (and, he would learn, in many other regards). In 2013, a grand opportunity to work together across all political and ideological lines presented itself. The county and country were in a recession and Rich was watching the evening news and heard the county leadership say that the county would have to tighten its financial belt by cutting services, mainly to the poor, like library and bus services. Then, in the next breath, the County Chairman announced that he had exciting news---the Atlanta Braves professional baseball team was relocating from Atlanta to Cobb County, and they were building a new stadium there. Then he launched a bombshell—the County, meaning the taxpayers, would be paying about 60% of the cost of building the stadium, to the tune of over $400 million dollars! This was incredulous to Rich as minutes earlier he heard they were hurting for money and had to cut back essential services. Plus, to make matters worse, the County Chairman said that the County Commission would be rushing a vote on whether to approve this in just two weeks--what's the rush---something didn't smell right! So, Rich immediately got on his computer and sent out to his extensive email lists, including one containing dozens of GOP and Libertarian members, the simple question, *"Does this announcement and proposed deal with the Braves, a billionaire owned team and organization, committing an exorbitant amount of taxpayer money during a recession when we are supposedly tightening our belt and cutting services, surprise and shock you, as it does me?"* The response he got was overwhelming and really the largest response to any issue email he had ever sent out, both in sheer numbers and in total agreement that this was incredulous. He immediately called a town hall meeting of those interested in exploring and possibly opposing this venture, at least until it could be vetted and approved by the taxpayers (who were having it shoved down their throats in an uncharacteristically rapid fashion, which smelled of shady back room dealing and corruption). The meeting turnout was not only large but the most diverse, not only racially but politically, gathering he had ever seen and attended in Cobb. He had finally found common ground with those who had considered him an enemy of the people in the past. At that initial meeting there were people sitting across the table from Rich who had incited violence against him in the past for his advocacy on behalf of immigrants and Blacks, so this was a perfect foundation for reconciliation—the goal of all "Kingian" (MLK inspired) activism.

They decided at the meeting to form a coalition--which local and national media would later call the most diverse, tri-partisan, citizens coalition they had ever seen--called Citizens for Governmental Transparency (CGT). Everyone agreed this was the least transparent and accountable massive commitment of taxpayer funds, without taxpayer input, in County history—and during a recession! Upon further investigation, they found that it was indeed a back-room deal conducted by the Chairman and one other Commissioner, without the other Commissioners even aware of it initially. They also learned that nearly every other similar stadium deal in the country with professional sports teams had fallen short of revenue projections, didn't pay for itself in new sales and other tax revenues, and left the taxpayers holding the bill. So, they said, *"Hell no", this* will not be ramrodded through without plenty of taxpayer forums and input, and possibly even a referendum or lawsuits, if necessary. The Chairman and his allies refused to deal honestly and openly with the issue, and he knew he had the votes on the County Commission to pass it without adequate hearings. When Rich and fellow coalition members attempted to speak at the one public hearing conducted, they were escorted out by the police, but not before shouting their comments which were heard and reported in the media. (After that, Rich become known for disrupting government meetings when they were not being responsive to the public, especially if they were trying to stifle or limit public comment.)

Ultimately, three plaintiffs, including Rich, filed suit in the Georgia Supreme Court to halt the deal, as it had so many improprieties. However, the Court ruled in the Braves and Cobb County's favor (even after the justices agreed that it was not done above board or properly, and was on shaky legal ground, so their decision was nothing but pure corruption as the Braves contributed heavily to the justices' campaigns).

Rich and CGT lost the battle but ultimately won the war, as they were able to clean the Cobb house by electing a new County Chairman and a couple of new Commissioners. (A few years later, it still appears that the stadium will not pay for itself, and the taxpayers will be on the hook—a perfect example of crony capitalism and corporate welfare.)[87]

The biggest triumph for Rich was the building of the diverse CGT coalition and making friendships with some "true conservatives" by working together. In our group, as well as in the country, Rich learned that there were two kinds of conservatives—those who were truly fiscally conservative and believe in smaller government and those who just use the label for political purposes. For example, one cannot claim to be fiscally conservative and support our massive military budget, expensive mass incarceration, crony capitalism and corporate welfare—which is common practice--- and other ballooning fiscal boondoggles. One cannot claim to want limited government and then be for government trying to control women's bodies, people's sexuality, immigrants, etc. And then there are the holier than thou *"Christian conservatives,"* haters who are not Christian at all, at least not Jesus Christ's brand of Christianity.

One thing that Cobb County, its elected and appointed officials, learned

[87] https://www.ajc.com/news/atlanta-news/years-after-opening-day-braves-cobb-stadium-deal-still-under-scrutiny/JQWOWCSRMNBHPA6DE4JF3J2SLU/

from CGT was that the people would no longer stand for a lack of transparency and accountability, and the old "Cobb way" of doing business behind closed doors was over forever.

Episode Seven: 2016 Election: American Aberration or Abomination?

Many alliances between parties, between the right and left, between races. cultures, genders, and anything else which makes America the "United" States, including Rich's local bi-partisan CGT coalition, were disrupted, or destroyed by the election of an abomination, and possibly an aberration, in 2016. He was, in Rich's opinion, not qualified to be a dogcatcher, much less president.

His motto of *"make America great again"*, apparently meant, by his words and actions both on the campaign trail and in office, *"make America hate again."* He and his most ardent supporters apparently longed for the bygone days when Blacks and other people of color, and women, immigrants, and anyone who was not a WASP ("white Anglo-Saxon protestant") shut up, knew, and stayed in their place of subservience and inequality, and were grateful to their elite white masters to have a place at all in this country. Hate crimes against those groups increased dramatically under his rule and incited by this hateful rhetoric.

Then, in 2021—the so-called *"Christian Conservatives"* should love this biblical parable--- a plague came (Covid), driving him and his followers out of power, and opening up the "Red Sea" so all the diverse peoples of this nation—BIPOC, LGBTQ, Muslims, immigrants, women, etc.--- could resume their rightful places as equals here. But no, his narcissistic and delusional self could not give up that easily or read the proverbial handwriting on the wall, *"YOU'RE FIRED."* He had to continue to manipulate his cult following, together with his fellow puppet-masters in the halls of Congress and on FOX News, to try and reverse the election, by any means necessary, including violence (recalling the fact that he had bragged when campaigning that he could do no wrong, even murder someone randomly in the streets and still not lose his followers: *"I could stand in the middle of Fifth Avenue and shoot somebody, okay, and I wouldn't lose any voters, okay?"* .)

It has been a bittersweet joy for Rich and his fellow activists to behold and watch that all unfold, though a lot of innocent people had to die or get hurt for this grand correction and redemption to occur. Unfortunately, that appears to be the choice of most Americans for change---unimaginable catastrophes rather than the consultative good will of coming together in collective responsibility to build "the Beloved Community" and rid the nation of its injustices and inequities that are preventing it from fulfilling its destiny of *E pluribus Unum*. If the scourge of that delusional, wannabe Hitler/tyrant and then the devastating Covid pandemic killing nearly a million Americans (more per capita than any other country) did not wake us up to recognize and learn our oneness and the need to work together to build community, together with the ongoing climate disasters-- then what will?

When that abomination was elected, Rich put out warnings to the Cobb community and to the White House and federal government that he and his bullying policies were not welcome here and, if they reached here, would be completely ignored, or vigorously opposed. (And Rich continues to emphasize to his family and all around him that any mention of this abomination's name in any positive light around him will be shut down as he doesn't tolerate serial bullies no matter what their title or position is, so forewarned is forearmed. *He is mega-EQualized!*)

Rich used to think that this dogcatcher (apologies to all the dogcatchers out there) and his rise to power were both an abomination and a temporary aberration however now that he sees Americans, at all levels, still supporting his racist, fascist, and delusional rantings and claims two years later, it is hardly temporary. Sadly, there are many Americans who are just as despicable and villainous bullies. They are the same ones who would bring their children and families to watch and applaud the brutal lynchings of the not-too-distant past. (To those who would say that this is just partisan politics, that is pure cow dung as it has nothing to do with politics but is about morals, ethics, and common human decency. Rich has voted for and supported people based on their policies and platforms who refused to bully and vilify groups of people, and for their servant-leadership qualities, both Republicans and Democrats, but would never support a racist bully, or anyone who refused to call out racist, bullies in their party.)

Episode Eight: Taking A Knee with Colin Kaepernick

Sometimes in history true leaders emerge bearing the qualities of servant-leadership. (Rich has been privileged to meet and/or learn from several, including some highlighted in previous chapters.) In August 2016, at the start of the National Football League season, one such servant-leader stood up and out when he chose to take a knee---then NFL quarterback, Colin Kaepernick. He knelt during the national anthem at the start of NFL games in protest of police brutality and racial inequality in the United States. This act of defiance and true patriotism, which ultimately cost him his football career, sparked a nationwide *"Take a Knee"* movement where both professional and amateur athletes in many sports and even cheerleaders in high schools and colleges supported and participated in this silent but powerful protest by "taking a knee" in their respective localities.

This drew the ire of racists and bullies at all levels, including the dogcatcher campaigning for the presidency at the time. And, as usual, many arrogant and supremacist white folks tried to tell people of color how to protest the racism and discrimination they experience daily in this country. ('Guess they prefer riots and violence rather than the peaceful taking of a knee.)

Locally, in Cobb, five Kennesaw State University (KSU) cheerleaders took a knee during the national anthem at a football game on September 30, 2017. The university president, a former GOP Georgia Attorney General, was pressured by the Cobb Sheriff (whose racist bullying and illegal actions have been documented and mentioned in earlier chapters), and a GOP State legislator (also known as a hater and bully) to punish the cheerleaders. They were then prohibited from appearing on the field during the national anthem at two subsequent home football games. Rich and his social justice and SCLC allies immediately jumped into action helping KSU student and faculty leaders form a coalition, composed of KSU students and student organizations, alumni, professors, and staff, as well as community members and organizations. That coalition, taking the name "TakeAKneeKSU", started a series of student-led protests and demonstrations on KSU campus in support of the cheerleaders, their actions, and the right for all to engage in free speech and protest. (This coalition and eventual student organization later became known as KSUnited and still exists on campus.) In less than three months, their actions, which sparked broad media attention and investigations, helped expose the lies of the three hater-bullies, one in uniform and two in business suits (who tried to cover up their communications which constituted illegal and unethical collusion), forcing the resignation of the university president, the full restoration of the cheerleaders' rights, and successful lawsuits against the university and the three haters.

What was most gratifying for Rich about this spontaneous movement is that the students got to learn first-hand the power of the people when unified and adamant regarding their absolute right to accountability, transparency, and justice from those in elected and appointed leadership roles. This was especially important to him, since it was Rich's similar experiences as a high school and college age activist (as highlighted in previous chapters) that provided him with a life-long confidence in his power as a citizen, not only of this country, but of the world, and has enabled him to become a *"Global Woke EQualizer"!*

Another of the slogans in the seventies, *"Power to the People",* meant to Rich at that time that "we the people" need to get power. But now he knows that we already have power and need to realize our power and speak truth to those who are in authority, vested in that authority by us, demanding just and equitable representation and servant-leadership. Our government is us, and they only do what we let them get away with doing. The vote is one of our powers, but it is not a "one and done" deal and doesn't stop there because whomever is voted into office, whether it is our choice or not, must be held accountable by our collective voices and actions, exercising our power.

When Obama was first elected President, and many of us were jubilant at the prospects for progressive change, he warned us that he was not king and could only make change if we the people helped him do so. Responding to that call, Rich had helped organize and moderate town hall meetings to get people together who wanted to work on the "Beloved Community" issues which Obama wanted to address, such as healthcare, poverty, housing, food, immigration, and mass incarceration. While some of these meetings were well attended, those who signed on to do the work were few, as they now had a leader in office whom they expected to do the work for them—a messiah, a superman, a prophet—to lead them to the proverbial holy land. That is not how it works. We are the "prophets"!

When Dr. King pressed the President at the time, Lyndon Johnson, for civil rights and voting legislation, Johnson told him that he and the people would have to force him to do the right thing because he could not do it unilaterally. Dr. King and his coalition, especially the Student Non-Violent Coordinating Committee (SNCC) and its founder, Helen Baker, mobilized hundreds, if not thousands, to take to the streets and risk violence and death to at least make it look like Johnson had no choice but to do the right thing. They did so on the streets of Selma and Birmingham and turned the tide.

Today, the right wingers and their cult leaders are good at forcing their elected officials to do the wrong things according to their misguided principles based on hate, fear, and persecution of other groups. If we want progressive, non-violent, change which is inclusive of everyone, we must fight for it and not sit back and expect our elected representatives to lead without our support and advocacy. If you complain that your vote doesn't count because those who are elected don't do anything for you, then YOU are the problem because you are not making them accountable to you. (You've heard Gandhi's famous call to action, *"Be the change you want to see in the world."* In the closing chapter and epilogue, we will list ways you can do that, as not everyone can or has to do the same things to effect change.)

Episode Nine: Time to Regroup, Reflect, Rededicate & Become Woke-- Globally

The latter years of this second decade of the new millennium, leading up to the fateful year of 2020, which would be another major turning point, was a time to regroup, reflect, re-educate, and then rededicate for Rich. He had plenty on his plate with all the social justice advocacy work in Cobb and the Atlanta metro area, with and through SCLC, CGT, BLM, Street Groomers, and the other organizations he was active in and sometimes called upon to serve (including Sharpton's National Action Network, Jackson's Rainbow Push Coalition, and Farrakhan's Nation of Islam, all of whom knew and respected his work). During this period, he was also honored with recognitions and awards by both non-profit and government organizations for his selfless work as a community advocate and servant. And he and V were blessed with six more grandchildren, totaling seven, so his family had continued to grow and occupy his attention, in addition to providing loving support so that he could continue to serve the community.

Rich always believed that his community building and social justice advocacy work is never really a sacrifice because the highest station we can attain, in his belief system, is service to others, and we get so much more in return than we give. This benefits family also, because without the village it is difficult to support and grow the family. This day, according to his beliefs which are partly derived from his Bahai and other spiritual studies, is one of "social salvation," not "individual salvation." In other words, the individual cannot ever be "saved" or reach his or her potential if others in the community are not being saved. Dr. King called it *"the network of mutuality."* He said: *"In a real sense all life is inter-related. All men are caught in an inescapable network of mutuality, tied in a single garment of destiny. Whatever affects one directly, affects all indirectly. I can never be what I ought to be until you are what you ought to be, and you can never be what you ought to be until I am what I ought to be... This is the inter-related structure of reality."*[88]

Rich also knew that his family will not be safe if the community is not safe. As Frederick Douglass, prominent Black abolitionist said, *"Where justice is denied, where poverty is enforced, where ignorance prevails, and where any one class is made to feel that society is an organized conspiracy to oppress, rob and degrade them, neither persons nor property will be safe."*[89]

With all his family activity and voluntary community service work, Rich's self-employment income suffered, but still covered their bills, with little or nothing left over. So, once when they needed a long overdue family vacation, Rich reached out to the community via email and social media, and they contributed the funds needed for his family's vacation retreat. (This is how the "Beloved Community" is supposed to operate, and Rich has been blessed to see and experience glimpses of it.)

However, although Rich's social advocacy work and family interactions were fulfilling, there was a gap, a hole—something major was missing. It seemed like Rich was spending a lot of time reacting to incidents of injustice and inequity rather than proactively building a fortress for well-being, the Beloved Community. And then he watched an interview (on Democracy Now progressive news program, on his favorite TV channel, "Free Speech TV") of long-time environmentalist, social justice activist, and anarchist, Scott Crow (who deliberately doesn't capitalize his name). Rich immediately identified with him having walked similar paths. Scott lamented the fact that he and similar activists have been reacting to injustices caused by this system

---

[88] — Martin Luther King Jr., Letter from Birmingham Jail: Martin Luther King Jr.'s Letter from Birmingham Jail and the Struggle That Changed a Nation
[89] https://advancementproject.org/9-greatest-frederick-douglass-quotes/

for decades, expending a lot of blood, sweat, and tears trying to fix the system and the people hurt by it when it is rotten and ready to crumble, rather than spending adequate time building the new system to replace it. He had learned that lesson when studying the effects of Katrina on New Orleans by going there in its aftermath to help the people, especially in the poor and Black neighborhoods. There he witnessed apocalyptic happenings including white militias randomly killing Black people to get their food, water, and other goods while the police did nothing to protect them and even sometimes joined in the chaos and violence against the people. The whole infrastructure had collapsed, and it was complete anarchy for days, so Scott and his fellow activists, including some ex-Black Panthers, formed an armed militia to protect the people, and then a relief organization, Common Ground Collective, to feed, house, and heal the people. This mission was so successful that the Red Cross channeled its aid through them. (This whole story is documented in Scott's book, *"Black Flags and Windmills: Hope, Anarchy, and the Common Ground Collective"*[90])

As soon as Rich read this story, he felt it needed to be shared widely, so he contacted Scott who graciously sent Rich a supply of both free and discounted books, which he promoted and distributed. The main takeaway from this story for Rich was the question of why we are waiting for catastrophes to do what we know we need to do now, form similar "Common Ground Collective" self-sustaining, grid-independent, cooperatives everywhere, NOW! We know that the government is not going to protect the people, especially communities of color and the poor, and we know that there are militias, mostly white nationalist ones, armed and ready to defend their areas and raid and ravage other areas for food and other resources. This is not science fiction or just in the movies and our only real defense is to build strong "Beloved Communities" that will wield not only practical but spiritual power.

So, Rich rededicated himself to spending at least the same amount of time building a new system as he was fixing the old system and rescuing people from the ravages of it. To that end, besides researching alternative, intentional systems and communities, he started writing about and forming new movements—first, the *Free States Collective Movement*, inspired by the *Free State of Jones* (in Mississippi), the libertarian *Free State Project* in Vermont, and the *Kansas Free-Staters* (anti-slavery abolitionists).[91] (He watched and was inspired by the historical movie, *"The Free State of Jones"*, in which white and Black residents united to drive the Confederate Army out of Jones County, Mississippi, and then declared it a sovereign state. He also read and studied the

---

[90] Read more about scott crow and his books at https://www.scottcrow.org/
[91] Read more about the three Free State movements at https://en.wikipedia.org/wiki/Free_State_of_Jones_(film) **https://en.wikipedia.org/wiki/Free-Stater_(Kansas)** ; **https://freestateproject.org** ;

book by Professor Ezra Aharone, head of "Sovereign Studies" in the political science department at Delaware State University, *"The Sovereign Psyche: Systems of Chattel Freedom vs. Self-Authentic Freedom"*, which taught Rich the history of sovereign, self-rule and self-determination mentality and behaviors, and how to revive that, especially among Blacks and other marginalized peoples today.)

Here is a description of Rich's "Free States Movement" from its Manifesto:

WHAT IS A *"FREE STATE"* AND SANCTUARY?

- A geographical area the inhabitants of which declare as an area free of hate, bigotry, corporatism, slavery, and dependence on existing local and/or national governments, and their oppressive, unjust, and corrupt policies; where a community will be built based upon "Beloved Community" principles serving to eradicate the Triple Evils of Racism, Poverty, and Militarism. This is not new as both historically and currently there have been and are "free state" initiatives.

- Also, a "sovereign" state of mind which embodies the principles above and extends beyond geographical borders connecting "Free Stater freedom fighters" virtually without boundaries.

This *"Free State"* movement and concept gained some supporters and even inspired the forming of a cooperative, eco-village and organic farm called *"The Free State of Palestine,"* near the town of Palestine in rural Georgia. To fulfill his goal of connecting with similar free-state type initiatives, Rich and some of his organizations joined the national Symbiosis-Revolution community, a *"confederation of community organizations across North America, building a democratic and ecological society from the ground up… by creating institutions of participatory democracy and the solidarity economy through community organizing, neighborhood by neighborhood, city by city."*[92] There he learned about the concepts of *"dual power"* (meaning working within the corrupt capitalistic and racist system to survive and channeling our collective action to fight it, while also building the new system to eventually become the governing structure of a new, liberated society), and *"municipalism"* (which concentrates power at the local, grass roots level through a true participatory democracy, and is explained in detail in the books of anarchist, author, historian, philosopher Murray Bookchin).

Through these groups and resources, Rich learned that America is not a democracy, or even a republic, but a plutocracy and oligarchy (a country or society governed by the wealthy elite or ruling class), and for that to change we must learn how to engage in self-rule and self-determination democratically and cooperatively. Through his participation in Symbiosis, Rich learned

---

[92] Read about and join the Symbiosis-Revolution at https://www.symbiosis-revolution.org/

that there are successful though embryonic initiatives to implement these liberating principles by exercising dual power strategies in various localities. These include *Cooperation Jackson* in Jackson, Mississippi, and the *Cleveland Model/Evergreen Cooperatives* in Cleveland, Ohio—signs of hope that the *"Beloved Community"* could be and is a reality in action and not just words or hopes.[93]

Incorporating the lessons learned from those initiatives, Rich formed *"Cooperation Cobb"* and linked up with similar cooperative, community-wealth building initiatives around the country through *Symbiosis* and in the Atlanta metro area, including *Community Movement Builders, Regenerate Atlanta,* and the *Tear Down Community.*[94] He understood that in order for there to be system change leading to self-determination, from the grassroots up rather than from the top down, it had to include a new economic system with a radical change in values that placed cooperation above competition and people above profit and property. As Dr. King said, *"I am convinced that if we are to get on the right side of the world revolution, we as a nation must undergo a radical revolution of values. We must rapidly begin the shift from a thing-oriented society to a person-oriented society."* (It doesn't matter if you call it democratic or libertarian socialism, as they do in Europe, or regenerate or progressive capitalism, as some American reformers do, the principles are the same—an end to gross inequities, poverty, materialism, and other economic and social injustices, all caused by and inherent to the current American economic system.)

---

[93] Read about Cooperation Jackson and the Cleveland Model at these sites: https://cooperationjackson.org/ and https://community-wealth.org/content/cleveland-model-how-evergreen-cooperatives-are-building-community-wealth

[94] Learn more about Community Movement Builders, Regenerate Atlanta , and Tear Down Community at these sites: https://communitymovementbuilders.org/ https://www.ohrdemocracy.org/programs/alternative-institutions https://www.theteardown.org/

The chart below, contributed by Symbiosis member and founding member of Cooperation Tulsa, Native American Roberto Mendoza, compares indigenous, cooperative values with existing corporatist, capitalist extractive ones:

INDIGENOUS (COOPERATIVE VALUES)	CORPORATE CAPITALISTIC VALUES
Generosity. Sharing, hoarding.	Greed. Hoarding, profit, taking more than you need.
Cooperation. Working together. Mutual aid.	Competition. 'Dog eat dog'. Losers can only blame themselves.
Community. We are all related, including plants and animals.	Individualism. Me first, pull yourself up by your bootstraps.
Reciprocity. If you take, you must give back in some form. Not just things, but also energy.	Exploitation. Of people, the Earth all living beings, plus the land, air and water.
Gender equality. Women respected as leaders. Lineage goes through the mother. Two Spirits Respected.	Patriarchy. Women subordinate to men, men control and use women and girls.
Commons. Belongs to everyone including communities — the land, water, soil. None of this can be bought or sold.	Private property. Owners can mark, then exploit/extract the commons for private gain.
Earth-centered spirituality. All living beings are sacred; nurtured and protected. Ex. Water is Life/Mni Wiconi.	Materialism/consumerism. The Earth seen as real estate, humans as commodities (slavery). Everything is bought and sold on the market.
Horizontal, direct democracy. Government by consensus. A balance between male and female leaders.	Hierarchy. Top-down, authoritarian governance. Representative instead of direct democracy, with men as leaders.
Restorative justice. No prisons. Wrongdoers and victims together to work out responsibility and restitution.	Retributive justice. Revenge, punishment, isolation. Mass incarceration, private prisons; war on drugs/militarized police.
Food sovereignty. Locally grown organic gardens/small farms. Use of permaculture.	Industrial sized factory farming, Using pesticides, herbicides and antibiotics.
Autonomy. Self-governing neighborhoods, towns and cities. No hierarchical state.	Centralized hierarchical states/ Empires. Nationalism, Plutocracies and dictatorships
Equal Rights. Including LGBT people regardless of race or religion.	Racism/Otherism. Segregation/ sectarianism/classism.

Rich and his allies believe we need a new system based on the indigenous, cooperative values outlined in that chart. They say anything less is barbaric.

Part of Rich's re-education included Ibram X. Kendi's book, *"How to Be an Antiracist,"* which re-framed the whole racism and antiracism discussion expertly by not allowing anyone, any longer, to claim he is "not a racist". In America, Kendi says we are all either racist or antiracist, and likely both, as racism is such an insidious and pervasive factor of American society and life, infecting everyone and every institution. The only differences between any-one in America are those who are in denial of this fact and those who admit it and are antiracists working to eradicate it.

Rich felt that this book was such an important work that he produced an abridged version, extracting many of the most profound insights (which is available on the Global Woke Institute website <www.HowWokeAmI.org> under the Antiracism tab). He felt that one of Kendi's most profound insights was contained in his Chapter 12 on "Class", in which he writes: *"To love capitalism is to end up loving racism. To love racism is to end up loving capitalism. The conjoined twins are two sides of the same destructive body.... Capitalism is essentially racist; racism is essentially capitalist. They were birthed together from the same unnatural causes, and they shall one day die together from unnatural causes."*[95] **They are EQualized!**

Rich also realized that none of these profound truths about our history and society are taught in schools or any other institutions. That led him to begin writing and sharing them, mainly in articles online and in social media. And most recently, he started *"**The Global Woke Institute**"* to teach these truths. Plus, he began his second book under the general heading, *"Thug Nation"* and sub-headings and sections, *The Greatest Lie Ever Told: American Exceptionalism,"* *"Truth, Reconciliation and Revolution=System Change,"* and *"American Survival Manual: Surviving the Coming Revolution."*

And then 2020 happened…

Episode Ten: 2020: Turning Point or Tipping Point: Two Pandemics

In his bestselling book, *"The Tipping Point: How Little Things Can Make a Big Difference"* author Malcolm Gladwell wrote: *"The tipping point is that magic moment when an idea, trend, or social behavior crosses a threshold, tips, and spreads like wildfire."*[96] This is drawn from medical terminology where a tipping point happens when a relatively isolated illness becomes an epidemic, and possibly a pandemic (and is the source of the social media term *"going viral"*).

---

[95] Ibram X. Kendi, *"How to Be An Antiracist,"* p.
[96] More on "The Tipping Point" at https://en.wikipedia.org/wiki/The_Tipping_Point

Rich had been actively waiting and working for a progressive societal tipping point since the last one in the 70s when many profound positive changes took place society-wide. He had been hoping that the "millennial revolution" which spawned Occupy, Black Lives Matter, the Movement for Black lives, and the Climate Justice and Me-Too movements, would be the catalyst for a major societal tipping point, however that hasn't materialized to any significant extent. Though these movements have positively impacted many thousands if not millions of souls, they haven't produced many systemic changes to sustain that progress. (This is not to take away from all the noble and sacrificial efforts of all involved, not only on the front lines but in supportive roles at all levels. A point often forgotten is that those like Rich who are often on the front lines of social justice and societal changemaking could not do what they do were it not for the many who are supporting them from the relative shadows—the unsung heroes of the movements. Fellow activists who were arrested with Dr. King in the civil rights protests told Rich that, to this day, they do not know who bailed them out of jail after protests so that they could continue the work. (So, never bemoan or belittle your role, whatever it may be. However, on the other hand, do get involved in some way!)

Two favorite quotes in this regard:

--*"The ultimate tragedy is not the oppression and cruelty by the bad people but the silence over that by the good people."* --MLK

--*"If you are neutral in situations of injustice, you have chosen the side of the oppressor."*—Bishop Desmond Tutu

In 2020, two pandemics (and potential tipping points) began or came to light. One was Covid-19 and the other the ongoing pandemic of racism with the cases of police brutality and murder of mainly unarmed Black people--particularly George Floyd and Breonna Taylor.

The Covid-19 virus spread rapidly, growing into an epidemic. In March 2020, it was declared a global pandemic, afflicting and ultimately killing millions worldwide and in the U.S., disproportionately people of color and the poor. Due to lockdown attempts to quell the spread of the virus, many people were out of work, and out of food and other necessities, so people and groups arose to offer what became known as "mutual aid" providing necessities for the most vulnerable and also for those dispensing the aid. ("Mutual aid" is a reciprocal and cooperative term and concept, originating in anarchist and socialist circles, which means the voluntary exchange of resources and services between community members to provide support for those who need it.)

Just five days after the World Health Organization (WHO) declared the

Covid-19 virus a global pandemic, on March 11th, 2020, Rich entered the hospital with one of the first major cases in Georgia. (He had all the symptoms of bronchial pneumonia and went to the Emergency Room twice, on two consecutive days, each time finding it harder to breathe no matter what the treatment, and finally on the third visit, he was admitted. He knew he had Covid because it was much worse than the pneumonia he had previously.) Once admitted, even with oxygen provided 24/7 and both proven respiratory and experimental anti-Covid drugs administered, he still could not breathe adequately. So, he asked, and the doctors agreed, though reluctantly, to place him on a ventilator—which was a last resort since the Covid survival rate once placed on the ventilator, unbeknownst to him at the time, was only about 50 percent. While he was in the ventilator intubation, sedation-induced coma, Rich's family was updated each day on his progress, which fluctuated. When he finally awoke from the coma, he thought he had been out for a day or two but was shocked to learn it was seven days. His entire care team was very encouraged about his lungs' recovery while on the ventilator, so they began to wean him off it, sooner than most. He still had to relearn how to talk, swallow, and breath on his own. That was a challenge, and at one point he even begged to go back on the ventilator as it was difficult to regain his basic bodily functions after his body became used to mechanical life support even for that short period. However, he made good progress and was able to shed the ventilator relatively quickly. Rich was discharged and on his way home a few days afterwards, making his hospital stay and life-and-death struggle with Covid only 19 days (which, he later learned, was minimal when compared with many others, especially those over sixty like him). Rich's doctors and care team were openly jubilant about his recovery, from the point he emerged from the medically induced coma until his discharge, because, at the time, this was all new to them and he was one of their first success stories (so much so that they coined the term *"The Pellegrino Pathway"* to recovery, which they shared with other patients who were also struggling). As he was discharged and wheeled out of the hospital by his daughters, the hospital staff lined the halls clapping and bidding him farewell, as this was a victory for them as much as it was for Rich!

Some of Rich's takeaways from this experience, include:

1) Breathing is essential. This may go without saying but it must be emphasized because we take it for granted. (And unless we learned how to breathe properly, it is likely that we are not getting the full benefit, meaning we are taking half-breaths, not full breaths. Rich felt lucky that in his youth he learned full breathing in yoga and martial arts. But unless you are in certain sports, like swimming, or are a

singer, or practiced yoga, you may not have ever learned to breathe fully or reap the physical and mental health benefits of doing so.)

In the social context you've heard the phrases *"please give me room to breathe"*, or *"please let me catch my breath"*, but imagine if the answer is "no" and the pleader is physically strangled to death, as we have witnessed unarmed Black men like George Floyd and Eric Garner killed by police, and the many women killed by abusive men in that manner. *LET THEM BREATHE!*

2) Rich's Covid care team of about 15-20, including doctors, nurses, therapists, orderlies, dietary and sanitary staff, was the most diverse group possible, composed of Africans, Asians, Middle-Easterners, Latinos, and American-born whites and Blacks---truly a "united nation", beloved community of healers and Rich's heroes who worked together to help save his life. They all worked under the harshest conditions, confronting an unknown and highly infectious deadly disease with the utmost grace and courage. And Rich was not an easy patient, with a long-time distrust of the medical profession in this country. He wanted to know every detail about what was going on with him. Even when he couldn't speak, he would write questions and expect answers, while the staff had their hands and the ICU full of Covid-afflicted patients, many in worse condition than him. They treated him and his requests with respect and dignity. (He no longer distrusts the medical professionals but the system which abuses them and us, the professionals, and the patients—the same capitalistic system which places profits before people and why we as a nation have the worst health and medical outcomes of any developed nation.) Rich grew to admire and respect all the workers on the care teams, from the doctors down to the sanitary workers, as they have built in their respective hospital wards an example of the Beloved Community in action.

So, after being discharged, Rich was determined to support them in any way that he could, which he has continued to do. First, he partnered with a local café to provide sixty box lunches to the ICU and critical care staff as a small token[97] of his appreciation. Then he partnered with the hospital foundation to raise money for the critical resources the care teams needed, including tablets for the nurses so that they and their patients could communicate with family members via video chat during their hospitalizations.

---

[97] Red the whole news story at https://www.11alive.com/article/news/richard-pellegrino-covid-survivor-gives-back-hospital/85-95360493-7811-49ee-aaf0-c217baa4786c or just google 11 Alive Atlanta Pellegrino

3) Since no visitors were allowed due to the highly infectious nature of the disease, Rich's smart phone was his lifeline--- especially the ability to text and post on social media—since he was too weak to speak. This enabled him to keep in touch with family, friends, and his many virtual cheerleaders--friends who he didn't even know he had. Word spread of his battle with Covid throughout his national faith and activist communities and he was deluged via text and social media with well wishes, healing vibes and prayers for his recovery—basically telling him, *"Rich, you got this!"*. Sometimes when your body is weak, especially when you can't breathe, you want to give up and that attitude of defeat delays or prevents your healing and allows the illness to win, but, as the tv news story covering Rich's recovery headlined, *"'If people aren't giving up on me, I can't give up on them': Community activist opens up about his COVID-19 battle"*[98]. That is how Rich felt, and he attributes at least 50% of his recovery to those prayers and words of encouragement coming from his many cheerleaders, including and especially his large family---wife, children, and grandchildren. Now Rich makes sure that he does the same for anyone and everyone he discovers going through an illness, no matter how minimal or severe, to let them know that he is pulling for them and to encourage them to fight back. Spiritual, mental, and emotional support helps and is just as important as medical intervention!

4) Our healthcare system is corrupt---not most of the people who work in it and want to help and heal, but the system that limits what they can do, based on income and race, giving people of color and the poor less than adequate care and shortening their lives. (Rich, as a white male, realizes he was and is treated with unearned privilege by every institution in this country, including healthcare.) There MUST be equity in healthcare, as in every other issue, and the ONLY way to begin to address that is to provide free healthcare for all, just as other countries, which have less resources than America, are able to do. It is not a matter of economics but of priorities and valuing all human lives over material things. As a society, we lament the rise of one-parent and even no-parent families, however we are killing off parents at young ages due to inadequate healthcare and leaving children motherless or fatherless. Then we blame them when they act out or commit crimes when it is our fault because we let the wealthy elite and corporations manipulate government in their favor and against social safety nets and literally get away with murder. How barbaric and uncivilized we are! ***We are EQualized!***

---

[98] Read the whole news story at https://www.11alive.com/article/news/health/coronavirus/community-activists-fight-against-covid19-in-icu/85-d86ace3e-389b-42fd-a87a-73663bb2629b or just google 11 Alive Atlanta Pellegrino

Upon discharge, Rich was provided with a nurse for home visits to monitor his recovery which involved getting his breathing back to normal and physical therapy to strengthen his body. He spent his days in front of the tv practicing "chair yoga" on YouTube and being nourished by the healthy and mostly vegan foods provided by his wife and family. As a result, his nurse and doctors marveled at how quickly he fully recovered and was back to normal activities.

What helped Rich through this whole ordeal, and really saved his life, was the fact that before becoming sick he had worked out daily, was an avid skater, and had a healthy diet and lifestyle (all of which he resumed soon after discharge, and still does). It is often not the sickness that kills you, especially when on a ventilator, but the shutdown of vital organs which were not healthy before the illness. So, within a couple of weeks he was back to relative normalcy. And due to the widespread publicity of his illness and recovery and the lack of knowledge and resulting fears experienced by the community regarding the pandemic, he started receiving and agreeing to requests to speak to community groups and organizations about his ordeal so that others could learn how to avoid Covid and deal with it if they or family members contracted it. It was the least he could do with his new lease on life.

Then, just a few weeks after his discharge from the hospital and just when he had regained his capacity to breathe fully again, George Floyd happened. On May 25, 2020, George Floyd, a 46-year-old black man, was murdered in Minneapolis, Minnesota, by Derek Chauvin, a 44-year-old white police officer, who brutally used his knee to choke Floyd to death while he screamed that he couldn't breathe. This, combined with the police shooting death of Breonna Taylor, an unarmed Black medical worker who committed no crime, in her own home, was a breaking point for Blacks and people of goodwill in America and the world and highlighted the most virulent pandemic of racism which has plagued this nation for centuries.

Episode Eleven: Black Lives Matter, Still: Breonna Taylor and George Floyd

The police murders of Breanna Taylor on March 13th, 2022 (two days before Rich was admitted to the hospital with Covid), and George Floyd, on May 25th, 2022 (a few weeks after he was discharged), were a breaking point, not only for Black Americans but for people of all backgrounds and all nations worldwide. Organized and spontaneous protests, some with thousands and some only two people with signs on their neighborhood street corners, sprung up everywhere. Since it had finally become apparent that Black lives didn't matter in America, *"Black Lives Matter"* became a rallying cry worldwide in rallies, marches, demonstrations, protests, posters, murals and even on neighborhood yard signs, including in predominantly white neighborhoods.

Rich wondered if this was going to be the turning or tipping point he was eagerly anticipating, and though not fully recovered from the aftereffects of Covid, he had to join and support the Atlanta and Cobb area marches, some of which were organized by diverse groups of young people who had never organized anything similar before. Besides getting caught up in the euphoria of people of all types arising in unity to seek social justice and call for systemic reforms, one of Rich's main objectives was to find those among the organizers and protesters, especially the young ones, who would be there after the dust settled to help sustain the gains made and truly make it a *"movement rather than a moment"*.

"Defund the Police" became another battle cry of the movement, a slogan that supports divesting funds from police departments and reallocating them to non-policing forms of public safety and community support, such as social services, youth services, housing, education, mental healthcare, and other community resources. (To the movement's credit, some major police departments have started hiring or working with mental health professionals to go out on calls involving a mental health crisis.) There was (and still is) a tremendous backlash against this movement from the right and white supremacist organizations, the police unions, the GOP, and even some moderate Democrats, however they offered no alternative solutions.

In areas where the police were overly aggressive and oppressive in their protest management tactics, the protesters became overly aggressive in return, sometimes damaging and burning property. Atlanta was one of those places, and Rich found himself in the middle of it. On May 29th, he, Brother Haroun, and other Street Groomer members participated in a massive protest march in downtown Atlanta in which thousands of protesters took over the streets and shut down a major part of downtown. Before the protest march ended, Haroun and Rich became tired and decided to leave along with another Street Groomer, Pat. However, when Pat tried to drive them to Rich's car, they ended up on a barricaded street near the CNN Center with a huge and growing police presence, including armored cars. They wondered why all the heavy artillery and were worried that there was going to be a violent confrontation and needed to warn the protest organizers, so they parked and walked back to the protest which was now contained in one area between Centennial Park and the CNN building. The police had placed barricades blocking the streets where the protesters were about to resume their march, but now found themselves blocked and penned in, and were not very happy about that. Here was a diverse crowd of thousands with a lot of pent-up anger and frustration protesting police brutality and murder of people not only nationwide but also in their own community, as Atlanta had a string of unadjudicated police murders of unarmed Black folks. Someone in the police command had foolishly decided to declare the protest to be over, and to confront rather than deescalate, but the protestors were having none of that.

Meanwhile, Rich, Haroun, and Pat, quite by accident, found themselves wedged between the police and the protestors, so they demanded an audience with the command staff, including the Chief, as they could feel the tension rising and wanted to help avoid a violent confrontation. They tried to advise the site commander to deescalate, pull back, remove the barriers, and let the protestors continue to blow off their steam and rage by marching for another hour or however long it took, as it was late night already and there was no disruption of commerce or traffic any longer. They warned police leaders that any further escalation, especially with their SWAT teams in armored trucks and militaristic troops in riot gear amassing on the street facing the protesters, would ignite a powder keg ready to blow. When Rich and team saw that the police were not listening and were just trying to use them to try and calm the increasingly agitated crowd of protesters, they decided to dash back to their vehicle to get out of the area as fast as they could since they saw even more militaristic police troops marching in and knew that would spark a conflagration. Sure enough, soon after they left, all hell broke loose when the police tried to disperse the protesters and that area of the city was burned, along with some police vehicles. Later, the authorities, and even some of the more moderate Black activists, blamed white Antifa and Anarchist members for the violence, but Rich and team saw firsthand that it was an equal opportunity riot with all stripes participating. When the Atlanta Mayor and Police Chief blamed the protesters, Rich and the Street Groomers went to the media and told the true story---that the police needlessly escalated the situation and provoked the riot. (And they knew, from colleagues around the country, that wherever there was similar violence at the protests the police had provoked it, and that some white supremacist groups, like the Proud Boys and Oath Keepers, had infiltrated the protests and instigated violent acts as well. It is interesting to note that when those two groups and others violently stormed the Capitol on January 6th, 2021, the Trump insurrection supporters tried to blame the violence on Black Lives Matter and Antifa infiltrators, who were not even present. *They are EQualized!*)

Rich and the other local social justice coalition coordinators who had captured the contact info of hundreds of Cobb County-based protesters and organizers, mostly young, reached out to them to discuss how the movement could be sustained locally, building upon the work which had already been done and continuing with their new energy and creativity---and they heard crickets in return-- nada, nothing. The protests ended just as abruptly as they had started, apparently not a movement but a moment, though a powerful one. So, Rich and company went back to helping the community survive the ravages of Covid, still hopeful but skeptical that the moment could still become a movement. (This is not to take away from the positive impacts and changes that the protests and protestors made in the lives of some and helped to address and bring more awareness of the systemic nature of the racism and oppression.)

Episode Twelve: Mutual Aid/Housing/Survival/Family/Intentional Community

The pandemic had exposed the gross weaknesses in the system, especially regarding healthcare and the necessities for survival of food, water, and shelter, and the role that both societal mutual aid and government aid could play in addressing those weaknesses. These weaknesses were evident before the pandemic however the pandemic brought them into the full light. People and non-government organizations of goodwill everywhere arose to provide mutual aid, and the government printed and disbursed aid money (just like it prints trillions for military weapons, bank bailouts and other corporate welfare and subsidies) for the social safety net that provided extra food stamps, rental and mortgage assistance, and free and subsidized healthcare for pandemic related sickness prevention and treatment. (Medicare paid $180,000 of Rich's $200K Covid hospital bill, the hospital wrote off the rest without any hesitation, and he also applied for and received both rental and food assistance, and helped many others do the same.) And the federal government even placed a moratorium to halt evictions and prevent further homelessness. In other words, the government did all the things which it could have been doing before the pandemic and, in doing so, provided a model for an ongoing social safety net (which Europe and Canada has provided for years).

But, just as in police brutality and racism reform, the moment didn't become a movement for economic equity and stability, and the country went back quickly to pre-pandemic business, inequities, and corruption as usual, with housing and other costs skyrocketing out of the reach of millions.

So, Rich, through the SCLC and other organizations, helped form an "affordable housing coalition" to try and keep people housed. Even before the pandemic, according to a Brookings Institution study, Atlanta rated worse in the nation for income inequality, and an Urban Institute study rated Cobb County the worse in the nation for lack of affordable housing;[99] Things were no better and actually worse now. The new civil rights struggle was for the right to shelter in the so-called richest country in the world, and as usual, corporate profits and private property rights ruled over human rights as companies started buying up the housing stock, especially anything remotely affordable, and then charged a fortune for rents. Meanwhile, people of who own their homes (really, bank-owned) and are worried about property value

---

[99] https://www.atlantamagazine.com/news-culture-articles/report-cobb-county-tops-the-list-of-places-where-the-rent-is-too-damn-high-for-poor-people/

become "nimby's" ('not in my backyard') fighting down efforts to build affordable housing and homeless shelters near their neighborhoods. Much of Rich's time was spent helping individuals navigate the difficult housing market and options to avoid evictions and foreclosures and just stay housed.

People wonder why there is rising crime and violence—when there is massive inequity, when people don't have hope and when youth see their elders place profit and property before people and principle---it is a recipe for disaster. This is happening especially in the cities where people are piled on top of each other, and gentrification is pushing the poor out. Mass murders are on the rise, occurring at least weekly, including horrific murders of school children, with no end in sight and only a milk-toast response from elected leaders who are bought and paid for by the gun lobby. So, it is time to face the facts: America is a country which has been born, bred, and sustained on violence; guns are worshipped more than gods though it has been proven that the proliferation of guns increases violence. Add to that the rampant mental illness epidemic with suicides at all-time highs, especially among white youth and veterans. And the gap between rich and poor ever widening. This is a recipe for disaster which we experience daily in this country and have become desensitized to believe that this is somehow normal and civilized, when, in fact, it is barbaric. We need to humble ourselves and learn from other societies which have reduced violence by limiting and controlling gun possession and by increasing the social welfare safety net. **We are EQualized!** (Is there a place for guns in our society? Yes, in the hands of trained law enforcement, the national guard and military, and "well-regulated militias" whose mission is to protect their communities from violence, like the Black Panthers, Deacons for Defense, Common Ground Collective, and similar groups. Also, each family or household can have an armed protector who is well trained and licensed—a license which cannot be obtained without stringent background checks, training, and testing, just as is required for a driver's license, with a provision for revocation of such license for abuse or misuse of the weapon or the commission of other crimes. No one else should have or need a weapon. Anything less is barbaric.) After recent mass shootings of children in Uvalde, Texas, and of Black seniors in Buffalo, NY, which outraged millions nationwide, including gun owners and enthusiasts, Rich joined the mainly youth-led organizations fighting for stricter gun control and removal of military-type assault weapons and ammunition, including March for Our Lives, Sandy Hook Promise, and Everytown, and formed a local coalition against gun violence. (At a local March for Our Lives rally which Rich and the coalition organized, he said: "Because our elected politicians are too weak to stand up to the corrupt and terroristic gun lobby, and many have been bought by that corrupt group, we the people are taking matters into our own hands and will be demanding that our local gun suppliers stop selling military assault weapons and ammunition and that they institute stricter screening of all gun buyers. If they refuse to comply, we will consider direct and disruptive, non-violent actions against them. ***They will be EQualized!"***)

Rich and family had seen all this American societal breakdown coming for some time and had started laying plans, once again, for an intentional community--- a cooperative eco-village and model for sustainable and equitable living in a rural area and not dependent on "the grid." They started to explore land purchase options, either on their own or with like-minded people and groups. One of those groups and projects is the Freedom Georgia Initiative, started by 19 Black families who purchased one hundred acres in central Georgia to build their vision of "the Beloved Community", fearing for their Black children's lives in the wake of the police murders of George Floyd and Breonna Taylor. Now they have diversified and purchased an additional 400 acres for residential and commercial development, open to participation by like-minded souls.[100] (Other examples of intentional "beloved communities" formed or forming are at both of these websites: www.ic.org/ and www.symbiosis-revolution.org/.)

While always avoiding insularity and continuing to fight for those who are embattled by the existing corrupt system (almost daily in his role as SCLC field director and related roles, known in the Cobb community as a go to person, especially when all other avenues have been exhausted), Rich gets calls from and tries to help families who need housing, are about to be evicted or facing homelessness, or have a loved one languishing in jail and need assistance, as well as other injustices or inequities meted out to people of color and the poor regularly in this county and country.

Rich realized that he already had a large intentional community including immediate family (numbering twenty-one, including grandkids and their parents), and many more including extended family of close cousins, aunts, and uncles. And more again, including close friends of all the above. (Many of his kids' close friends often expressed interest in being part of his family because of its size, closeness, welcoming spirit and "beloved community" principles of oneness, justice, and equity. To Rich the ultimate form of love, whether familial or societal, is a commitment not to abandon each other no matter how tough the going gets and to ultimately and eventually work things out. That may take various forms and occur at various levels which the participants must willingly agree to and is always a work in progress. And that doesn't mean that you have to tolerate bullying and abuse of any forms—in which cases one may have to apply "tough love" tactics, letting the bully and abuser know that you are not going to allow or enable their abuse, however when they are ready to change and abandon that bullying then you still love them and are there for them; that is a high form of love, both self-love and

---

[100] https://thefreedomgeorgiainitiative.com/

other-love.) Rich also realized that he was among the wealthiest and luckiest people in the world due to both the spiritual and practical richness of his family who give him the love, support, inspiration, guidance, discipline, humor, fun, constructive criticism and every other positive vibe and value so that he can serve the community and humanity. Introducing the original ten members of the Pellegrino "intentional beloved community" (in age order):

Rich: *"The Woke EQualizer;"* Father (of eight); grandfather; activist; coalition builder; revolutionary; entrepreneur, skater; NY Italian. *Libra*

Woman King V: Mother (of eight); grandmother; rock of stability, loyalty, and motherly love; talented and capable in many skills; healer; entrepreneur; vegan; tennis pro; West Indian. *Aries*

Queen L: First born; protector; counselor; first college grad; married; entrepreneur; hr professional; visual artist; dog enthusiast. *Libra*

King L: Father; entrepreneur; counselor; college grad; protector; designer; sports/soccer enthusiast. *Aquarius*

Queen M: Mother (of three); visual artist; management professional; organizer; debater; counselor; runner; hair artist. *Sagittarius*

Queen T: Mother (of two); married; nursing professional; college grad; entrepreneur; political debater; counselor. *Leo*

Queen B: Free spirit; hippie; organic farmer; vegan; singer; healer; massage therapist; counselor. *Gemini*

King A: Father; entrepreneur; vegan; author; gaming enthusiast; healer; traveler; activist. *Scorpio*

Queen R: Free spirit; dental professional; world traveler; fitness and volleyball enthusiast; entrepreneur; party planner; gift designer; hair artist. *Aries*

Queen A: Organizer; administrator; activist; nursing professional; interior decorator; dog whisperer. *Gemini*

All the Pellegrino "intentional beloved community" immediate family members reside within minutes, or less than four hours, of each other. However, a community doesn't require living on the same plot of land or in proximity, especially in this virtual age. That broadens the prospects of forming your own intentional beloved community. Maybe you are already part of one, for example, a Greek sorority or fraternity, or other close-knit regional or national organization, or your own extended family and network of friends. (Remember, as Rich says, *"the strength of the wolf is in the pack,"* so either start one, or find one you can be part of.)

Rich and family still plan to acquire arable land, with adequate water supply, in order to learn how to survive *"off the grid"* because of their belief that the current system is unsustainable with the likelihood of collapse. They may, if the land is spacious enough, invite like-minded others to join them just as the Freedom Georgia initiative is doing. (Stay tuned and check out the Epilogue for ways you can get involved.)

Episode Thirteen: The Global Woke Institute/Woke EQualizers/Woke Warriors

Since his own awakening (or, more appropriately, "awokening") in the seventies, Rich has been teaching others what he has learned about the realities of our oneness and the need for us to build the Beloved Community upon that oneness. He has done this in many venues, nationally and globally, whether in formalized classroom settings or informally on the streets and in the neighborhoods (sometimes literally on the street with a bullhorn in hand or knocking on doors).

Two realizations in 2021 inspired him to form a more organized motivational and educational initiative, *"The Global Woke Institute"* (www.How-WokeAmI.org), and the action-oriented offshoot of that, *The Woke EQualizers"* practical action group:

1) Most Americans, including many of those whom Rich considers *"woke"* (meaning, in his definition of the term, aware, awakened, enlightened, and anti-racist, anti-poverty, anti-militarism, while trying to build "beloved community) are not necessarily *"globally woke."* In other words, when many "woke" Americans say *"Black Lives Matter"* they are really saying *"Black AMERICAN Lives Matter"* unaware of the realities and plights of Black Africans, or Black Mexicans, or Black Brazilians beyond our borders. And when they are advocating for BIPOC folks' rights, they are really saying *"American Black, Indigenous, and People of Color"* because they are unaware of BIPOC folks' plights around the world. Why is this an important distinction? Because in this global society, which due to ease of travel and the internet is now a global neighborhood, many of our smallest daily habits, practices, and actions here in America have significant and profoundly negative impacts upon people, mainly BIPOC folks and the

poor, worldwide. Especially our materialism, consumerism, and consumption—what we eat, clothes we buy, waste and pollution we generate, directly or indirectly, causes the continued triple evils of racism, poverty, and militarism around the world. For example, some of the products we buy, including but not limited to some brand name clothing and shoes, and knockoffs, chocolates, coffee, diamonds, gold, beef, etc., are produced by slave and child labor, and rape the environments and economies of other countries. Our wasteful habits—leaving lights on, cars running, water running---and the tremendous dumping of waste in landfills and the oceans, not to mention nuclear waste, contributes disproportionately to climate change, causing drought, famine, violent storms, and other climate catastrophes worldwide, killing millions of innocent people, especially children. Many of the company stocks we own and other investments we hold also contribute to these travesties and tragedies. **We are EQualized!**

This is easy to forget because we have been trained and conditioned as "American supremacists" to be wasteful polluters and consumers purchasing items way beyond what we need. Because this conditioning—really brainwashing—is so ingrained in us, we need to remind ourselves of these facts daily, so three of Rich's daily affirmations are: *"Live simply so that others may simply live;" "Let your vision be world-embracing";" Think globally, act locally."* And therefore, we need a re-education such as that provided by *"The Global Woke Institute"* and similar global organizations such as *Global Citizen (https://www.globalcitizen.org/en/)* and Avaaz *(https://secure.avaaz.org/page/en/).*

2) Very few Americans, including many of those who Rich considers as "woke", realize that the American economic system is unsustainable, has been on the brink of collapse for years, and was virtually beyond repair before recent pandemics and climate disasters, which have only weakened it further. In his opinion and belief system, these are warnings from whatever Higher Power you believe in---nature, the universe, God—of its imminent collapse. And most Americans, even those who are affluent, are dependent on this failing and faulty system for their basic needs, including food, water, and shelter. In this divisive political and racial environment there is no government leadership that will provide adequately or equitably in times of disaster, especially for BIPOC folks, just as government failed to do so in New Orleans after Katrina causing catastrophic loss of life there, mainly Black lives, and failed to do so during the pandemic, causing nearly a million lost lives needlessly here (which is more per capita than most other countries in the world). And all relief efforts, under

the weight of increasing climate disasters, are starting to show signs of imminent collapse. The wealthy elite and right-wing survivalist groups, both of whom only care about themselves, are building self-sustaining off-grid bunkers, shelters, and communities to prepare for this impending and inevitable collapse. Woke people of goodwill, who will care for and protect each other rather than kill each other in such disasters, need to learn how to do the same. (That is part of building "beloved communities" now, which will be taught through Rich's Global Woke Institute—survival and sustainability, in the face of calamities.)

EPILOGUE

How to Become a Woke Equalizer Warrior and Peacemaker.

So, here we are at the end of this story and, hopefully, the beginning or revitalizing of a new chapter in yours. The main question to ask yourself now is, what are you going to do about it and where do we go from here? Yes, we are all connected in a *"network of mutuality"* however everyone must make their own choices on how "woke" and, more importantly, how "actively woke" and connected they want to be.

Using the analogy of sleep and wakefulness, some people go through life sleeping, whether naturally or drug induced, with an attitude that *"ignorance is bliss "*or, for whatever reason, they just don't care, while others just want to get enough sleep to have an awake, active, and fulfilling day. And some like to lie in bed awake afraid to get up to confront the day and act on their wake-fulness. All three of those states indicate different levels of laziness and self-ishness. Likewise, we are all at different stages in our journeys to self-deter-mination and fulfillment, which equates to happiness. However, one of the major lessons Rich learned throughout his journey is that we cannot be truly happy or fulfilled if we are not *"actively woke"*, in some way, shape or form. That means getting enough "rest" (both spiritual and physical) to actively face the challenges of the day, but in a "woke" manner. That doesn't mean you have to be on the protest lines, or shouting in the face of elected representa-tives, or in radical underground or above ground groups, but maybe you can confront and dismantle bullying or racism (a form of bullying) at work or school, or teach your or other children to do the same. (*"Woke parenthood"* is one of the highest levels of servant leadership, and woke parents, especially mothers, are true warriors leading the way. And not only biological parenting but parenting the "children of the village.) Treating others fairly and calling out systemic bullying, inequities, and oppression when you see it. All and any of that is **Woke EQualizing**. Anything we do to teach children woke, one-ness principles, including how to stand up to bullies is the Woke EQualizing and servant leadership work of the highest order, as the "village" is the "be-loved community."

The first stage of *"woke warriorhood"* is knowledge and awareness. You have no excuse for not knowing, as knowledge is all around and readily accessible. If you are reading this, you have been exposed to the most important knowledge about yourself and life---our essential oneness with each other and with all living things—our "network of mutuality." Everything else---equity, peace, justice, love, anti-racism, beloved community—can be built on this foundation of oneness. Any other foundation is faulty and destined to fail.

So, the question is, will you become a *"woke warrior"* for oneness in your personal, family and community life? As mentioned above, there are many ways to do this. One is to enroll in our **Global Woke Institute** to gain a deeper knowledge of these concepts, and to join our **Woke EQualizer** warriors/peacemakers' movement to put these concepts into action. In the former, we will learn together spiritual and practical strategies for survival and sustainability in this chaotic world transitioning from the realm of the Triple Evils to the Beloved Community we are engaged in building. In the latter we will help protect others around us from the ravages of the Triple Evils and the bullies and haters who promote them. And the **Woke EQualizers** warriors/peacemakers will also have children and youth activities and groups to start them young in these noble endeavors since they are attracted to super-heroes, and that is who those fighting bullying and the Triple Evils are.

To join either or both, or for more information, use the contact form at www.HowWokeAmI.org or email us at globalwokeinstitute@gmail.com.

In closing, we offer one last challenge. Do you know the difference between a prophet and a philosopher? A prophet has and shares lofty ideas, principles and visions and puts them into the realm of action providing an example for us to follow, while a philosopher shares similarly lofty and poetic ideas however doesn't act upon them, so they begin in words and often end in words. Yes, some philosophers' words and ideas inspire others to action, however they often live and die an unfulfilled life because of their own inaction and inability to apply their own lofty ideas to their own lives and that of those around them. Which would you like to be? Our goal at the Global Woke Institute is to help you to be a prophet. And, as we've stated, that can take many forms—the main thing is we don't want anyone to feel or be alone in this struggle to survive and thrive holistically, both within ourselves and with each other, as, once again, *the strength of the wolf is in the pack, we are one human family in a network of mutuality and oneness, and this is the day of interdependence—a graduation from the stages of dependence and independence.*

We also want to help you experience and utilize your true power: "*Power, when understood as a scarce resource and a means of domination and division, is used to perpetuate racism and other forms of oppression. Such power is hoarded, jealously defended, and susceptible to the corrupting influence of vested interests (like political power). (Spiritual education) raises our awareness of other forms of power—moral or spiritual powers—which give us the capacity to transform our social worlds. These powers of the human spirit are limitless and accessible to all. They include the power of unified action, the power of love, the power of justice, the power of truth, the power of pure deeds and sacrificial service, and the power of divine assistance and confirmation. Awareness of these powers opens trans-formative possibilities. We have the capacity to build new social realities that can supplant the current social order with its competitive and conflictual uses of power."* (From the Dialogue on Race & Faith's statement "Overcoming Racism")

Last but not least, one of our favorite quotes to live by, from historian, activist, author, professor, prophet Howard Zinn[101]: *"TO BE HOPEFUL in bad times is not just foolishly romantic. It is based on the fact that human history is a history not only of cruelty, but also of compassion, sacrifice, courage, kindness. What we choose to emphasize in this complex history will determine our lives. If we see only the worst, it destroys our capacity to do something. If we remember those times and places—and there are so many—where people have behaved magnificently, this gives us the energy to act, and at least the possibility of sending this spinning top of a world in a different direction.*

And if we do act, in however small a way, we don't have to wait for some grand utopian future. The future is an infinite succession of presents, and to live now as we think human beings should live, in defiance of all that is bad around us, is itself a marvelous victory."

---

[101] To learn more about Howard Zinn: https://www.howardzinn.org/about/biography/

Photo Erik Voss 2013

ABOUT THE AUTHOR

Rich Pellegrino has extensive professional multi-media sales and market-ing experience, as well as a former career as an Addictions Counselor/Therapist/Treatment and Prevention Program founder and manager. He has self-published and mass-distributed a book, *"Immigrant Survival Manual"* (in both English and Spanish), has written many articles published in newspapers and magazines relating to both spiritual personal transformation and social justice issues, including some of his most recent writings/essays found on the web-site and blog of the organization he recently founded, The Global Woke Institute, at www.HowWokeAmI.org . Presently he serves as Field Director for an Atlanta area chapter of the SCLC (Southern Christian Leadership Conference, national civil rights org founded by MLK), among many other roles in various civil and human rights organizations, both in Atlanta and nation-wide. Finally, though he still fits in a couple of paid hours daily as a marketing consultant for a couple of clients, his main labor of love is doing just about anything with his multi-racial family of seven grandchildren (so far) and eight grown children (yes, he's also a "recovering catholic"), and he often tries to rope them into joining him at the roller rink as he still tries to skate an hour daily, even at the ripe young age of almost 69 .

Made in the USA
Columbia, SC
22 February 2024

31856894R00111